90+5

OUR TIME HAS COME

Sport Media

*This book is dedicated to the
memory of Jack Reyna*

If you'd like to donate to the Making Headway Foundation –
dedicated to care, comfort and cure of children with brain and
spinal cord tumours – please go to www.makingheadway.org

Sport Media

90+5

Written and compiled by David Clayton

Editing & Production: Adam Oldfield
Jacket Design: Colin Harrison
Images: Kevin Cummins

Published by Trinity Mirror Sport Media
Executive Editor: Ken Rogers
Senior Editor: Steve Hanrahan
Editor: Paul Dove
Senior Art Editor: Rick Cooke

First Edition
Published in Great Britain in hardback form in 2012.
Published and produced by: Trinity Mirror Sport Media,
PO Box 48, Old Hall Street, Liverpool L69 3EB.

ISBN: 978-1-908695-36-9

Additional photography: PA Photos

Printed and bound by CPI Group (UK) Ltd, Croydon, CR0 4YY

Contents

CONTENTS

CONTENTS

Acknowledgements

Thanks to Will Beedles, Steve Hanrahan and Paul Dove at Trinity Mirror for all the patience and encouragement to get this book from the idea stage and onto the shelves. Thanks to all the staff who helped transcribe some of the older interviews for me, too. Also my editor, Adam Oldfield, for the fantastic job he's done assembling the 95 interviews that follow into a coherent and enjoyable read. Thanks to Kevin Cummins for allowing me to use his brilliant photography in this book, and thanks to all the contributing writers who have assisted in the writing of some of these interviews and, of course, the players themselves.

Introduction

A plethora of City books hit the shelves after our momentous title win in 2012. Every man and his dog, it seemed, wanted to share their epic journey; watching City go from playing York City to Real Madrid in little over a decade.

What there wasn't, as far as I could see, was the story of the players who were involved in helping transform the Blues into one of the best teams in Europe. Enter 90+5. In the following pages, you'll find all the major players from the last decade and hear their views through a series of features that first appeared in various magazines and newspapers, but mostly the City Magazine.

Excerpts from lengthy interviews, snippets and news items of the day, 90+5 begins managerially with Kevin Keegan and ends with Roberto Mancini. It shows how the attitudes changed from 2001, where promotion was a necessity, to the present day, where expectations are, shall we say, a little higher.

The calibre of the players ebbs and flows as the money flows in, then out, then further out before flooding back in and then taken away until Sheikh Mansour finally transported the club onto an unchartered plain.

From Nicolas Anelka to Hatem Trabelsi and from Bernardo Corradi to Sergio Aguero – the thoughts of the players and management at the time – this is the story of the last decade, all to the backdrop of a minute-by-minute breakdown of the title-decider against QPR.

Enjoy the ride…

Talking In A Keegan Wonderland

This was a big deal for me. I was thrown in at the deep end with City's new manager and it wasn't just anyone — this was Kevin Keegan. I couldn't mess this up. I waited three hours outside his office before being asked in...

Kevin Keegan shook my hand, settled behind his desk at the Carrington training complex and offered me a seat opposite. I sat down, turned my recorder on and glanced at my notes. I looked up and was about to ask my first question when it finally sunk in…Kevin Keegan, manager of Manchester City Football Club. It has a nice ring to it, don't you think? I'm not after brownie points here either, but you just get the feeling he is the man who can take us on to win trophies and bring exciting football back to Maine Road. It only takes a minute or two in his presence to feel some of his enthusiasm rubbing off on you. The man has an aura that is almost tangible.

He looks tanned and relaxed from his recent holiday and, more importantly, he looks very much at home. His office overlooks the gym and the training pitches. The smell of fresh paint (pale blue, of course) is everywhere at Carrington – the place belongs to City now after the recent move from Platt Lane and Keegan is keen to make sure everyone feels at home. It's still pre-season and there is much to be done, so, with that in mind, I begin…

I ask him how he feels about the task ahead. He looks into the mid-afternoon sunshine and smiles, contentedly.

"Well, we've had, what, ten days now and the attitude's been terrific," he begins. "I couldn't fault that at all. You'd be disappointed if it wasn't, because you have to think about when a new manager comes in, it's a clean piece of paper for everybody. The players who've played well need to continue to impress and the ones who feel they've been shoved out of it, for whatever reason – maybe the manager played a system that didn't suit them or if they've been out injured or maybe they weren't Joe's type of player – a million different things, they have to show what they can do. So everybody thinks 'wow, I've got a chance here' and they've all worked like they really want to be part of it and trained really well."

Keegan wasted no time in finding a respected leader on the pitch. The decision to bring Stuart Pearce to the club was wise and shrewd with the former Nottingham Forest and England skipper looking for one last challenge before hanging his boots up for the last time.

I ask if he is already having an influence on the squad.

"Definitely," he smiles. "Everywhere you look. On the field, which is most important, he is a quality player with vast experience and you can tell he has the respect of the players. I felt we just needed a leader and this is something I've done at all my clubs. I've always tried to bring in someone who will help you manage the players. In other words, I can tell Stuart 'this is what we're thinking, go and see what the lads think about it'. He's formed a committee with Shaun Goater and Steve Howey, and they're the three that can represent the rest. If the training's too hard or too easy or the travelling could be better, they can give me feedback."

I ask if any of the current squad have pleasantly surprised him – as well as whether he felt some had been underachieving.

"Well I hope there are some that have underachieved so far because it's my job and the coaching staff's job to find something more in every one of them," he said. "If you look at Danny Tiatto, who had a great season last year in what was a poor season, the challenge is still there for him to do it again, and for the ones who've underachieved last year, for whatever reason, to put that behind them. I'm sure all City fans would prefer us to be in the Premiership. I'd prefer to be looking at a fixture list that took us to places like Highbury and Old Trafford, but in reality it doesn't. It's a bit early to be picking people out, but we've mixed the young lads in with the training and some of them have done really well and others have struggled a bit, but that's to be expected. The attitude has been great and though I don't want to single anyone out, Shaun Wright-Phillips and Terry Dunfield have been very impressive of the younger ones. That won't be a surprise to City fans because Shaun played a few times and Terry's played for 60 minutes in the first team."

Keegan has built a career on making an impact almost from the word go. He did it at Liverpool, Hamburg, Southampton and Newcastle – so who inspired him? Where does that ability come from?

"Bill Shankly, my dad…you know, everyone motivates you if you're that type of person; you find something in everybody," he said. "Even people that you don't particularly like that have got strength; players that you don't particularly get on with, but you learn something from them. Inspiration-wise, I would have to say Billy Wright – not through knowing him – but through seeing a small guy play centre-half because I was always told 'you're too small', so all the way along your life I think you have to keep finding inspiration. Bill Shankly was tremendous, though; he made you feel ten feet tall, even if you're only five feet seven."

Sustained City possession is ended when Ferdinand intercepts a pass and clears downfield. A one-two between Zabaleta and Tevez fails to come off and QPR win a throw. The ball goes back to Kenny who is quickly closed down by Aguero, but he clears in time...

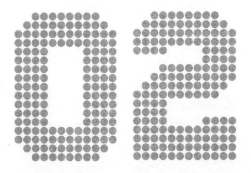

Floats Like A Butterfly

After watching Ali Benarbia make his debut against Birmingham, I couldn't wait to meet the man who has become an instant crowd favourite. His was a special talent. We met up at Carrington after training...

It wasn't only Kevin Keegan who was pinching himself after Algerian international Ali Benarbia signed a two-year deal. Around 31,000 City fans were doing the same. His first game against Birmingham City must rank as one of the best debuts by a City player ever, and it left many people wondering how the Blues could get so lucky.

On deeper examination, it would be insulting to Kevin Keegan and Arthur Cox to say that Ali simply fell into their laps, for they were well aware of his abilities and moved quickly when the chance arose. Had Sunderland realised just how good Benarbia was, they would surely have snapped him up, but they didn't, and he's now wearing the No.44 shirt of Manchester City.

When you consider the French invasion of British football over the past few years, it seems incredible that no club brought Ali, now 32, to England sooner, though he was a wanted man elsewhere.

"I stayed in France because all the major teams in France wanted me to play for them, but now I think it is a good time for me to see another country and I prefer England because all the people love their football," he said.

"I had to think, 'which team can give me a challenge?' I knew of Manchester City and how they want to win the league and, for me, it is very important to play with a coach who likes players with spirit and more technique. To work with Kenny Keegan is wonderful."

City now have a growing list of international players, and maybe this makes it easier when foreign players arrive than it might have been several years ago. Ali has been impressed with what he has seen so far.

"I've seen in training how all the players respect each other and listen to the coach, which is very important. They are very professional and when they played the first game with me, they made it easy for me to fit in. It was a dream and wonderful to play in England, especially so at Manchester City because they are such a big club."

Ali was substituted on his debut and received a standing ovation from all four sides of the ground. Was this adulation different from his time at Paris St Germain?

"It is very different to France and I never imagined the fans would give me a standing ovation like they did. It will help me to have a good season. I have to give thanks to all the players for helping me by giving me the ball and allowing me to express myself. It has made things very easy for me. It was a wonderful way to start my City career."

Ali is familiar with several City stars and he's getting to know some of the ones he didn't know beforehand quite quickly.

"I already knew of Paulo Wanchope, Shaun Goater, Laurent Charvet, Stuart Pearce and Eyal Berkovic. Now I see the other players like Dickson Etuhu, Danny Tiatto, and I think we have a very good chance to win this league."

With Eyal Berkovic sidelined with a hamstring injury, most City fans were left dreaming of an Ali and Eyal dream team in the middle of the park, but Benarbia is keen to emphasise that all the squad have their part to play.

"We have many players who are good and there are many, many games. In one season, you have 46 league matches and we need all the players to win this division. Maybe I play with Berkovic, maybe I don't play every game, or maybe I play with Tiatto and other players; it is no problem. The most important thing is to win and for all the players to be happy when we are promoted."

Kevin Keegan heaped the highest praise on Ali by saying that he could well be one of the best players to wear a City jersey since Colin Bell.

"It is very good to be compared to one of Manchester City's best ever players," said Ali. "It is very important to give pleasure to the fans that come to see me, not just to win; they want to talk about the game and see something special or different. Fans' lives may be good or their lives may be bad, but when they come to the stadium, they want to be happy. It is important for me to make the fans happier, and if I can do that, it will be my contribution to the team."

Ali was born in Algeria and moved with his family to France when he was just two years old. He has lived there ever since. His career has been spent entirely in France. Recent signing Alioune Toure shares the same agent and this appears to have been a key factor in the move to Maine Road.

Ali asked to go to Sunderland for talks on a possible move, but was only in England for two days and they wanted extra time to look at him.

"I came for only two days," Ali explained. "Sunderland were playing Blackburn, so the coach didn't see me. He asked me to stay longer so he could see me play and I said 'no – you know me and I can't just stay for you to see me' so I left and Kevin Keegan, who knew me and how I play, invited me to lunch and then signed me shortly after."

Sunderland's loss is very much City's gain.

City win a corner but it's cleared at the front post by Hill and then further away by Cisse. Wright-Phillips wins a free-kick for QPR in his own half...

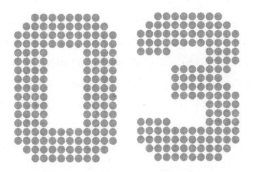

The Flying Dutchman

Everybody liked Gerard Wiekens. Dependable, no frills and a nice, relaxed guy off the pitch. Interviewing him was always a pleasure...

Gerard Wiekens has repaid City's £500,000 investment many times over since he joined the Blues back in 1997. He is now one of City's longest serving players and his level of consistency has made him a firm favourite among City supporters and the managers that have had him in their employ. Uniquely, Gerard has never played successive seasons in one division while at Maine Road – a record that all Blues fans hope will continue at least for one more season!

The affable Dutchman is arguably one of the club's most underrated performers and has filled a succession of roles for the team including sweeper, central defender, midfield and midfield anchorman. Born and raised in the flat lands of Holland, Gerard recalled his early days in his home country.

"I was born in the north east of Holland in a place called Groning. It's about fifteen minutes from Germany – just a few miles from the border. It was a very small village, very rural. For a kid, it's a great place to grow up. Comparing my hometown to places like Manchester or any of the big cities in Holland that are so crowded with people is hard to do. The place I lived was all detached houses with big gardens."

He laughs when I ask him if there was a big German influence on his village.

"I think the closer you live to Germany, the more you don't like them. The petrol is a lot cheaper in Germany, as are the groceries, so people would go over the border to do their shopping or fill up their cars and then come back as quickly as possible!"

Gerard's love of football began with his local side, FC Groningen, who play in the Dutch Premier League. He explains – in perfect English, of course – of the days when he was just a football fan, much like the rest of us.

"Holland is defined into 12 smaller parts, much the same as England is with the shires. I'm from Groning and the capital is called Groningen – this is where the team is based. They've always been in the highest division, except a few years ago when they went down and came back up again.

"I was a big fan of them in the Eighties," he continued, "and they played in Europe against the likes of Atletico Madrid and Inter Milan – both of whom they beat – and then I think they went out in the next round of that particular competition. The Koeman brothers, who both represented Holland in the 1988 European Championships, started with FC Groningen. They had a good team back then, but after playing in Europe, they didn't seem to do so well and struggled at the bottom of the Premier League."

Gerard had the shirt as a fan and almost had the opportunity that every schoolboy fan dreams of – playing for the team he supported.

"When I was about 14 or 15 years old, I was playing for an amateur side and Groningen asked me to have a trial with them. There was also another club interested and they acted much quicker because there was no trial involved. I gave Groningen a week to decide and told them if I didn't hear during that time, I would sign for Veendam. I didn't hear from them, so I made an appointment to sign for Veendam. About one hour after I'd arranged to sign, Groningen contacted me to sign for them. I was a little bit disappointed at the time, but I think I made the right decision."

Gerard would go on to play for Veendam for nine years, playing the first two in the youth team and the remainder in the first. Veendam were actually closer to where Gerard lived, but were only a First Division club.

"It was easier for me to make the first team at Veendam because they were a smaller club. When I was only 17 years old, I made the first team and became a regular. It's good because I was young and played a lot of matches – if I'd signed for FC Groningen, I don't think it would have been the same."

It must have been a little odd for an English side to come in for Gerard as he was relatively unknown outside his own country, but English football and English clubs are no mystery to the people of Holland, as Gerard explains: "In Holland, we have the BBC on normal television – you don't have to pay extra for it – so we always watched Match of the Day. A lot of Dutch players started moving to England and I knew there were some clubs interested in signing me, so when I found out one of them was an English team, I was interested."

"I can't say it was always my dream to play in England," he admits, "but I'd made my mind up that if I left, I would go abroad, especially England because we know the language and it's not far from Holland. It was an easy choice and I'm just pleased City came in for me."

Only Richard Edghill, Jeff Whitley, Kevin Horlock and Paul Dickov have been at City longer than Wiekens in this, his fifth season at Maine Road, something Wiekens is only too aware of.

"It's a long time in football," said Gerard. "When I signed a four-year contract, I didn't expect to play the four years at City. Maybe two or three years and I would see how it went, but I really enjoyed it and had a good time. Every season we've had something different – we went up, we went down, and we'll see what happens this season."

His family has settled over here and he enjoys the different way of life – especially the social side of English life, which he is becoming quite accustomed to.

"In England," he begins, "people like to go out with friends to a pub and then out for dinner. In Holland, you tend to invite people to your home and spend the night there. Here, you go to a restaurant, which I find more enjoyable. Different surroundings, nice food, so that's really cool."

Indirect free-kick taken by Kenny. Clichy picks up the clearance, the ball finds Barry who plays a 30-yard pass aimed at Silva but Taiwo reaches it first and concedes the corner. The ball is cleared and Wright-Phillips wins a free-kick in his own half...

A Mystery Wrapped In An Enigma

Nobody could deny Paulo Wanchope was a talent, but you never knew which Paulo would turn up on the day. Frustrating and exciting in equal measure, I found him to be quiet, a bit shy and a little distant at times...

Costa Rica is a beautiful Central American country sandwiched between Panama and Nicaragua. On one side of the country is the Atlantic Ocean and on the other is the Pacific. The Spanish-speaking population of 3.7 million is among the friendliest in what can be a somewhat unstable region, and with a low crime rate and booming tourist industry, Costa Ricans – or Ticos – as they are also known, enjoy a healthy standard of living.

The country is so peaceful – it doesn't even have an army, would you believe? With all these facts in mind, should we be surprised that City's Costa Rican star Paulo Wanchope has such a laid-back nature? It is obviously in your blood to stay cool and chilled out when you come from such a peaceful background – something that perhaps fans at West Ham and Derby maybe never fully understood or appreciated, but in joining Manchester City, Paulo may have found his spiritual home.

His older brothers, Javier and Carlos, who both play professional football in Costa Rica, heavily influenced their younger brother. He was born on July 31, 1976, in a small town called Heredia, which is surrounded by tropical rainforest and even has several active volcanoes nearby. "They are very beautiful places to visit," Paulo tells me. "It is a very beautiful country."

Despite living amid such spectacular scenery as a young boy, Paulo was only interested in playing football whenever and wherever he could.

"We used to play in the street every day. Everyone knew each other. It was a very close, friendly neighbourhood," he remembered. Was it here he developed what is quite an usual, even unique style? He thinks all players are unpredictable to some extent.

"I think every player has to do things differently – if we all played the same, it would be very boring. My style of play comes naturally to me."

Watching Paulo play football is anything but boring. He is one of football's true entertainers. As a toddler, he had a very happy upbringing with everything a youngster could want. He had many toys, but his favourite game was always playing with a ball. He smiles as he recalls his early years.

"In Costa Rica, football is very big. Of all the things my mom used to buy for me when I was small, it was a ball that I used to like playing with the most. I used to play with my older brothers in the house, outside the house; wherever we could, really."

There must have been some fairly high calibre knockabouts in the Wanchope household seeing that all three boys now earn their living playing professional football!

Being only 25 years old, and so far from home, it is no surprise that Paulo misses his home comforts.

"I do miss my friends and family and, of course, the weather, but it's okay because I like it here and enjoy the football," he said.

Paulo isn't alone in England – he has his girlfriend with him, and his family has visited him regularly since Jim Smith signed him for Derby County in 1997 from his hometown club, Herediano. "I've been in England for four years now and my family came over when I was at Derby for two or three months, and then my brother stayed with me when I moved to London and he helped keep me going," recalled the striker who set the Copa America alive in the summer.

Paulo's season as a West Ham player was, without doubt, the toughest time he has spent in England. The Hammers fans didn't take to Paulo's laid-back style and were rarely off his back during a turbulent 12 months. His record at Upton Park was impressive enough and he scored more than his fair share of goals – 12 in 35 league appearances.

West Ham's loss was very much City's gain and Paulo began his City career with his first senior hat-trick on his home debut. If people were wondering how City fans would take to the talented Costa Rican, the answer was crystal clear after just two games in a City shirt –they loved him.

Living in Manchester is a million miles from life in Costa Rica and it's easy to forget sometimes that foreign players have to adapt to the food, weather and culture, as well as trying to adapt to the pace of the game over here. Paulo, however, doesn't complain about life in the North West – except for the rain, maybe!

"Yeah, it's different in England, but the people are very nice to me, so they make it very easy to live here. I don't like the weather, though. I hate the weather! With all the rain and cold," he says with a charismatic grin, "however, when you are among good people, you could be anywhere in the world."

Paulo is settled at Maine Road and he is continually amazed by the City fans and their attitude towards their team.

"They're great. I've never known support like theirs. Even when the team are playing badly, they always try to lift you up – that's nice. I think they are the only supporters in the world who can do that. I've played in many countries and, for me, they are the best."

Whenever Paulo plays, you can bet a fair amount of money that the word 'unpredictable' will rear its predictable head, but he is a little mystified as to what exactly people are trying to say.

"When they say unpredictable, what does that mean? What about Zidane – is he predictable? Luis Figo – is he predictable? Every player is unpredictable in their own way," he insists.

Yet it is not only Paulo's unique ability that sets him apart from many other talented strikers. He has had to adapt from the more patient style of Central and South American football to the hustle and bustle of the English game – something few players from his region have managed to do. In Costa Rica, they say he has 'survived' the English game, so how does he feel about being labelled this way?

"You have to combine the style of your game," he says. "It's very fast and some players just like to run and run, but you have to just relax sometimes. People want to see a fast game, so when you stop and look up to see what's around, you may get people saying 'pass the ball, pass the ball!' That's normal. Sometimes you have to play fast and quick and have to fight. That's how football is."

Paulo's performance for the Costa Rican national team – for whom he is fiercely proud to play for – in last summer's Copa America, made him the subject of intense transfer speculation, with a host of top European clubs said to be monitoring his blistering form in Colombia. He scored six goals and was at the very top of his form, and it was a relief for many City fans when he reported back for pre-season training. He has always maintained that it was nothing but newspaper speculation and has stated on more than one occasion how happy he is with life at Maine Road.

As a young player, he must be looking forward to the World Cup in Japan and Korea next year when he could well become an international superstar now Costa Rica have qualified.

"We're looking forward to playing in the World Cup, and now we're there, I can concentrate solely on Manchester City. The first thing is to get back into the Premier League because that's the main target for everyone. It would be great for me to score a lot of goals, but the main thing is for the team to do well."

With his frequent trips over the Atlantic, events in New York on September 11, 2001, had a profound effect on Paulo. I asked him how difficult it was to go and play a football match after such traumatic events earlier the same day. "What happened was horrible. It could have been me or any one of us, but you have to go on," he said.

City have begun this season by scoring goals for fun and it is Paulo's blossoming partnership with Shaun Goater that could well fire the Blues back to the Premiership next May. He likes Shaun and enjoys playing alongside him.

"He's a great striker and a funny guy to be around. All the players are very good and the spirit is great and so is the manager, too. It's all looking very good for the future," he concluded.

Kenny takes the free-kick and plays it downfield,
Lescott leaves the header and Hart picks it up on
the bounce in his own six-yard box...

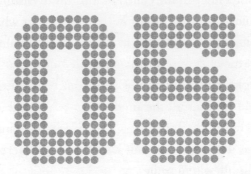

Tower Of Strength

*With promotion secured and the Division One title in the bag,
City began looking for bigger names. It was time to kick on and
ensure we didn't go straight back down again, though with the side
Keegan was assembling, there was no real danger of that. Sylvain
Distin was a man-mountain who grew tired of Newcastle's
dithering following a loan period and signed for City instead...*

The first thing that strikes you on seeing Sylvain Distin, is how
tall he is. Slim and lean, yet powerfully built, it wouldn't be
hard to imagine him shooting hoops for the Los Angeles
Lakers or maybe running the final leg of the French Olympic 4x100
relay team – he is, after all, one of the fastest players in the Premiership.

He is a natural-born athlete and it's a fair bet that the majority of Premiership strikers will not be looking forward to a 90-minute tussle with City's new No.5. He follows in a great tradition of defenders to wear that particular number on his back – Sam Cowan, Dave Ewing, Dave Watson, Tommy Booth, Mick McCarthy, Colin Hendry and Keith Curle have all served the club proudly in that shirt.

Happy playing either in the centre or out wide, Distin is expected to slot into the role vacated by Stuart Pearce. Signed for what could prove to be a bargain price of £4 million, the 24-year-old already seems to have settled at the club and is relaxed and happy.

"Everyone told me," he said looking at the blue skies outside, "that it rained in Manchester all the time and that it's cold and grey most of the time." He squints in the glorious sunshine flooding in the room. "But every day has been like this since I arrived here. Warm, blue sky…" he trails off with a smile.

I didn't want to burst his bubble, so I say nothing.

Sylvain Distin will be a big hit with City fans this season. He was very popular with Newcastle United supporters, too, and when he signed for the Blues instead of the Magpies, it was the board that was criticised, not the player. Radio phone-ins were full of disgruntled Geordies for days after the news broke.

"I had a discussion with the chairman of Newcastle and we couldn't agree, and after that, I don't know what happened," he revealed. "You would have to ask him, I suppose.

"After I'd had some contact with Manchester City, I decided I wanted to come here and play. Ali Benarbia told me all about the club and the supporters and it was an easy decision to make."

Distin was part of a Paris St Germain team that included Ali Benarbia and Nicolas Anelka – not a bad trio to build a team around. It's only when you think of them at another club that it hits home that players of such high calibre are now wearing the laser blue of

City. Sylvain is also aware of Ali's standing with the Blues faithful.

"Yeah, I know how popular he is here," he said. "I can see his face is everywhere! Everybody knows him and, as I said earlier, I spoke with him before I came. I knew Nicolas from playing in the same PSG side and we met in Paris just before he signed and we spoke a little about the club.

"It's nice to know other players at a new club, but I've only been here a week and it's not difficult to get on with all the players here because everybody is very friendly. So even if Ali and Nicolas weren't here, I would still be happy. It's better for me because they are here, but I would feel at home and content anyway."

He's not had chance to have a look around the city yet because he's only just unpacked his belongings, but he's in no rush. He put pen to paper on a four-year deal and has plenty of time to discover the delights of his new surroundings, and besides, what he has seen so far, he likes.

"Yeah, it's nice, the places I've seen so far. I've seen only a bit of Manchester and a little of Altrincham where I'm going to be living, but having just arrived, my stuff is all in boxes, so I've not really had any spare time," he revealed.

With no international recognition to date, he knows there is plenty of time to break into the national side. His first concern is success on the pitch for the Blues, and whatever else happens in the future, happens.

"I've only been a professional for two years and I am only 24 years old," he reasoned. "There are players in the national squad of the same age as me who have been professional for four or five years, so if they are ahead of me at the moment, that is not a problem.

"I'm just happy to be here and I want to work hard for Manchester City and I think about the club first. If everything is good here, the rest will follow. If I do get called up for France, I am ready. I want to show the lads, the staff and the fans that this is my club now and this is where I want to stay."

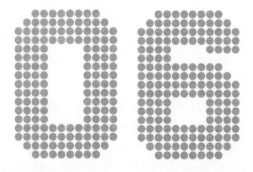

Renaissance Man

The City fans called him 'Super Kevin Horlock'. A great servant on the pitch, Kevin was also the life and soul of the party off it. Every team needs a Kevin Horlock...

Kevin Horlock has played in every game since winning back his place in the 2-1 defeat at Crystal Palace in early December, and it is no coincidence that boss Kevin Keegan has opted to use a three-man midfield consisting of Horlock, Eyal Berkovic and Ali Benarbia as the Blues' promotion push takes off.

Playing alongside creative talents such as Berkovic and Benarbia has meant that Horlock has had to curb his natural attacking urges, instead concentrating on winning the ball, running the engine room and setting forward raids in motion.

It is a niche, though, that suits him down to the ground. And with City flying high at the top of the First Division, it is not surprising to learn that he can't wait for the next fixture on the list to come up.

"Everything is going brilliantly at the minute and I am really enjoying my football," he enthused.

"I've managed to get a sustained run of matches and the added bonus has been the great run of form the team have been in. It's all rosy at the minute.

"I'd like to think that where I am playing now is the role for me. I'm playing with confidence.

"It's brilliant playing behind Eyal and Ali. Even though they aren't the best defenders in the world, you have to give them that leeway because they create so much and are a joy to watch."

The situation for him at present is in stark contrast to the beginning of the season. He had worked hard to regain his fitness after his Premiership campaign was curtailed when he broke his ankle in a freak accident against Charlton.

But for all his efforts in pre-season, Horlock struggled to break into Keegan's starting line-up.

Alhough he began matches against Burnley and West Bromwich Albion in the league, as well as the Worthington Cup victory at Notts County, the 29-year-old found himself relegated to the bench when Benarbia arrived from Paris St Germain.

After being given a chance, more frustration followed when he was sent off in the bore draw with Sheffield United.

"It couldn't have come at a worse time," he admitted, "as it just looked like I was about to get a run in the side."

And it looked as though he was being pushed even further down the pecking order when Christian Negouai arrived from Chaleroi in early November for £1.5m.

Indeed, it was rumoured that Crystal Palace and Birmingham were ready to tempt Horlock away from City with bids in excess of £1m.

Ironically, though, a suspension to Negouai re-opened the first team door, and the former Swindon and West Ham man had no hesitation in jumping through it.

"My ankle wasn't perfect at the beginning of the season, I have to admit that," he said. "It was also hard because as everyone knows, I wasn't as involved as I would have liked to have been.

"I was desperate to be a part of a side that was going in the right direction, and when I wasn't, I went to see the manager to see where my future lay.

"But he assured me that it was at Maine Road. That's one thing you know you'll get from the manager – honesty. I appreciated that.

"True to his word, he has put me back in the team and given me a defined role. Hopefully I have started to repay the faith that he has placed in me."

Barring the slip-up at Selhurst Park, the Blues won seven of their following eight fixtures in which Horlock figured and has also chipped in with a number of vital goals against Wolves, Bradford and Swindon.

"Perhaps things didn't go as well for Christian as they might have done," the father-of-three went on. "It could have been difficult for him settling into a new club and a new country.

"The manager decided to change things around and I had to grab the opportunity. Things happen like this all the time at clubs.

"When you do get put back in the frame, you have to make sure you take that chance as you never know when the next one will come."

The fear of losing his place, Horlock reckons, has spurred him on to producing a sustained high level of performance.

With confidence high in the camp, and every squad member wanting to be a part of the team – not to mention competition to take free-kicks – he is well aware that one small slip-up could lead to yet another spell on the sidelines.

He is, however, adamant, even after playing a key role in two successive promotions, that this is the best he has performed during the five years he has been with the Blues.

"When the manager makes a signing, you know that whoever he brings in will have a part to play," he explained. "I know that there are players here who can already take my position, so I've just got keep doing what I'm doing.

"It's been nice scoring. Every player loves getting on the scoresheet, and I'm no different. But I'd settle for not scoring, the team winning, with me being a part of it.

"Now and again I'll practice free-kicks after training, but it's becoming harder to take them during a game because Eyal and Ali want their chance to show what they can do, and Stuart Pearce wants a crack as well – there's a dash for the ball every time we get one now.

"But I'd say that I've done half decent in my time here, but I would say that, at this moment, I am playing as consistently as I have ever done."

The Real Deal

For me, this was our first real superstar signing – at least since Trevor Francis arrived in 1981. Anelka dressed like a rock star and was coolness personified. This was the first of three interviews with Nico. He was a million miles away from the guy the press called 'Le Sulk'...

Nicolas Anelka has been given such a bad press over the years that after just five minutes in his company, you are left wondering why. Friendly, charming, polite and almost painfully shy, is this really the multi-million pound superstar that has made life difficult for the managers of top clubs throughout Europe? If it is, he's doing a fantastic impression of somebody who is completely the opposite.

Perhaps his reluctance to seek the glare of the media in some of the biggest cities in Europe, like London, Paris and Madrid, has created the myth of Nico being moody and sullen, when, in reality, all he's ever wanted is a quiet life. It is almost impossible to live a normal, everyday existence when you are as famous as he is – the lack of a private life comes with the territory, just as the fantastic trappings of wealth do – but you can't help feel that sometimes the anonymity afforded to the general public is something Anelka covets.

Maybe that's why Manchester is the perfect place for the French superstar to rediscover the form that made him one of the most sought-after strikers in the world. His South Manchester home may not sound as glamorous as his apartments in Madrid and Paris, but at least it affords him the opportunity of walking to the corner shop for a pint of milk without a pack of photographers watching his every move.

His early form suggests exactly what Kevin Keegan has been saying all along, that at £13 million, City have a real bargain on their hands. His goals in the opening matches – a volley, a header and a long-range drive – carry the hallmarks of a player who can do pretty much everything you could want a striker to do. He was cruelly robbed of the deflected free-kick against Everton, but he doesn't plan to appeal against the somewhat harsh opinion of an official panel.

"If they want to take the goal away from me, that's up to them. It would be nice to have been given it, but if they want to give it somebody else, I've nothing to say about it," he declared.

It was amusing to hear the commentators on Sky Sports covering the Arsenal v City game last month say that Nico had never scored a header in England just moments before he nodded Benarbia's cross home past a static David Seaman. He ran past the Arsenal fans urging them to stay silent, a wish with which they were happy to comply.

Anelka had been given plenty of stick by the Gunners faithful on the night, despite scoring 23 goals in 65 Premiership appearances for Arsenal. Football fans, though, rarely boo a bad player. And it must have been sweet to score his first header at Highbury. Anelka admits he enjoyed it.

"I have scored headers elsewhere in the past, but this was the first time I'd actually managed it in England," he said. "I think the Arsenal fans were the way they were because they don't understand why I left Highbury.

"I went back there twice last season with Liverpool and the reception from the fans was okay, but I don't care about that. I have got on with my life and Arsenal fans should forget. I forget their whistles and only think about the good times. They are an awesome side and they still have the desire and hunger to win more.

"Arsene Wenger was a big influence on my career and I am full of admiration for what he has done at Arsenal. He had confidence in me when I was a teenager and I had confidence in him. He helped me as a 17-year-old and I helped him by doing my best on the pitch. He trusts me and I trust him."

His time at Real Madrid yielded only two goals in 19 appearances before he returned to Paris St Germain in 2000. He remained there until his loan move to Liverpool last season, where he added four goals in 20 appearances for the Anfield side. While it seemed almost certain he would join Houllier's men, he was surprised and disappointed when the Reds boss decided against the move.

Anelka recently said of Houllier that 'he imagined future problems and imagined the worst.' Privately, the young striker must be hoping to make the Liverpool boss regret the decision. But their loss is City's gain and he has surprised many by not just his prowess in the penalty area, but his all-round work rate, which is something he admits is a new side to his game.

"It was not part of my game when I was at Arsenal where I was an out-and-out striker and a scorer of goals. But, first at Real Madrid and then at Paris St Germain, I learned to play behind the strikers. Now I do both for the side, and I like that a lot. I am a better player now. I am older and wiser. Many things have happened to me in my career since I was at Arsenal.

"I feel I have different dimensions to my game now and I am a more complete player because of it," he continued. "When I was at Paris and Madrid, I learned how to play as a forward coming from deep and to play behind the strikers, and it made me a better player.

"I am enjoying playing for City, but we all know we need to improve. I feel very settled and the supporters have been behind me from the very first game, which I appreciate a lot."

In the car park after the interview, Matias Vuoso walked to Nico's Ferrari and pretended to get in before shrugging his shoulders and walking back to his more conservative Peugeot and a laughing Paulo Wanchope. It's nice to know even professional footballers have a wish list, just like the rest of us.

Wright-Phillips dribbles the ball forward before being tackled. Aguero reaches the ball before Taiwo takes it off him and concedes a throw...

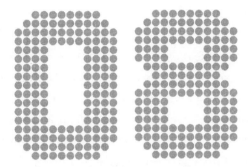

Great Dane

Despite his United connections, Peter Schmeichel was warmly welcomed by most City fans — he would be the first in a succession of top names who were mostly past their sell-by date, but Schmeichel was still a commanding presence nonetheless and had started his career with the Blues in impressive fashion...

You can't help but be a little in awe of a man like Peter Schmeichel. He's done almost everything there is to do in football and is arguably one of the greatest goalkeepers of all time. Now aged 38 years old, he is coming towards the end of a memorable career, but if his current form is anything to go by, he could be around for a few more years. Hopefully, that will be as a City player.

Looking extremely relaxed and settled, it's hard to believe that this is the man who can turn defenders into jelly with his verbal scalding. Fresh from watching Europe regain the Ryder Cup at The Belfry, he admits to liking golf, but more for relaxation purposes than anything else.

"I do enjoy playing golf," he admitted. "It's a nice way of getting out and getting some fresh air, and with the level my golf is at, it is always a challenge to play. I like watching the game, too. I know one or two players on the PGA Tour.

"A few of them are fellow countrymen and through them I've got to know a few others. At the World Championship in Ireland last month, there were only three countries with more players than Denmark. We had five players challenging and it is something we are very proud of as a nation."

He laughs at the suggestion that he might be a dark horse to join up with future Ryder Cup squads and replies: "Only if they need a good caddy."

City fans have taken to Peter Schmeichel in a big way and he is now officially an adopted Blue after a series of top-notch displays for the club, and he's been given a warm welcome from the very first time he played for the club during the close season. The reception has not been lost on one of the greatest goalkeepers of all time and he recently commented that he "loved it" at Maine Road.

Schmeichel's achievements with the Reds are well documented and somewhat painful to read, so let's not dwell on them. He left in 1999 to join Sporting Lisbon but returned to England with Aston Villa after two successful years in Portugal. John Gregory's exit from Villa Park resulted in Graham Taylor returning to the Midlands club and Schmeichel deciding to pursue his career elsewhere.

That led to Kevin Keegan snapping him up on a free transfer after allegedly taking just 20 minutes to agree a deal. Just as Stuart Pearce did the previous year, Schmeichel has been a vital leader on the pitch in the early matches for City.

"It is important to have a manager who is inspirational," declared the Dane at the time of signing. "Kevin Keegan is a fantastic person and a great motivator. You can see that from what he has done and where he has been. It is mainly down to that reason that I made the choice to join City."

City slowly build up the play before Nasri picks up the pace and runs directly at the defenders before firing a pass into Tevez, who has his back to goal…

Gone In 60 Seconds

Darren Huckerby had just enjoyed the best season of his career, but the arrival of Nicolas Anelka and others threatened his place in the first team – he wasn't someone who hid his feelings…

Pity the poor defenders at Manchester City. If it's not bad enough for them going out each Saturday knowing they have to mark lighting quick forwards such as Arsenal's Thierry Henry, Michael Owen of Liverpool, or Newcastle speedster Craig Bellamy, think about what they have to deal with every single morning.

Neither Nicolas Anelka nor Darren Huckerby would look out of place were they lining up in the 100 metres final of a major athletics event, as they have shown when zooming in on goal.

So just imagine how Steve Howey, Sylvain Distin, or Jihai Sun feel when they have to give chase to either of City's strikers on the Carrington training pitches when they hare after a pass.

Before Anelka's £13 million transfer from Paris St Germain, Huckerby was recognised as being the quickest man on City's books. That, though, has been thrown into doubt with the arrival of 'Nico' and Distin, who is no slouch, either.

But Huckerby, who diplomatically acknowledges that his strike partner can move a bit, still believes that he is the man to catch if a sprint were ever to develop.

"There hasn't been a race yet, but Sylvain isn't in our league, and he knows that as well!" joked the former Leeds man. "Nicolas and myself are both pretty quick and just lucky that we haven't got to mark each other!"

Though it is still very much early days, Huckerby and Anelka have shown the first signs of developing a fruitful partnership, given the way they like to race onto passes from deep and run at defenders.

While conceding that there is a long way to go before they have a telepathic understanding, the 26-year-old reckons the initial signs that they can both work together are good.

Huckerby was on a summer break when he learnt that boss Kevin Keegan had splashed out a considerable amount of cash to make Anelka a Blues player in June, as well as Argentinian Matias Vuoso, but was in no way disheartened by the news.

Though he recognised it would make it tougher for him to secure a starting place, given that there would be six strikers competing for two places, Huckerby admits that the extra challenge will spur him on to become a more able striker.

"You don't mind players coming in if they are top quality, especially someone like Nicolas," Huckerby, who scored more than 25 goals as the Blues raced to the First Division title last season, declared.

"He's an established international and he's won the Premiership, the Champions League, and he's no mug. We're very lucky to have a striker of his quality here.

"We play a similar type of game to each other, so it might take a little bit of time to gel. But we'll work on these things and hopefully something exciting might develop.

"Myself and Shaun Goater know that Nicolas is always going to be first choice, so when we get a chance, we know that we have got to take it, and it's the same for all the other players in the team.

"When you are out of the team, you have got to do everything you can to get back in as quickly as possible. It's up to the manager who plays. I'll be rooting for whoever is in the side if I'm not," he said.

"I had a couple of holidays with my wife and children, but other than that, I trained virtually every day over the summer to get myself ready for the season.

"So it was disappointing to be left out against Leeds because I thought that I had done well in pre-season. I was feeling strong and had kept myself as fit as possible, so it hurt when I wasn't involved.

"The gaffer had made it clear before that game that he wanted to play with just the one man upfront and to see how it would work out. Thankfully, I didn't have to wait long for my chance and it was nice to score the only goal in the following game against Newcastle.

"But I should have had three or four, really. Shay Given was excellent, and if it wasn't for him, I think I'd have had a hat-trick."

That swashbuckling performance against Newcastle is something that City's management, players and supporters are eager to see reproduced during the coming months.

The End Game

Life is full of 'if onlys' — that the Blues had Ali Benarbia at the back end of his career, left City fans wondering what might have been if Ali had signed five years earlier. As it was, the pace of the Premier League was catching up on his ageing legs, though class never dies...

If you had suggested to Manchester City supporters last season that Ali Benarbia would find himself relegated to the bench after just 10 games of the new campaign, chances are your sanity would have been questioned.

After all, the talismanic midfielder had helped transform the Blues from promotion hopefuls to runway First Division champions, turning in a string of mesmeric displays that had the Maine Road hordes drooling with delight.

Nevertheless, just as Kevin Keegan's side have found difficulty adapting to life in the Premiership, so too has the 34-year-old Benarbia. Only on fleeting occasions has he show shown the brilliance that earned him the title of Player of the Year.

The shuffles and shimmies which made him impossible to mark in the realms of the Nationwide, have not – as yet – had the same outcome in the top flight. But such is Benarbia's ability, it still came as a surprise when boss Keegan moved him to the bench for the Blues' 2-0 away win against Birmingham last month.

He is the type of player who can turn a game with one moment of magic, or switch defence to attack with one swoosh of either foot. However, the Blues chief chose to go to war without his alchemist and it was a decision that caused Keegan a great deal of angst, but one the player took on the chin.

Despite that setback, and his side's unexpectedly low position in the table, Benarbia still finds himself happier now than at any stage of a decorated career which saw him win the Le Championnat in France, play in the Champions League as well as being named France's Player of the Year.

"I have never been at a club like Manchester City because the staff do everything they possibly can to make things easy for you. It is the same for every player here. It is special that people want to help you in that way.

"It is like going to see your family every day. All the players believe it is a family club and now we have to show to the fans when we are on the pitch that we are like a family. That spirit will be good to help us.

"I am looking forward to the rest of the season and every game will be a big one from now until the end. Manchester United is just one of many to look forward to. We will just have to be at our best to stay here."

After beating Everton in August, results nose-dived dramatically and defeat against Chelsea at Maine Road in October saw City plunge into the bottom three – not exactly what supporters had anticipated at the beginning of the campaign.

Benarbia, though, has a pragmatic view of the situation. He was never carried away by the bright opening the Blues made to the season, nor has he become too concerned about the dip in form that has stalled progress.

As he sees things, just as boss Keegan has continued to stress, the most important thing for Manchester City this year is to stay in the Premiership and then look forward to progressing next year.

Then they will have a glittering new stadium to move into, more money in the coffers to improve the squad again, and a heightened sense of awareness as to what it will take to succeed against the very best teams in England.

"People were saying after the first three or four games that we were a very good side, but I always said we would have to wait 10 games before we should be judged, and things have been a little difficult," Benarbia reasoned.

"Others have been saying that we can get into the top six or top ten, but, for me, I think it would be very good if we just stay up and then next year, when we have the new stadium, then we can really start to go forward. We will be a very good team then.

"You can have many good players, but not a good team. Other sides don't have a lot of great players but are very difficult to beat. I think we have to find a balance in between that and show how hungry we are to stay in the Premiership.

"I have always played for sides that have been challenging for championships, so this is a bit different, but I am still enjoying it very much. We have to be very determined to get as many points as we can.

"The quality of players isn't different in the Premiership; it is the quality of the teams. Every side has many great players in lots of different positions and that makes them stronger.

"We have had a lot of players coming in and sometimes it may take 10 or 15 games for them to get used to playing together. I think we have to stop making mistakes like we have done in order to take off. Together we will then become stronger than the others."

Onuoha gives away a throw-in just inside the City half. City begin to make QPR sit deeper and the ball is switched from Zabaleta to Clichy before Nasri picks it up and attempts a shot but drags it a couple of yards wide of the post...

Let The Sun Shine

Jihai Sun arrived at City as our first Chinese player – a lovely guy, few realised he would stay at City for six years...

I didn't recognise Jihai Sun when he wandered past me in the reception at Carrington. With his fashionable clobber, floppy hat with expensive shades on, it could have been anybody. The man I had interviewed a year ago was very quiet, dressed conservatively and was flanked by his interpreter when he needed to communicate with anybody.

That was then, this is now.

The Jihai Sun of today could be a completely different person and, in many ways, he is exactly that. Twelve months ago, he seemed more than a little lost and undeniably homesick. I wondered at the time how long he could continue in a similar vein for any great length of time, and thought it might be the first and only time I interviewed the popular Chinese international.

His absence from the side for much of the second half of last season also indicated all might not be well for the defender, but he battled back to first team action towards the end of the 2002/03 campaign and enjoyed an excellent pre-season in the summer.

He carried that form into the current campaign and is showing the kind of ability that makes it easier to understand why he is so popular back home. 'He's the Chinese Beckham' and other such lines came out when he first signed from Dalian Shade 18 months ago, and this writer used the same hackneyed comparison in my first feature on him.

He's not David Beckham, but that's just fine. He probably can't pick a 60-yard pass with quite the same unerring accuracy as the England captain, but then Becks can't run up and down the pitch with the same energy as Jihai, or put in half a dozen crunching tackles during a game, either. He's Jihai Sun, he's very popular in his homeland, and that just about says all that needs to be said.

Jihai sits on the couch next to me and makes himself comfortable and I ask if he's okay for half an hour or so.

"Yeah, no problem," he replies. "But it's best if you ask me questions slowly because I'm still learning the language."

Learning he may be, but his progress since our last chat is as commendable as it is impressive. His whole demeanour and body language suggests that his form on the pitch is largely due to the fact he is becoming used to life in Manchester. He agrees fully.

"Everything has settled down," said Jihai. "I've got a lot of good friends now and my family are here, and everyone at the club, from the players through top the coaching staff and manager, have all helped me adapt and feel at home.

"My English is much better now, and that obviously helps a great deal, too. I think I had some problems on the pitch with communication, especially with David Sommeil who arrived last year speaking little or no English at all, just as I did.

"With his problems and mine, it made things tough at times last season, but I feel I am improving, and so is he, and despite our difficulties, football is a language everyone can understand, so it hasn't been too bad. I take lessons and listen to English tapes at home, which all helps a great deal."

Will this lead to a Manchester accent to accompany the Manchester look he is currently sporting?

"I hope not," he laughed. "I want to speak properly with no accent at all."

So not much chance of Jihai greeting me with a Gallagheresque 'Yer all right, our kid?' when we next meet, then. Maybe that's not such a bad thing. Another becalming influence in his life – or disruptive if the sleep patterns of the junior Clayton clan are anything to go by – has been the birth of his first child, Jing-Ying Sun. She was born a year last July and is quite clearly the apple of his eye, but hopefully not the eye that is currently bruised with three stitches above from a nasty clash of heads at Chelsea three weeks earlier.

His wife and mother also ensure that if he wants a reminder of China once every now and then, he has two expert cooks on hand to recreate dishes that most Mancunians would give their right arm for. Jihai adds he is useless in the kitchen, just for good measure.

He has also struck up a strong friendship with Everton midfielder and compatriot Li Tai since the pair arrived in England at roughly the same time. Li Tai (incidentally, also dubbed 'the Chinese Beckham') has not had quite the same impact for Everton as he had last year, and has hardly featured in David Moyes' starting eleven this season, but Jihai believes his friend will bounce back given the chance.

"I see Li Tai at least every couple of weeks and we get along very well," he declared. "He travels to Manchester to see me and the family, and though he hasn't been playing, I believe he will do very well for Everton if he is given time to adjust. I was told 300 Chinese million people tuned into the City versus Everton game last season because it was the first time two players from our country had met in the Premiership."

I tell him to ensure the next meeting is pay-per-view and that he and Li Tai take £1 from every subscription. "Good idea!" he laughed.

Jihai's popularity at City has increased a lot over the past year, too. It was unusual to see a Chinese player in England and, without meaning to be disrespectful, something of a novelty. There were a couple of songs chanted about him including one that was borne out of typical City fan humour, but nothing more.

Jihai battled on despite all his off-field problems, and never gave less than his all every time he pulled on a blue shirt; and now he has the form to match the incredible fitness he displays week in, week out in the Premiership. The novelty factor has gone, replaced by respect from all at the club and particularly the supporters.

City fans love nothing more than a wholehearted performer, and Jihai Sun expels a jet engine's worth of energy with each appearance – part of his game he acknowledges he has worked hardest on.

"I take extra training during the summer months," he revealed. "I train with my father who is a fitness coach at Dalian Shade and he pushed me hard to build up my stamina. I train hard here, too, and do extra sessions so I can maintain a high level of fitness out on the pitch.

"My father never played football as such but was a decathlete at amateur level, so he is an expert at many different disciplines which we mix in with my training. I enjoy playing at right-back because I have played in this position for a long time and it allows me to use my fitness to good effect. I try and get forward whenever it is feasible."

Indeed, he has become a potent weapon in the Blues' attack this season, scoring a couple of goals, winning a couple of penalties and also providing the odd pin-point cross for the likes of Paulo Wanchope to profit from.

"I've scored two so far," he acknowledged, "but in my position, it's difficult to get goals. I just want to help the team to do well and my first priority is to defend. I hope I can get many more goals in time, but as long as we are defending well, that's good enough for me.

"As for the two penalties, I suppose they were carbon copies of each other with me running around the back of a defender and being pulled down. Obviously, this isn't something you can practice – I just saw the defenders coming at me and knew that if I touched the ball at the right time, they would probably make contact as I went past them – then it is up to the referee to decide."

If the City fans have taken Jihai to their hearts over the past 12 months, the feeling is mutual.

"They are absolutely wonderful," he said of the Blues faithful. "They sing all the time and get behind you. The Chinese fans are different from here in England. Here each player has a song – I like the 'Sun Jihai! Sun Jihai!' chant the best.

"When I hear my song, it makes me feel excited and gives me more energy than ever. Sometimes when I'm out around the town centre, City fans recognise me and come up to talk with me. They don't ask for anything, they just want to wish me luck. It's very good and it makes me feel great.

"In China, fans sing songs, but not together. I think if they can sing like the fans do in England, it will create a much better atmosphere for the club sides and the national team. They need to improve their singing."

His success with the Blues has not gone unnoticed back home – as highlighted by the 300 million viewers that saw him in action last season for a Premiership match – and add another 198 million for the Fulham v City clash earlier this year. When Jihai first arrived, there was a posse of Chinese journalists covering his every move, and while it hasn't been quite as intense this season, the interest is still huge. While we're on the subject, I ask just how big a star he is in his homeland?

"The press back home keep updated on how I'm doing," he revealed. "Sometimes I read the papers via the Internet and there will be stories about City training and team news and suchlike. As far as me being famous, that's tough for me to answer. There were an awful lot of people who watched me in a few live games, but I don't know if it's anything to gauge my popularity by."

One would assume that should his current performance levels continue over the next couple of seasons, it will make him an automatic choice when China do get down to the serious business of World Cup qualification in 2005. And if his fame continues to rocket here and in Asia, perhaps if David Beckham decides one day to exploit his popularity over there by signing for a Chinese team, the press in Peking may get the opportunity to call him 'the English Jihai'.

Lest we forget that City's favourite Sun is also China's favourite son.

Kenny takes the goal-kick but it falls straight to the City defenders who pass it around at the back and then bring it out before the ball ends up with Silva in the centre of the pitch...

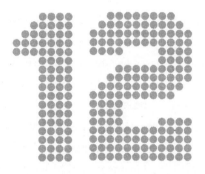

Finding Nico

Nicolas Anelka had given City fans a glimpse of a possible future that didn't include Lincoln City and Barry Conlon. Anelka was settled, scoring goals, and the fact he was playing for the Blues proved we were capable of attracting A-list talent. He'd started the season so well, it seemed well worth another interview...

Settled off the field in a luxury apartment in Hale, a very content Anelka has terrorised Premiership defenders since the opening day of the campaign at Charlton. Here is a man who is enjoying life to the full.

In fact, he's been so settled that City fans are perhaps seeing the best of the much-travelled Frenchman. There are reasons, of course – there always are, and Anelka is happy to share his happiness.

"At this club, it doesn't matter whether you are French, Dutch, English, German or whatever," explained Anelka as he takes off his trademark Ray-Ban glasses and stretches back into a blue armchair.

"It is so easy to be the same, and we are all friends. That is not the case at all clubs. Here, though, it is the best. It is very easy to be accepted. This atmosphere is different to anywhere I have been. In Spain with Real, going into the dressing room is like entering into a family environment. If you are a stranger, it takes time to be accepted and it is hard to get inside that inner circle.

"It is not like that here. Straight away you are made to feel welcome, and players enjoy it. There are no reputations to get past. At Real, you have to wait to see if you are accepted.

"A manager like Kevin, though, helps bond the players together. He smiles all the time, even when you miss chances. He will always have a laugh and a joke and a smile is never far from his face."

Nor is it from Anelka's. It appears the more he smiles off the pitch, the better he becomes on it. Already into double figures for the season, there are few strikers in the Premiership who can match his form in front of goal. A seemingly unquenchable appetite to add to his tally, added to a multitude of jet-heeled performances, has led his colleagues and manager tipping him to become the best frontman in world football.

Chew over this suggestion from goalkeeper David Seaman, who remembers Anelka from his time as a rough around the edges 17-year-old. What he sees now on the training pitch and in the Premiership is a polished gem.

"When Nicolas first joined Arsenal, he was a young lad and had a problem with the language," Seaman recalled. "So, obviously, he would close ranks with the older French players, but straight away you could see he was a quality player. Since I have come to City, you can see that he is a totally different player. I know he is only 24, but he has matured so much. He knows what he wants and knows how to get it. He has been on a great journey. I keep telling him that he has been around a bit and that he has played football in some wonderful places. Now he has come back here to the Premiership and you can see he has more of that quality.

"Thierry Henry is all pace and strength over long distances, while Ruud van Nistlerooy is more of what you would call a box player. Nicolas is really a mixture of both of them and it is great to see that he has so much enthusiasm."

Keegan, on the other hand, is of the opinion that Anelka has already done enough for City to play his way into the pantheon of great City strikers. Quite simply, he feels 'Nico' is the club's new talisman.

"I don't think there will be many Manchester City fans who remember a better centre-forward than him," Keegan mused after Anelka's two-goal salvo during the 6-2 demolition of Bolton last month.

"They will have their favourites from the past, people who scored goals in different ways, but as a thoroughbred athlete for the modern game, he and Thierry Henry would be the computer-produced prototypes.

"You can, I believe, compare the two of them. Nicolas' finish for his second against Bolton looked simple, but it was absolutely world class. You looked at him closing in on goal and you knew he was a man in control of the situation. When he gets to 27 or 28, you will see him convert even more of those chances. He will convert two or three out of five rather than one or two. That is what experience does. When Nicolas fires, we fire as a team."

Such praise, especially coming from Keegan, must surely make a player feel 10 feet tall whenever they go on to the pitch. Not Anelka.

Almost blushing at the praise bestowed on him, he feels he must always improve on his last performance.

"When I play, I just try to do my best all the time," he said, half apologising for the praise that has come his way. "That has always been the case. When Kevin says he can make me the best, I just try to get on with things and hope to prove him right. Sometimes it works, sometimes it doesn't. But when I go on to the pitch, I only ever think about being as good as I can."

And here are some words to fill defenders with dread. "I think I will be playing for another 10 years, so I will get better," he continues.

"When you are training, you must always try and progress. Every year you must try to get better and better. Even if you have scored a lot of goals one year, it doesn't matter. When the season finishes, the challenge is to do it again the next. Every team you play is different. If you beat a smaller team four-nil, it means nothing when you go out and play better opposition. You have to improve all the time and think how the team can move forward."

A bright start to the season has captured the imagination of the Blue hordes and left them dreaming of a future festooned with silverware. Anelka, however, feels the biggest challenges have yet to be scaled.

"There are four big clubs," he pointed out. "Arsenal, Manchester United, Chelsea and Liverpool are always going to be around the top four. Maybe they are better than Manchester City at the minute, but we are a new side and you never know. Look at what happened in Spain. It was always Real Madrid and Barcelona, but then Real Sociedad came from nowhere to get into the top three. If we keep trying to play better and better, it will come.

"But we have to look at what the four sides in the Premiership have done and find that consistency to get us in there. We can definitely win something, and the players want to do that. The problem with cup games is that little teams can surprise you.

"I have to say thank you to the supporters here. They accepted me very quickly and I am always happy to play for them. They are simply the best I have ever played in front of.

"Since the start of the season, I have been happy with the way things have gone. And I am really happy here, the happiest I have ever been. When you have travelled around places like England, France and Spain, you get to see what things are the best.

"For a player, England is the best. When you leave training, you are left alone and you can generally do whatever you like. That is not always true in France or Spain, and you can't walk around like everyone else in the street."

Happily, though, in Hale he can meander around the streets in peace. Relaxation is very much a priority of his and invariably he spends free time in front of the television or perusing the latest high street fashions.

"It is hard when you have people following you around all the time," he said. "But when you are happy off the pitch, it makes you play better on it. That is how I feel now and it is very important to be that way. Sometimes I go shopping. But most of the time I like to just go home and watch a video or DVD and just relax. I like to chill out as much as I can."

The latest hip-hop sounds, such as Dr Dre and Snoop Dogg, can often be heard emanating from his beatbox. But he passed up the opportunity to see 50 Cent when he was in Manchester recently as he was indulging another of his passions.

Anelka is keen on basketball and recently paid a visit to his hometown to watch the San Antonio Spurs take on the Memphis Grizzlies in a NBA exhibition match. Central to his attentions was France's latest sporting phenomenon – Tony Parker, who plays for San Antonio.

"I love basketball and like to play sometimes," he said. "But I also like tennis, and when we do not play football, I play that on my holidays with my brothers and friends. It is good because we usually have about two months off. On holidays, I usually go to Miami or Spain. One of my brothers has a house in Madrid, so it is a nice place to go and relax. You are so busy during the season, it is just nice to go and do nothing when the season ends.

"Miami is not far from where my family comes from in Martinique. It is only two hours away and it is hot. I go back to Paris whenever we have Monday's off. It is only an hour from Manchester and my house is not far from the airport.

"It is a long time away, but when I finish, I think I would like to have a house in Manchester, a house in Miami and one in Spain. Spanish life suits me because the people are so laid-back.

"But at the minute, I am only thinking about Manchester City. I am happy here and hope it continues like that for a long time."

Nasri gives possession away but the ball is cleared straight back to the City defenders. City threaten down the right with Zabaleta before Toure misplaces a pass which ends up going for a QPR throw-in...

The Indomitable Lion

I liked Marc Vivien Foe from the moment I met him. Always smiling, he insisted he looked at the picture the photographer had just taken as he came off the training pitch. 'It looks okay,' I suggested. He smiled at me and said, 'It's shit,' winked and walked off to get a shower. Within a year of this interview, he was dead. It remains one of my favourites...

In his floppy Stone Roses-style hat, stylish clothes and baggy jeans, Cameroon international midfielder Marc Vivien Foe – 'Marco' – to his team-mates, already looks like an adopted Mancunian. Tall and slim with a cool demeanour, this is a player whose style off the pitch matches that on it, and he has the pedigree to become a big favourite over the coming months.

He arrived at Maine Road in July this summer on a 12-month loan from French champions Olympique Lyonnais. The deal will cost the Blues £550,000, but it could well prove to be a small price to pay for such an experienced and influential player. He's played Champions League football and appeared in two World Cup Finals for the indomitable Lions – and he's still only 27 years old.

City will have the initial option of making Foe's transfer a permanent deal at the end of the loan period, and with praise from Kevin Keegan still fresh in the memory, the ball-winner has every chance of becoming a regular fixture in the Blues' engine room for many years to come.

"I'm committed to playing a certain type of football, and that is why Foe's signing is very important," enthused Keegan. "You've got to have someone in there to marshal the troops, and Marc is a player who will certainly do that."

Foe is one of Cameroon's most experienced players, having won his first cap aged just 18 years old. The total of 60 caps he has won is all the more impressive when it is taken into consideration that he missed out on many more due to a nasty injury.

Indeed, he could even have ended up playing at Old Trafford after actually putting pen to paper on a non-binding agreement with Manchester United in 1998.

A broken leg meant that because the United deal had not been fully finalised, it consequently fell through and it also put paid to his France '98 World Cup ambitions. It must have been a particularly crushing blow for Marco to take, especially as he had earned his living in France for much of his career, but all the disappointment is now confined to the past.

He finally ended up in Manchester – this time the right half of the city – and his early performances for the Blues suggest he will be a tremendous asset to the club in the tough months ahead.

He was just 19 years old when he played his first World Cup at USA '94, and is undoubtedly the driving force behind the Cameroon side. He helped Lens win the French League before an 18-month spell in the English Premiership with West Ham United. His arrival at Upton Park was overshadowed slightly by controversial Italian striker Paolo Di Canio joining the Hammers at the same time.

Marco never really settled in London and was on the verge of a move to Liverpool in 1999, but, like the United deal, it fell through in the latter stages. He returned to France in a £6 million deal that saw Freddie Kanoute travel in the opposite direction. A tough-tackling, athletic footballer, Foe was a key part in helping Olympique Lyonnais to win last season's championship.

A veteran of the Japan/Korea World Cup, where he played all three games, and a key member of Cameroon's successful African Nations Cup defence earlier this year, Marco brings the kind of ability with him that caused Keegan to say he was an absolutely crucial signing. He has set himself high standards and was none too pleased with City's opening defeat at Leeds.

"Of course, everybody was disappointed about what happened in the first game. Not winning the game was a bad thing, but we all need to keep smiling and think about the next game. We have to be strong," he said.

Fellow countryman Lucien Mettomo is now in his second season with City and it seems pertinent to suggest that he may have played a large part in Marco's arrival at the club, but surprisingly, it didn't.

"Not really, because I knew a lot of people at City already," he revealed. "I know Eyal Berkovic, Stuart Pearce and Paulo Wanchope from my time at West Ham, and I also know Ali Benarbia and Nicolas Anelka because we used to meet up a lot in Paris.

"I am looking forward to the season ahead with City and feel fresh and ready to go. I haven't had as long a break as some players because of the World Cup, but I feel great and I am a professional. I already knew Manchester before I signed for City because I spent 20 days here when I signed for United.

"It was a nice place then, but in four years it has changed a lot. It seems to be a much bigger city now. I'm looking forward to learning from a man like Kevin Keegan, who was a great player, and it will be a very good experience for me to be around him."

Marco's wife and children will be joining him in Manchester shortly. They are in the process of finding a house and he is understandably keen to have his family alongside him as soon as possible.

His two youngsters, Scott and Leslie, aged seven and four years old respectively, love sport, but he doesn't believe they are likely to follow in his footsteps.

"They prefer basketball," he says with a broad smile, "but then, I love baseball as well. The New York Yankees are my team."

Foe was only recently cleared to play in the opening games for the Blues after initially being handed a four-match ban. He was sent off twice while he was with West Ham, but that was more than two years ago and the FA finally agreed City's protest should be upheld because such bans last for no longer than a year.

Foe is a strong believer in teamwork and aims to let his efforts out on the pitch do the talking for him in the coming months.

"The most important thing for me, is that we play for each other," he said. "I think we have to fight for each other because as long as we all stick together, we'll get some good results.

"My job is to work hard in midfield, and I'm happy to have players like Ali and Eyal around me. I have to work hard for them so that I can get the ball to them to score and make goals. If you want to be successful, you have to work hard. I think we will do well this season."

We Need To Talk About Paulo…

The cool and laid-back Paulo once had a training ground fight with Andy Morrison, who was less than impressed by his time-keeping. Thereafter, Paulo changed his ways and was largely a different character at work. We spoke for a second time on October 2003, not long after he'd returned from a lengthy lay-off…

If you were to find out in advance that the game you were playing in would be your last league match for 18 months, you'd want to sign off with a bang, wouldn't you? Of course, Paulo Wanchope had no idea the February 2001 clash with Preston NE would conform to that exact scenario, but his cracking 25-yard goal against the Lilywhites proved decisive in a 3-2 win and was his sixth strike in five games.

How cruel, then, that the Costa Rican's red-hot form should be curtailed by a knee injury that was bad enough to leave question marks over the payer's future. He worked hard to regain his fitness and was passed fit to play in the 2002 World Cup when he showed himself to be among the very best in the world with a goal against Brazil.

The knee injury resurfaced, perhaps aggravated by the hard pitches in Japan and Korea, and he was forced to sit out the entire 2002/03 season and undergo operations in the United States. He may have made the back end of last season, but his bad luck returned as he built up his fitness when he dislocated his shoulder in training and again had to rest and recover.

Paulo was declared fit for pre-season and looked as sharp and inventive as ever, but it was his promising link play with Nicolas Anelka that must have most pleased manager Kevin Keegan against Villa in the middle of last month. Paulo finally made his long-awaited return to the starting line-up and gave the Villa defence plenty to think about.

Hopefully, the injury jinx has come full circle and the enigmatic striker can resume his City career in this, his fourth season with the club. The match with Villa was his 150th career game and he clearly enjoyed being back upfront and entertaining the supporters with his – at times – jaw-dropping skills.

"Yeah, I enjoyed it a lot because I have been waiting so long for that moment," declared the 27-year-old. "Things are easier when your team-mates are playing well and there is a good atmosphere in the stadium, as was the case against Villa."

Those team-mates Paulo referred to are almost an entirely different set compared to his last game against Preston. The only other survivor from that day is Shaun Wright-Phillips and though he has trained with the squad regularly for several months, it must still be a case of 'getting to know you' when it comes to competitive match action.

"It's different from the last time I played," he admitted. "There are many new players and a new home, but the mentality is still the same – to improve the club and win things. There may be new players, but the attitude is the same. We all want to do the best for our club and for our fans. This last year has taught me just how big this club is and we now need to transform that grandness to the pitch."

With so many strike partners in his time with City, it is interesting to find out what he thinks of departed forwards such as George Weah, Paul Dickov and Shaun Goater, and how did it feel to play alongside Nic Anelka for the first time in a competitive fixture?

"All those players mentioned have different abilities and strengths that complemented my style in various ways. I have my own way, too, but they are all great, great players and it is always easy to play with such talents.

"Football is like that in respects of the playing staff changing all the time. Players come and go, but the club always stays the same."

Paulo could have easily become withdrawn and sullen during his lengthy lay-off, but he kept a positive attitude at all times and has always had a smile on his face, even when it must have been difficult to face another day of gruelling knee-strengthening exercises.

That the injury came when he was reaching a new peak in his career must have been even more frustrating, but he says that feeling sorry for himself would have been the worst thing he could have done and has taken many positives from his enforced absence, including becoming a dad for the first time with his little girl, Pamela, now nine months old.

"When you have this kind of injury, you have to always believe you will be fine and be positive and strong mentally, otherwise you will never get back," he said. "It's good that I was able to think that way and focus on getting back into the first team by working as hard as I could and be involved with everything possible. Those were my aims and that's what kept me going.

"The time I've spent recovering has made me realise that football is not everything and there are many things you can do in life. It has made me appreciate my family much more and the value of being close to them.

"It was great for me that my daughter arrived when I was injured because I've spent so much quality time with her, and I suppose if there is such a thing as a good time to be injured, this, for me, was it. I've just enjoyed my life more and made the most of the time.

"I need to concentrate more on my club now and, as I've said before to the journalists in Costa Rica and to the manager and the FA back home, I need to focus on Mancheser City more than ever because I've been out almost two years.

"I must thank the fans, too, for the reception they gave me because they are easily the best supporters I've played in front of. They always try to lift the team when things aren't going well and I said to the boss that this is the only place to be and to win things with. The stadium itself is fantastic and everything is there for us to keep getting better.

"Football is not for life and these are the things I will remember when I retire. One thing I've learned during my time out is what is really important to the City fans. Having watched so many games from the stand, I feel I really understand what they want to see and what they are looking for in their team, so I will make sure I put that into practice when I play."

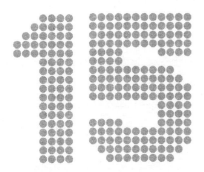

Captain America

When the Blues signed USA skipper Claudio Reyna, nobody knew that much about the former Rangers midfielder. He settled in quickly and proved a steady influence in the middle of the park. He was a good guy off the pitch, too. This book is dedicated to his son Jack, who tragically lost his battle with illness in 2012...

The USA soccer team is no longer the butt of jokes in the world of football – far from it – today's side is one of the most respected and upcoming teams in international football and they almost made it to the semi-finals of the World Cup in 2002, narrowly losing to Germany in the last eight. Reyna captained his country during that tournament, without a doubt the highlight of his career thus far and a million miles from his sleepy hometown of Livingston, New Jersey.

It's perhaps not that surprising that Reyna became a footballer considering his parents are from two football mad countries – his dad is Argentinian and his mother is Portuguese. But life as a kid is different in the States, with baseball, basketball and American football the dominant sports in school and on the sports field. But things are changing and that is thanks to the likes of Reyna and a host of other top American footballers plying their trade around the world's top clubs.

I ask if his dad was a footballer and he smiles with a look that suggests he's thinking 'aren't all dads great footballers in their son's eyes?'

"Yeah, he played a bit," he said. "He grew up in Argentina and played for several amateur sides and also Independiente's youth team. Then he moved to America and continued playing as a non-professional for various teams."

Reyna spent several months in his father's homeland as a youngster and is fluent in Spanish and Portuguese as well as being able to speak several other languages, which has served him well in his playing career. It will also give Paulo Wanchope – who Reyna has played against many times in the USA versus Costa Rica clashes – the chance to have a chat in his mother tongue, should he wish.

"Football is growing in popularity in the States all the time, but it is growing in the right way," declared the 30-year-old midfielder. "There's much more played than you might think with the many junior sides and a lot at 16-18 level. In fact, it's the biggest youth sport – along with basketball – in the country and it's equally popular with boys and girls.

"I'm not saying that basketball, American football and baseball aren't still as popular as they've always been, it's just that football is growing all the time. If you drove around a few blocks, you would see kids playing football everywhere – parks, streets – anywhere.

"It just hadn't taken off at a professional level and that's what everyone judges it by, and for a long time there wasn't really a league that was flourishing and the other sports are massive at professional level.

"The North American Soccer League was huge in the 1970s, but it became too big, too quick and now they are just trying to get it right and steady and aim for the right markets and pace things so they don't become a victim of their own success and suffer financially. The NASL worked for a while, but it was a bit too jazzy and had cheerleaders and suchlike, but the players were overpaid."

Reyna remembers the halcyon days of New York Cosmos and their 70,000-plus crowds, and admits they helped him along and it soon became clear he had a glowing future in the game. He left high school for the University of Virginia where he was inspirational in helping them win the National College Championships a record three years on the bounce. He was also named young American Player of the Year for 1992 and 1993 and was soon playing for his country at senior level.

"College sports in America are really big," he explained. "It's all at an amateur level and something similar to us winning the FA Youth Cup. You get sent to the schools that are the best for the scholarship you've earned, and Virginia was the best for soccer.

"From Virginia, I played for the national team in the 1994 World Cup which was held in the States. I'd played for the US in the lead-up to the finals and I guess Bayer Leverkusen had been scouting me because that's the club I signed for after the finals.

"I was 20 and it was a big challenge for me to move to Europe and continue my football education."

Reyna has also represented the USA in the Barcelona and Atlanta Olympics, scoring in the first minute of his first Olympic appearance against Argentina who had a very strong side out. It must have caused some mixed feelings for his father, but he says he was as proud and happy as always.

He was loaned from Leverkusen to Wolfsburg in order to gain valuable first team experience, and played 48 times for the Bundesliga outfit between 1997 and 1999.

"I was building up to the '98 World Cup and I wanted to go to a club where I was virtually assured of playing. Wolfsburg were a newly-promoted side whose aim was to survive the first season, but we kicked on and finished sixth, qualifying for the UEFA Cup," he continued.

"Then I was transferred to Rangers in 1999. The biggest difference was the size of the club and the crowds. The move meant I would be playing in Europe every season, which is something I really wanted. Every home game we had about 45,000 fans watching and Rangers are a worldwide club with fans all over the place. Everywhere I go I bump into Rangers supporters, no matter what part of the world I'm in."

While with the Glasgow giants, Reyna became the first American to captain a side in Europe – another accolade for the boy from New Jersey who takes it all in his stride.

"It was nice and definitely an honour for me. The best thing of all was to be the first American to be selected in the FIFA All-Stars side because other players picked me and that makes it a bit more special than just a coach appointing you captain. When it's your peers that pick you, as in this case, it means more in terms of respect.

"The European nights were fantastic at Rangers and we made the Champions League three years in a row, with full houses each game at Ibrox always being extra special. We played the likes of Bayern Munich, Valencia, Parma, Monaco and PSV – all the top teams. It was a good time for everyone at the club."

At this point, Reyna had been earning his living outside his homeland for eight years and admits to missing home.

"I missed the lifestyle more than anything and still do to a certain extent," he confessed. "I miss the weather and, of course, family and friends, but I've been away for 10 years in total now, so I just have moments when I feel a little homesick more than anything else. In terms of work, this is the best place I could possibly be.

"The great thing about moving to Manchester is there is a direct flight to Newark, New Jersey, and therefore I hope to have a lot more visitors from home than I've had before."

Reyna still has a house in Springfield, but he also has an apartment in New York City and a beach home in Westhampton. From his home in Springfield, just 23 miles outside Manhattan, he could see the World Trade Centre's twin towers every morning from his front doorstep.

Imagine, then, how he felt on September 11, 2001, when the tragic pictures of destruction and death were relayed to the rest of the world. For an American living abroad, it must have been a very tough time and he admits that pretty much sums everything up.

"I grew up seeing the Towers every day, so I know the people around there and also some of the ones that died as well," he reflected. "For two or three months, it was never out of my mind. Football is probably the only thing that helped me get through it. It is still horrible to think back and I want to forget about it in many ways, but then again I want to talk about it, too.

"We (the national team) went to Ground Zero as the clean-up began, and it was horrible – there is nothing that could describe it and it is something that the whole country is mourning about. It didn't matter where you were from in the world, it was terrible, but being from there, and being brought up nearby, just hit home for me all the harder.

"I used to get the train to the World Trade Centre every day when I was younger and it's hard to think it's not there anymore. The skyline has changed and everyone still thinks about what happened all the time. I try not to talk about it when I go home, but it's hard not to.

"For a couple of weeks after I was completely numb and couldn't train or do anything – it was a really tough time and everyone throughout Britain was very supportive, but they were sad, too. So many British people died in the tragedy that it probably helped to be here and see it wasn't only America that felt the devastation."

Still The Real Deal?

Steve McManaman was a likeable guy and, together with Robbie Fowler, he was part of an off-field double act that was never dull to be around. After a career with Liverpool and Real Madrid, the question was, did he have much more to give? In a double cover issue of the City Magazine (Claudio Reyna on one cover, McManaman the other), Kev Cummins came up with the headline 'Hey, Macca Reyna' – I doubt it will ever be topped...

It's an autumnal Wednesday afternoon in early October and Manchester City's Carrington training headquarters is a buzzing hive of activity.

Press officers run around trying to catch members of Kevin Keegan's squad for weekly interviews; journalists frantically pace up and down steps yapping into their mobile phones, while players go through the task of signing balls, cards and shirts.

Just standing in the midst of the commotion is enough to make one dizzy. One man, however, exudes a calmness and composure that is juxtaposed with the scene that unfolds around him.

Dressed in a baggy green jumper and a pair of dark blue jeans, Steve McManaman nonchalantly eases his way through the packed corridors, as he would through opposing defences, and puts his signature to the various souvenirs in his path.

Quite clearly, this is a man whom nothing flusters. Be it Champions League finals, media inquisitions or the headaches of moving from one country to another; not even a bolt of lightning could knock McManaman out of his long, languid style.

But this, remember, is a player who was Man of the Match for Liverpool by some distance in the 1992 FA Cup final. Even when he was just a spindly-legged 20-year-old, the big stage didn't hold any terrors.

Think of his virtuoso performance three years later when Liverpool won the Coca-Cola Cup final against Bolton that had the legendary Sir Stanley Matthews looking for superlatives to describe his two goals.

Then contemplate his mesmerising display in a star-studded Real Madrid side which waltzed away with Champions League in 2000 after beating Valencia 3-0 in the Stade de France.

Few players attempt to find the net with scissors kicks in such important games. Even fewer actually score. McManaman did try – and scored. That's why he is English football's most successful ever export.

Now, though, he is a Manchester City player, enticed back to the Premiership by Kevin Keegan's promise of helping the ultra-ambitious midfielder take his career onto a new plain.

Sitting down in the same room he was unveiled as Keegan's last summer signing, McManaman puffs out his cheeks, takes a gulp from his cup of tea and talks about the whirlwind that has been his last four weeks.

"As you can imagine, what with moving from Spain back to England, it has been a bit hectic, but my wife, Victoria, has been fantastic and helped a great deal, letting me concentrate on my football," said the Blues' new number 20.

"In that time, things have gone very well. We have got some good results and, bar a little tweak to my hamstring, I am feeling really good and enthusiastic about what lies ahead for the club and I.

"I am staying in Liverpool now, but I am looking for somewhere to live a bit closer to the training ground. Although Liverpool isn't that far away, it is just far enough to be a pain in the winter mornings.

"Travelling on the motorway, you never know what could happen, so I just want to find somewhere that little bit more local. It is nice to have come home, though, after what were four magnificent years with Real."

When leaving Liverpool after 364 games and 66 mostly spectacular goals, he embraced the challenge of life in La Liga with El Galicticos with both hands. Rewards came almost instantly.

"When I made up my mind to leave Liverpool, I knew I could have gone to another club in England, but I didn't really see the point in that because I had experienced almost everything and wanted to broaden my horizons," he recalled.

"Real fitted in perfectly and both myself and Victoria didn't have anything to tie us down and that made the move to Spain a lot easier for us and we learnt to speak Spanish almost immediately.

"That was a fantastic side when I first arrived, with players like Ivan Helguera, Raul and Fernando Redondo. We won the Champions League that first year and it was some way to finish."

That night in Paris clearly stirs his emotions. Having seen the replicas of the European Cup in the Anfield trophy room, to get his hands on it was something special.

"I had as many of my family and friends at the game as I possibly could," he said. "I scored the second goal and things went according to plan. The next thing I knew, I was standing there with this massive silver trophy in my hands!"

McManaman's arrival in the Spanish capital coincided with some of the most amazing transfers of the decade as President Florentino Perez set out to accrue the best players on the planet. No matter what the cost.

"The year after, we bought Luis Figo, who had just won World Footballer of the Year; 12 months later it was the same with ZZ (Zinedine Zidane) and then last year the same again with Ronny (Ronaldo)."

The mention of those three supremely gifted artists is enough to stir even the most cynical observer. Far from being overawed by their presence, McManaman made it his business to learn off them.

"They are all great blokes and good friends," he said. "But I have never been the type to be daunted by anything. When I was an apprentice at Liverpool, I used to clean John Barnes' boots and Peter Beardsley was there. They were both world stars."

Spanish life clearly suited McManaman. Though the media spotlight is intense, sports journalists do not scrutinise the lifestyle of the men they write about. Away from the pitch, he was left to his own devices.

"I loved Spain," he enthused. "I will go and live there again one day, maybe not Madrid. Even though I love it dearly, it is perhaps just that little bit too hectic to live there. But Spaniards are similar to me.

"They are very relaxed and like to take things easy. They eat late, they drink late. It is just a very sophisticated country. Players are treated like Gods and it was just an amazing experience."

Wherever he has been during his glittering career, awards have followed apace. As supporters of Real Madrid, Liverpool and Manchester City can testify, an on-song Steve McManaman is a sight to behold. Whether he can turn back the clock for the Blues remains to be seen.

Joey's First

I can clearly recall meeting Joey Barton for the first time – there was a real look of determination in his eyes and something that set him apart from any number of hopeful youngsters I'd spoken to before. He was a decent lad, too, and this would be the first of a number of colourful interviews over the years...

Few players hit the headlines before they've even made their first team debut, but young midfielder Joey Barton had the misfortune to do exactly that when he was poised to make his bow at Middlesbrough last November. He warmed up along the touchline and then was told by Kevin Keegan to get ready to go on. A vital piece of kit, however, was missing – his City shirt.

"I was told I was going on, so I went to warm up," said the likeable 20-year-old. "When I came back the boss told me to get stripped, so I put my pads on and went to put my shirt on, but it wasn't there. I think one of the Middleborough fans must have leaned over and took it because they were so close to the bench and it would have been easy.

"I was heartbroken. It meant I couldn't go on and my chance had gone. I didn't say a word on the coach home – I couldn't; the other players were telling me not to worry about it, but I was too gutted to talk. It was the realisation of a dream to play and to have it taken away like that was too much.

"It's up to the player whether you have your shirt already on under your tracksuit – some do, some don't – there's no rule as such, just whatever suits the individual. The ribbing I've had ever since, as you can imagine, has been unbelievable.

"They're all as bad as each other and the boss is one of the worst! The coaching staff are no different. The next reserve game I played in was probably as bad as it got. My shirt went missing four times off the peg, even up to half-time. It has helped ease the pain, but until I actually make my debut, it will always be hanging over me.

"Maybe in a few years I'll look back and have a laugh about it myself, but until I do, I'll have to put up with the stick."

Even when Joey later went outside to have his photograph taken, the players were leaning out of the rest area windows telling him not to forget his shirt, and half a dozen other bits of advice. It's likely he'll never really be able to forget it, but such is the healing process within a football club, making light of disappointment is the way of things, from pub players to those at top Premiership sides.

"Maybe it was down to fate," he reflected. "Maybe if I'd have gone on that day, something bad might have happened. I believe in all that stuff, so who knows?"

The set-up from the Academy and reserve set-up is helping Huytonborn Barton develop both as a player and as a young man. Clearly popular among his team-mates, he realises the demands that go with training with the first team squad and the spotlight it constantly puts him under.

"You have to be so much better as a player at this level," he admitted. "both physically and mentally, you have to be quicker in your mind as to what you're going to do next. When the ball comes to you, you have to know where it is going straight away because you don't get as much time on the ball.

"The players I'm surrounded by are quality internationals, and by training with them every day, it can only improve me as a player. Most of the senior lads are only too happy to pass on advice like Ali Benarbia who tells me certain ways to approach things on the pitch, and Shaun Goater who advises me on how to conduct myself off the field.

"I watch other lads, like Eyal, who have a certain skill or a way of doing something that I don't do, and try and learn from them. I've tried a few tricks and flicks that I've picked up from Eyal and Ali in training and even tried a couple in a reserve match, but the coaches didn't like it and told me – well, I won't say exactly what they said – let's just say they advised me not to mess about!"

Joey's former team-mates in the Academy have progressed well in their leagues and the FA Youth Cup this season, but he hasn't been able to watch them at all due to his elevation to the first team squad. He still lives on Merseyside and this restricts his opportunities to watch City's Academy teams in action.

"I haven't been to any games so far," he said. "I still live in Liverpool and because I don't drive, it's hard for me to get up and see them in action, but I know most of the lads and they've got a great side and have done really well. They were unlucky not to win the FA Youth Cup this year, but I'm sure they'll be even stronger next year."

It's a tough time to be an English youngster because of the direction football has taken in this country. There are so many quality foreign imports at almost every club; homegrown talent has to fight tooth and nail to first earn their chance, and then make sure they stay there. The Blues have seen a number of young footballers make the fringes of the first team but not quite break through. Chris Shuker, who was loaned out to Walsall last month, is a case in point. Barton is well aware of the challenges ahead but is unfazed by it all and certainly has confidence in his own ability.

"I think that when I get my chance, I will show the City fans and the manager what I can do. My style is more defensive, like that of Roy Keane or Patrick Viera. I graft more than the attacking midfielders and like to play just in front of the defence. I think if I do play, I will stay in the team because I have something to offer. I don't think there is anyone who plays the way I do, so I can offer a variation. You just have to prove you can do it in the Premiership. I've got to keep working hard and wait for my chance."

Kevin Keegan has hinted he may well blood some of the youngsters at his disposal in the final weeks of the season. Both Barton – an Everton fan as a lad – and Mikkel Bischoff have been praised by the manager and should see some action before the end of the season. Another scouser, Robbie Fowler, gives Joey a lift to Carrington from their homes in Liverpool, not a bad way to get to work!

"He gives me a ride in and is a great lad. He's an Everton fan and a Liverpool legend, which is a bit unusual when you think about it," acknowledged Barton.

Away from football, Barton is gaining a reputation as a promising golfer and claims he has to give Gerard Wiekens lessons because he is so poor. He urges me to describe just how the Dutchman is at golf, but there are kids that read this interview! He admits it is tough for any 21-year-old in the game to keep his feet on the ground, but a tight-knit group of family friends ensure he remains his old self as he attains more publicity.

"What hit home for me was when I was arriving for training recently and a young lad said 'Alright Joey' and I hadn't a clue who he was, but he knew me. It made me think that wherever I was, out with friends, playing golf or whatever, people would be watching me and how I acted, and I suppose it made me grow up a little quicker," he concluded.

"My dad and mates are the first to give me a ribbing if something has gone wrong, so because of the background I've come from, I don't think I could change much as a person. The coaching staff and players at the club would never let me get away with it anyway!

"I just hope I get a chance to play at Maine Road for the first team before the club moves to the new stadium. I'm desperate for that to happen so I can say I played there in years to come. That's my ambition at the moment."

Zabaleta plays the ball inside for Silva, who is put under pressure and concedes a throw. City win the ball back, Tevez slides in Silva on the left-hand side and he plays a cross deep into the QPR box, but the danger is cleared to Barton who is fouled...

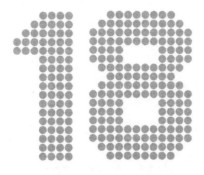

The Magician

When Eyal Berkovic signed for City for just £1.5m, Kevin Keegan had unearthed a genuine bargain. A brilliant footballer and often a class apart, it was a pleasure to catch up with the Israeli genius who always said things exactly the way he saw them...

Eyal Berkovic arrived at Maine Road in the summer of 2001 costing Kevin Keegan just £1.5 million from Celtic. After successful spells with Blackburn Rovers (on loan), Southampton, and particularly West Ham United, the Israeli midfielder's career went on hold with the Glasgow giants where things just didn't work out.

City offered him the opportunity to re-establish himself as one of the best playmakers in Europe and he has done exactly that by making his transfer fee look like peanuts. There a few players who have the ability to dominate a game the way he did at Old Trafford last February and as he deservedly picked up his Man of the Match award, he was busily telling everybody he could improve!

"I'm probably playing as well as I did when I was with West Ham," declared the hugely likeable Berkovic. "I played well against United but I can still improve by scoring and making more goals. If I can do that, I will be at my very best. It's all about teamwork.

"It was nice that people said I played well at Old Trafford, but it wasn't my best game for City, in my opinion. As a team, we only really performed in the second half, but because it was United we were playing, the headlines were bigger. I'm happy that the fans are happy."

Eyal is very much a team player and when he first arrived at Maine Road, he was keen for people not to make comparisons between himself and Gio Kinkladze, claiming he was a completely different footballer.

After almost two years with the Blues, the difference is obvious. Kinkladze was a great individual player, whereas the Israeli star is the beating heart of the City team and is literally everywhere during a game. His stamina levels are incredible and he covers an amazing amount of ground during a match.

He is on course for his best ever tally of appearances this season since first arriving in England back in 1996, and despite a niggling stomach injury, he puts his improved fitness down to hard work.

"I've been working really hard on the training ground this season," he revealed. "I give one hundred per cent to keep my fitness because it is such a big part of my game. I like to see as much as I can of the ball during a game and keep moving around the pitch for 90 minutes.

"I've tried to avoid injury as best I can but I've been a little bit unlucky lately with my stomach muscle problem. But I'm not letting it stop me and will train and play through the pain."

Moving to Manchester has suited the Berkovic family well and Eyal promises his young son, Lior, will be a big City star in the future – remember the name. They are very settled in the city and Eyal's on-field form reflects his happiness off the pitch. He is also one of the most popular players at the club.

"When you are happy, it makes it easy to come and train and to get along with other players and the staff, and that is how I feel. Everything is very enjoyable for me here, and if you feel happy and settled off the pitch, it is a great help when you are on it."

One of his trademarks is the gloriously threaded passes he regularly makes inside defenders for the forwards or wing-backs to move on to. I ask if such a skill can be learned, but Eyal is not so sure…

"This is what God gave me," he said with a broad smile. "This is the only thing God gave me, though. All the rest I worked very hard to achieve. Every footballer has a special talent and mine is balance and vision, but there are also a lot of things the manager doesn't like! I have plusses and minuses.

"I'm pleased the City fans are happy with my performances. I always try my best for them and give one hundred per cent every time I go on the pitch, but sometimes I know that they don't like it when I don't tackle, but I'm trying to do this more often now.

"It has improved over the past few months and the coach Derek Fazackerley told me I made eight tackles against United and I won most of them, so I must have improved! I know this isn't the strongest part of my game.

"My strengths are to be creative within the side and use my vision, but I need to tackle as well because it is part of modern game."

Berkovic has scored some fantastic goals in his time with the Blues. The solo effort against Norwich, the superb strike against Burnley and the exquisite volley in the FA Cup tie at Ipswich last season were matched with a cracker against Crewe and Bolton this campaign. Doesn't he ever score tap-ins?

"Not really, no," he replied, honest as ever. "This is why I don't really score a lot of goals, because I don't go looking for the tap-ins. This is something I don't like in my game and perhaps I should be a little greedier at times and shoot more often, but it's difficult to change how I play because I'm always looking to pass the ball all the time."

Like everybody else connected to the club, Eyal is excited about City's move to the City of Manchester Stadium this summer and there are few who would disagree that it is a worthy stage for his sublime skills.

"I have been only once to the new stadium and it's magnificent," he declared. "I'm really looking forward to playing there and it is a dream of every footballer to play in a stadium such as this and I'm sure the City fans will create a fantastic atmosphere for every home game."

The talented Israeli is a huge star back home where he is also known as 'Kosem', which translates to 'The Magician', and he acknowledges City are probably the most popular Premiership team in his country.

"Every City game is live in Israel." He revealed. "There are a lot of City supporters there now. I know quite a few and some are mad Blues, travelling to Manchester to watch the games whenever they can."

He is only 30 years old and is at the peak of his game. The matching of player and club seems perfect and all City fans will hope he is in the team for many more seasons to come. Ali Benarbia has proved it is possible to perform to high standards into the mid-thirties and there are a whole host of other examples around the world. The question is, how long does Eyal Berkovic want to continue with the Blues?

"Ask the manager!" he said with a beaming smile. It is patently clear that the player would like to remain with City for many years to come, and if he continues to perform as exceptionally as he has this season, he may well walk away with the Player of the Year award for the first time, too.

In Safe Hands

David Seaman was a larger than life character — he seemed to enjoy every moment of his time with City, even though he knew it would be his last season as a professional. We spoke at a photoshoot at City's new stadium in the warm Manchester sunshine...

If laughter is the best form of medicine, then it is little wonder that David Seaman is contemplating extending his top-flight career to a 20th season.

Genial, humorous, not to mention one of the best keepers in English football, a smile and a chuckle is never far from the lips of the City's number one — even at the most testing of times.

There have been certain members of the media who have seemingly had a vendetta against Seaman ever since an outrageous Ronaldinho free-kick during England's 2002 World Cup quarter-final defeat to Brazil beat him.

Since leaving Arsenal to replace Peter Schmeichel for City, his every move has been scrutinized. Those vultures have been ready to pick on the slightest mistake. For some people, that attention could prove too much. Not Seaman.

Having experienced every spectrum of the footballing world during a career that has taken him from Leeds to Eastlands via spells at Peterborough, Birmingham, QPR and Arsenal, the 40 year-old takes the brickbats and bouquets in equal measure.

Happily adjusted to life with the Blues following a glorious 13 years at Highbury, Seaman admits that things have gone like clockwork from the time he took up Kevin Keegan's offer in June.

"It's been great," admitted Seaman, who serenaded City-supporting ex-colleague Lee Dixon with a unique version of Blue Moon when he found out he would be signing for the Blues.

"There has been a bit of stick flying around, as usual, but other than that, everything has been fine. Obviously, it was difficult to leave Arsenal, but I have come to an absolutely quality place.

"The training centre is superb. Arsenal's was excellent and I wondered what this place was going to be like. But, to be fair, it was just as good. This is where we come every day to do all our work, and it is great that everything is catered for.

"The icing on the cake is that we get to play in a stadium as good as the one we do every other week. So from that point of view, it has been fantastic. I've found somewhere to live and my family is up here regularly, too, now.

"It's a new challenge and you've got to win over a new set of fans. Some people had a go at me after the Lokeren game, but they are entitled to their opinion. If they feel that I have made a mistake, so be it."

For a man who has won three league championships, as well as a glut of other trophies, David confesses that the thing that has taken him the longest to get used to is City's age-old idiosyncratic tendencies.

Brilliant some games, baffling in others, the Rotherham-born stopper has been perplexed at how certain occasions – and in the space of 90 minutes – City have looked both like Champions League contenders and cannon fodder.

The challenge now, as Seaman points out, is to find the consistency to make the Blues into a genuine top four side. Though it won't happen overnight, he reckons the nucleus is there for a bright future.

"The strange thing for me is that things have been so unpredictable, and it hasn't just been for one game to the next," he agreed.

"We can play really well for some periods during the games but, in other parts, drop off. Charlton away on the first day of the season is probably the most consistent that we have played.

"We have been scrapping through here and there, getting points and wins. I just feel that there is so much more to come. It is heartening because we have got so much quality here. It's just a case of getting it all together.

"If we have a game on the training pitch, I want to win, no matter what. If you get the competitive edge up in training, it serves you well in the big games. If I can spread some of the winning mentality we have at Arsenal, I will have achieved something.

"The good thing is that everyone mixes together. Yes, there are little groups, but it's not as if you can't go and sit with those people. There are no cliques or animosity. All the lads enjoy taking the Mick out of each other. It's good banter.

"I haven't started looking back on things just yet – that's for when I retire. But it is nice to have the feelings of going up to pick up trophies like I have done. It's one hell of a feeling, I can tell you."

Away from football, David's ideal form of relaxation is to spend as much time as he possibly can camped out on the riverbank, angling, just like team-mates Paul Bosvelt and Nick Weaver, once Britain's Best Young Angler winner.

"I haven't found anywhere to fish around here yet where you can catch the really big carp. When I go fishing, I do it properly. I'll take a tent and go overnight. I'd go all week, given half the chance!

"The really good anglers go all day and all night. Places like France, Bulgaria and Romania are the best. Again, though, that's all for when I retire. Summer holidays are just for the family!

"Bosvelt is more into his fly fishing, but I have done that as well. And yes, Nick has told me all about the prize. He's even shown me a picture of the fish! I suppose he thinks he'll be able to show me a trick or two when he gets the chance!"

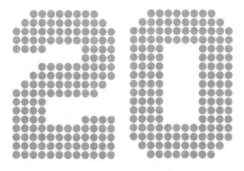

German Precision

Michael Tarnat was another player many City fans wish had come to the club long before he had. Nearing the end of his career, he was a class act with a thunderous shot on him. For a free transfer, he was terrific value...

It didn't take long for City fans watching the TNS match to work out that new German signing Michael Tarnat is a class act. Defenders of his quality become available for free very rarely, and he looks sure to become a crucial part of the first team in the coming months.

His debut against the Welsh minnows last week was not merely restricted to polished defending – the accuracy and pace of his cross-field passing was quite magnificent and the rapturous reception he received when substituted showed what an impact he'd made on the home support.

A new stadium, new team-mates and a new country – quite a lot for the eloquent former international to absorb in one go, and a big difference from this time last year.

"I was thinking that I would play for two more years and then retire," said Tarnat. "Then Munich told me I could go after last season, when I had found another club. Then Kevin Keegan came to me and asked me if I could play for Manchester City and I said 'of course!'

"For me it was a dream come true to come and play in England, and now my dream is just beginning."

Tarnat is well aware of the strong links between City and Germany. Bert Trautmann, Uwe Rosler, Maurizio Gaudino, Eike Immel and several others have represented the club over the years with distinction, and he is keen to join the list.

"I had heard of City and knew of the strong links with my country. There is a great tradition of German players coming to Manchester City and it is a big challenge for me to continue that successful relationship.

"I spoke with the manager before I signed and he told me that he thought my vast experience of European football would benefit the club both in the Premiership and in Europe. If I can use the experience I have gained over the years to help my team-mates, it's not a problem. I want to help as much as I can.

"I think we have a good team, with some great new signings and a very good set of players already here. I think we have a good chance to do well in the Premier League – last season the club finished ninth and I believe we can definitely improve on that and aim for fifth or sixth.

"As for European competition, we need to learn as we progress and see how far we can go. If we win through to the third or fourth round, you would have to say you never know what can happen from there.

"I've enjoyed my first few weeks in England and I like the fact the crowd are so near to the pitch. In Germany we have running tracks around many grounds and most of the stadiums are old. In England, every club has a nice stadium and there are big crowds with a good atmosphere.

"The atmosphere in the City of Manchester Stadium against Barcelona was okay, but I think most people were watching the stadium rather than the football! I enjoyed it against TNS but I'm really looking forward to the Premiership games because I think it will be much better."

Michael has been compared in some quarters to City coach Stuart Pearce, but he says he isn't aware of that, but doesn't mind, all the same!

"I didn't know that!" he laughed. "But it is a big compliment for me. I played against him in the World Cup semi-final in 1990 and people in Germany said Stuart Pearce was crazy! However, he is a legend in England and to be compared in any way to him is nice for me."

Tarnat believes his English isn't too good at the present, but he speaks very well and seems very relaxed and settled at the club already. His left-foot thunderbolts have already had the other City players commenting that they wouldn't like to be lining up in a defensive wall with Michael preparing to take a free-kick.

All in all, a tidy piece of business by Keegan.

QPR struggle to clear the cross and City pick the ball up on the right-hand side with Zabaleta. The ball switches flanks from right to left and then back to right before Zabaleta drills in a right-footed cross, but it eludes everyone including Aguero and goes out for a throw-in...

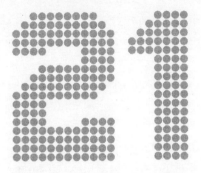

Best Defence

The thought of City's defence without Sylvain Distin as part of it had become unthinkable. A beast of a defender, the classy Frenchman had everything in his locker to become one of the best in the world. This was the second interview I had with him and he was a really likeable guy, too...

It was on a hot summer evening in Odense when Sylvain Distin's name was entered permanently into City's history books.

Emerging from the tunnel, leading his team out to battle, the elegant French defender wore the captain's armband for the first time as sole proprietor and thus joined a select band that included legends such as Colin Bell and Tony Book.

With Ali Benarbia and Peter Schmeichel both retired, boss Kevin Keegan had no hesitation in making Distin – whom he signed for £3.5m from Paris St Germain just 12 months earlier – his new leader. He had already sampled the captain's role at the end of last season in the absence of Schmeichel and Benarbia.

Distin admitted to being surprised when he was informed of the decision. Having only been at the club for 12 months – indeed having only turned professional at 22 – the Frenchman was concerned that he lacked experience for the role. Not Keegan.

He was certain that in Distin, he had a player who was committed to the club for many years and, not only that, a supremely talented defender whom he could build his rearguard around.

"I see Sylvain as a leader by example," praised the Blues chief. "He has been 100 per cent committed to everything we do in training or in matches, and that is why he has got the captain's armband."

The season could not have started better for both City and Distin. An exciting brand of football was being played; a place among the Champions League challenger's beckons and Distin even scored his first goal for the club.

Autumn, though, unexpectedly provided the first major test of his captaincy. For players, management and supporters alike, a nightmare November and wretched December left them shuffling uneasily as the Blues slid down the Premiership.

It is testing times such as these that players learn more about themselves, and the former Newcastle man admits he found it difficult to take a more vociferous role in the dressing room. It is a challenge, though, that he has grasped with both hands.

"We have had a bad time of things lately, but we are trying hard to reverse it every day in training. We just keep on going," he said, eating segments of an orange while reclining on a plush couch at the Carrington training retreat.

"In some of the games, we hadn't really played that bad. It was just a case that the luck wasn't with us, but to cancel that, you just have to be a bit more confident.

"You always feel an extra responsibility. It is not just down to one man, though. It is the whole team that has to take responsibility. I am proud to be captain, but if I didn't have the armband and we were playing badly, I would feel the same.

"I would do all I could to help out. But as skipper, I say my bit and do everything to get the lads up again.

"That is something I have had to change in my game and I am not really used to doing that. Maybe I have been concentrating on the others too much and not on myself. I don't know. That is not an excuse, but I know I have to do more."

Reflecting on the moment that Keegan told him he would be his new skipper, Sylvain admitted it was a huge privilege to be given such a position having spent such a short time at the club.

"It was a great honour to be given the armband, I was very proud, in fact," he said. "I had only played two years in England, three in total as a professional, and then suddenly I was asked to captain the club.

"I have made a big jump, a massive jump, and I still have to improve. I haven't got a lot of experience, so with each game I am still learning more and more. Being made captain has made me want to learn about the game more quickly.

"It is hard being captain when you are in the middle of a bad run, but you have to get on with it. But it is good conditions to learn in and you get on with it."

News comes through that Manchester United have just taken the lead at Sunderland through Rooney's strike...

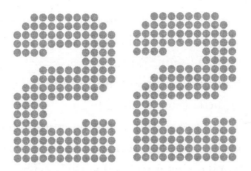

Mountains To Climb

It's hard sometimes when you interview a young lad and you can see the obstacles in his way. Kevin Stuhr-Ellegaard was a case in point. With a lot of experienced goalkeepers blocking his path to first team football, it was interesting to hear what he had to say and what his realistic ambitions were...

Kevin Stuhr-Ellegaard has come through a difficult start to his first team career determined to prove that he is a more than able deputy for David Seaman and a challenger for the former England goalkeeper's number one spot.

The last 12 months have seen Kevin move up in the first team pecking order in the most dramatic fashion, with Carlo Nash and Brian

Murphy both leaving the club and Nick Weaver possibly sidelined for the next year.

It's been a tough start for the young Dane and, in truth, he couldn't have won his first team spurs at a worse time, with City saving their worst display of the season for his Premiership bow against Leicester last month.

The 20-year-old was given little protection as virtually all the Foxes' on-target shots ended in the back of his net, but though his confidence could have taken a severe dent, he knows he has to get on with things and not let setbacks arrest his impressive progress.

"It was really disappointing," admitted Ellegaard. "It wasn't a good day for the team against Leicester, but I had to just put it out of my mind because it doesn't pay to dwell on games like that.

"It wasn't the best way to make my debut, but it was a tough game and we didn't play well as a team. I was obviously a little nervous about the occasion, but it happened so quickly that I didn't have much time to think too much about it.

"It was wonderful to play in the stadium in front of our own fans, but it was just a bad day at the office all-round."

David Seaman returned for the 3-0 defeat at Newcastle but Ellegaard was again on duty for City's next home game against Middlesbrough. The former Farum 'keeper must have felt the gods were against him when, despite one smart save from a right-wing cross earlier in the game, he was beaten by his own team-mate when a wicked low drive sped across the box and struck the boot of Jihai Sun for a bizarre own goal that he could do nothing about.

"Sometimes you have to learn the hard way," he said. "The first game I had three goals put past me and the second match we lost to an own goal. The odds seemed stacked against us in those two matches for some reason, but I've not been moping about it.

"Yes, I am inexperienced at the moment, but I'm not going to tell the defenders they have to take care of me out on the pitch because I'm young and relatively new to the Premiership. They do their best for me and vice versa, but things weren't going well for us at the time."

He showed his ability with almost the last touch of the game as he produced a superb fingertip save to Boudewijn Zenden's injury-time shot, but it was a match that the Blues could have probably played until the following morning without finding the net.

Ellegaard must have been cursing his luck again when City's woeful run continued at Tottenham, and again he was, for a period, fighting a losing battle with the Tottenham forward line who fired in shots at will.

"That game at Tottenham was awful," he recalled, shaking his head. "But it was just the first half that we were really poor and didn't look like a team at all. In the second half, I thought we played a lot better and got our passing game together, but the damage had been done.

"In that game, I actually had the chance to save some shots because we were under pressure for a while, and I admit could have done better with the first goal, but at my age, it doesn't pay to dwell on things like that – I just need to get on with things, let it go and make sure I do better next time. If you don't adopt that attitude, it could ruin your confidence."

With young Kasper Schmeichel the next in line after Ellegaard, is he passing on advice to the son of the man who inspired him to become a goalkeeper in the first place?

"Kasper has his dad to advise him, but if I see something I think I can help him with, I'll offer my help, but if he doesn't want to listen, that's fine," he revealed. "We're good mates and he knows when to listen to me and I know when he's not, so I just stop speaking!

"He wants to learn everything, and when his dad is not around, I'll pass on anything I know that he has passed on to me."

A bizarre twist in many ways, and not one he perhaps imagined when he was a junior at Farum, but then Kevin playing football for the manager he was christened after, Kevin Keegan, is perhaps even stranger still!

Silva attempts to weave through the QPR back line before the ball is cleared and Wright-Phillips drives forward and wins a free-kick in his own half. Cisse lifts the ball over Barry's head before being brought down; QPR free-kick on the edge of the City box...

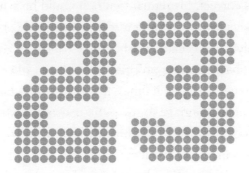

Onward Christian Soldier

Christian Negouai represented a shift in sights regarding player purchases – the Blues seemed to be bringing in free transfers and modestly priced talent. Negouai was unknown to City fans and his career would be brief. The momentum gained from promotion had subsided as the funds dried up...

Luck is not a word you would associate with Christian Negouai since his £1.5m move from Belgian club Charleroi. In fact, you could be forgiven for thinking that the quiet, Martinique-born midfielder had run over a pack of black cats, walked under a succession of ladders and had an argument with a dozen gypsies since signing for City. And that's just off the pitch! On it, he's been sent off and incurred the wrath of Rotherham United's players for scoring what was – at best – a dubious goal in a Division One match at Maine Road and goodness knows what else. Perhaps not that incredible in the grand scheme of things, but he's only played five games so far for the club!

It would be fair to say that the likeable Negouai hasn't really had the chance to show what he can really do, and if Kevin Keegan's assessment of his talents is correct, his return to fitness could be a huge bonus for City and he is keen start over after a nightmare couple of years.

"It's been really tough because I've been out so long," admitted Negouai. "I've only been back training properly a month, so I know I can't rush things. I need to get back to full fitness but I need to pace myself.

"I suffered cruciate damage to my right knee and had problems with my left knee, too. I've never been injured before, so to get two major problems at the same time is maybe a bit unlucky."

Christian spent three weeks relaxing on his home island of Martinique during the summer as he prepared mentally for the challenges ahead. He not only has to get back to where he was two years ago with his fitness levels, he also has to oust the likes of Paul Bosvelt and Joey Barton for a place in the first team.

"It was nice to see my family and friends and everyone knew about Manchester City, believe me!" he recalled. "I returned feeling refreshed and have enjoyed being part of the pre-season build-up."

Thousands of Blues witnessed Negouai in action at Oldham and his towering presence added a new dimension to the midfield. He almost capped an impressive match with a thunderous drive that hit the bar.

"I was just happy to take part," said the 28-year-old. "I know there are a lot of great players at the club, and I realise I have come from a modest club in Charleroi, but I hope opportunities will arise for me this season. I want to build-up my strength and see what happens."

The Iceman Cometh

Arnie Arason was another low-key signing – but was a decent guy, into his music and knew his first team chances were limited. He would have a couple of memorable games before moving on…

Arnie Arason was still attuning to life at Manchester City when he made his debut in the epic FA Cup fourth round replay with Tottenham last month. He had been a free agent following the completion of the Norwegian season in December.

He decided to leave Rosenberg after several successful seasons with the champions of Norway and an opportunity to play in Austria arose. That fell through and the Blues made their move. Since then, he's become an instant favourite with the fans and is hoping that he can remain with the Blues for the foreseeable future.

"It happened very quickly," said the Icelandic number one. "My contract with Rosenberg expired at the end of December and I was looking for a new club. I almost went to Austria, but that didn't happen, and then City came in and the thought of joining them excited me."

Capped 33 times for his country, he came initially on trial but had soon sufficiently impressed the coaching staff enough to be offered a deal until the end of the season.

"It was a week before the club offered me a contract," he revealed. "I'm really happy to be here. I've had approaches from other clubs while I was at Rosenberg, but I enjoyed playing for them so never talked to anyone else.

"As far as my career was going, I was playing Champions League football every season because Rosenberg always won the Norwegian title – always! But after six years, I felt I wanted to try something new, and so far, I've enjoyed my time at City."

While he kept goal for Norway's finest, former City player Aage Hareide – who now manages the Norwegian national team – coached him for one season. Did he mention City as a possible future destination for Arnie?

"No, because the season was over and the move had nothing to do with Aage," he declared. "I knew he had played for City and I've always followed English football, so I've a good knowledge of the game and teams over here because my dad is a City fan!

"I also realise I'm the first player from Iceland to play for City, which is nice, but I know the City fans in Iceland are even happier."

Toure dispossesses Wright-Phillips easily and then finds Nasri on the right-hand side. Nasri runs at Taiwo before drilling in a cross which Aguero nearly reaches but is blocked by the defender. Then Wright-Phillips handballs on the edge of his own area and gives away a free-kick in a dangerous position...

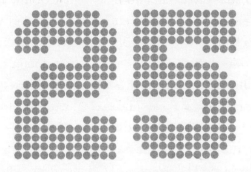

More Joey Wisdom

Having forced his way into the team, Joey was already soon making an impact – this brief interview was prior to the Manchester derby and he was keen to resume his battle with United's Roy Keane...

Joey Barton is champing at the bit to add a bit of balance to the Manchester derby bragging rights today after suffering two defeats to the Blues' deadliest rivals in the space of just two months.

Few would argue Barton was one of the few City players to come out of the Premiership United defeat with any real credit and he was again mixing it in the middle of the park with Roy Keane for the FA Cup tie last month. He was also a whisker from scoring an equaliser in the second half, but was denied by a breathtaking Tim Howard stop.

Those defeats are now confined to the history books and if Barton plays today, he will be as eager as any City supporter to compound the Reds' Champions League exit against Porto by all but ending their Premiership hopes with a home victory.

The young England midfielder is available again after suspension kept him out of the Liverpool and Birmingham City matches, but he sharpened his fitness with a competitive display in last week's reserve derby at Altrincham that ended 3-3.

Barton scored in that game with a drilled left-footed shot that can't have failed to impress his manager, who was watching from the stand.

"I don't get too many of those," he said. "I had a chat with the gaffer this week and he thought it would be a good idea if I played in the reserve match. I missed the Chelsea game because the team did ever so well while I was out. With no match last weekend, I haven't played now for nearly a month.

"So it was great to get out again and play a competitive game. It was just like the old days playing in the reserves. In the end, the lads did well to get a draw after playing 65 minutes with only 10 men."

If Barton does play, he may well be counting the bruises on his shins after the inevitable crunching clashes with Manchester United skipper Roy Keane. If, however, he has helped the Blues to a vital win and thrown a spanner in the Reds' title aspirations at the same time, chances are the warm victory glow will ease any aches or twinges.

City fans have always loved a performer who gives one hundred per cent every time they pull on the blue jersey and that's why Barton is one of the most popular players at the club. Quelling Keane and helping earn three points today will only enhance his profile among the supporters.

Dutch Courage

Paul Bosvelt was a fisherman, designer and owned a Harley Davidson. A typically laid-back Dutchman, he liked my shoes and asked where I'd bough them – next day he had a pair! A first! Although his best playing days had passed, he was a player who would give the club decent service...

Paul Bosvelt may not have enjoyed the most auspicious starts to his Manchester City career, but things have taken a marked turn for the better since he won his place back against Liverpool just after Christmas.

From a personal and international point of view, the timing couldn't have been better. Bosvelt has always maintained that the City faithful had yet to see the best of him and a combination of suspension, injury and squad rotation meant that he only made half a dozen Premiership starts in the first team in 2003.

For a player who has been a regular since being a teenager in Holland, sitting in the stand or on the bench was a new experience and not one he is desperate to repeat for any length.

"Yeah, I was out of the side for a while for one reason or another," said Bosvelt. "But I've been in the side for several games now and I feel I'm getting the rhythm and the fitness I need to perform the way I know I can.

"Watching from the sidelines wasn't easy but it definitely gives you a different perspective on the game. There will be times when you are on the pitch when you think the game is fast flowing, but, in fact, it isn't the case.

"It's easier to understand why the crowd gets frustrated at certain things when you are actually sat among them. You see things that you think you might do differently and it makes you more determined to get back and actually do that.

"But I had to wait for my chance and do my best in training to get my place back, which hopefully I've done at the moment."

Indeed, Bosvelt has become one of the Blues' most consistent performers in the last few weeks with some excellent displays as the midfield anchorman, and he also played a starring role in the Blues' last FA Cup tie at Leicester City. He has the art of breaking up play on the edge of his own box and setting counter-attacks into motion.

He needs this kind of form not only to keep his place, but to impress Dutch national boss Dick Advocaat if he is to book his flight for the European Championships in Portugal next summer.

"As I've said before," said Bosvelt, "the Dutch manager knows what I can do, but I have to be playing first team football to be in with a chance of being selected for the Holland team.

"Of course, I have ambitions to play for my country in Portugal, but that is only the second part of the equation. I want to be at my very best for Manchester City and a long run in the side will help me get my energy and rhythm. I've had to wait for my chance but now I aim to grab it."

Off the field of play, Bosvelt has settled well to his new surrounds, especially as he is now in his house. At least he now has a shed to call his own and a place to store his fishing rods, though his love of motorbikes is on the back-burner for a little while.

"I've always felt at home in England," he declared. "Even more so when I moved from the hotel to my house. The football side of things wasn't going too well, but things have changed now in a positive way, which is much better for me because that's why I came here, to play – not just for the nice weather!

"If I had to give my time so far at City a mark out of ten, I'd say it could have been better from a football point of view, so I'd give it a six."

15:27

Jamie Mackie brings the ball forward before winning
a throw-in in the City half...

An American Tale II

*More words of wisdom from the USA skipper who
had by this time settled in well at City. We spoke as the
Blues were poised for a European return against Welsh
minnows TNS. Real Madrid seemed a long way off...*

Claudio Reyna's path to the City of Manchester Stadium is a
little different from that of most footballers at the club. For
one, he grew up in a country where football – at least as we
know it – is not the national sport.

But with 96 caps under his belt, he's one of the most decorated
American footballers ever, with appearances in two World Cup finals
(he missed the 1998 tournament through injury), two Olympic Games
and he also became the first player from the USA to captain a side in

Europe while at Rangers and also the first American to be voted in to the FIFA All-Star side. That's a lot of firsts!

It was at the 2002 World Cup that he really excelled when he captained the States to the quarter-finals where they controversially lost 1-0 to Germany.

"The whole of that World Cup was definitely one of the major highlights of my career," admitted Reyna. "We finally came out on the biggest stage possible and made it to the last eight. It was also the manner we lost against Germany, too.

"We played well and everyone thought we deserved to win – even the Germans! We were so close to the semi-finals and we still think 'What if...?' but overall it was a great experience and for me to captain the team was really special.

"It was also nice because we put soccer on the map back home. We were front page news in the papers and on television and it was just what the country needed. The interest since has been really good and we get around 30,000 for our home games, which is double the gates of about ten years ago."

After being voted young player of the year twice (1992 and 1993) in his homeland, he was snapped up after the 1994 World Cup by Bayer Leverkusen. From there he was loaned to fellow Bundesliga outfit Wolfsburg and he was instrumental in helping them qualify for the UEFA Cup in his first season there.

He remained with them for another season before moving to Glasgow Rangers in 1999. Reyna had a successful stay with the Scottish Premier League champions, playing in the Champions League for three years running and making 63 league appearances for the Ibrox club before signing for Sunderland in a £4.5million deal in 2001.

He almost joined Fulham before the transfer window closed, but once he was made aware of City's interest, there was only one club he was going to sign for, much to the displeasure of Fulham boss Chris Coleman.

His experience in European competition will be invaluable for the Blues and along with Steve McManaman and David Seaman, he is probably one of the most seasoned players when it comes to top-level continental football. Though unavailable for tonight's game with Lokeren, he knows all about the potential banana skins that European football occasionally throws up.

"You can't take any team in European competition for granted," Reyna warned. "From my experience, the smaller teams are often the more difficult matches than playing some of the bigger clubs.

"For whatever reason, there'll be times when you go to a club with a small stadium in a country you've never been to and it's harder to get yourself motivated. There's no doubt that we will be a big scalp for them, so they'll be really up for it."

Cisse attempts to play a deep cross, however, Wright-Phillips fails to reach the ball and it goes out for a throw-in to City...

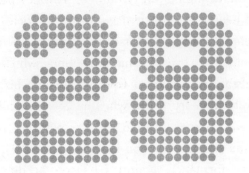

Mersey Paradise

Nobody doubted Robbie Fowler was one of the best natural goalscorers of his generation — but after leaving Liverpool via Leeds United, City fans were a little sceptical as to whether he still had it in him to score at the highest level — it represented another expensive Keegan gamble at best...

It is just over 12 months since Kevin Keegan drove down the M62 to Liverpool to persuade Robbie Fowler that his future lay with Manchester City. It could prove be the best two gallons of petrol the Blues chief has ever used.

After a slow start to life at City, when injuries and a lack of goals stalled his career, Fowler is now starting to hit top gear again. At his best, the

England international is certainly a Rolls Royce among strikers.

Much to Keegan's and the supporters' delight, Fowler has been hitting the net like he did during his pomp with Liverpool, with whom he won a clutch of honours and become one of the most feared strikers in Europe.

It is ironic, then, that while City's collective fortunes have not been the best since the beginning on November, Fowler's performances in that time have been excellent. Hard work and endeavour have been spiced with creativity. And, of course, goals.

This has all helped win over a demanding public, who understandably expected an instant return from Fowler following his £6m transfer from Leeds but became frustrated when he failed to find his range.

But if proof was needed how much his stock has risen, one need only think of the standing ovation he was afforded when substituted following his performance against Charlton at the beginning of January.

Settled in a new home in his native Liverpool and free of the injuries that blighted his days at Leeds, Fowler is moving with a noticeable spring in his step once again and a smile has replaced a once furrowed brow.

"It has been good for me recently," said Fowler, who was December's Player of the Month. "The start of the season wasn't too great and for 11 months things hadn't really been going my way, but once it all starts coming together, it's a big relief.

"Although results have been great for the last couple of months, from my point of view, it has been much, much better.

"I could understand the frustrations of the fans. When I first came here I was brought to score goals and I simply wasn't delivering. It has taken 12 months to win them over, but I hope I can keep doing that now.

"Although Liverpool is only 30 miles from here, I found it quite hard to settle when I first signed for the club. I have got used to the drive over now and I'm feeling settled and I think that is showing through in my football."

Clearly. During the early part of the season, when he was desperate to prove himself a hit with City supporters, Fowler started trying to do things he had never done before on the pitch.

Different moves, different runs, delaying shots that you would normally expect him to gobble up. The ball, however, would not run for him. This, in turn, caused much frustration in the stands and Fowler was aware how fans were nonplussed with him.

Happily, though, there were a few people to whom he was able to turn to in his hour of need. During his barren spell, his mobile phone never stopped ringing with messages of support from friends and former team-mates.

One man became a particularly frequent caller in that period. Liverpool legend Ian Rush – the man who helped polish Fowler's unique skills when they were together at Anfield – simply told him to get back to what he did best.

Once that lesson was heeded, the difference in Fowler's game was evident. Back came the zipping runs in behind bewildered defenders, the first time shots and – most importantly – a flurry of goals.

There was a clear zing in his game when he scored a superb header during City's 2-1 Boxing Day defeat at Birmingham and it was also evident when his former employers visited Eastlands two days later. Again he found himself on the scoresheet.

"I played for Liverpool from when I was 11 and to score any goal is great, but when you do it against your old club, it is that bit special," said Fowler. "Saying that, it could have been anyone that day, I just desperately wanted to score.

"I spoke to Rushie quite a lot. He is always complimenting me, giving me advice and telling me what I should and should not be doing. I always listen to what he says. There have been others, too, like John Aldridge and some other ex-Liverpool players.

"They have all been very helpful. But as for Rushie – even though he is now working at Liverpool – he still takes time out from his day to leave messages for me and that means a lot because he is a legend.

"He has achieved absolutely everything in the game. When I was at Liverpool, he was the one who did more than anything to help me settle in the first team.

"I was trying things and they were things that I wouldn't normally do on the pitch. Because I was having a bad time, I'd try them even more and no matter what I did, it would all just backfire.

"I just wanted to try and impress the fans, yet nothing seemed to go right for me. I could sense there was one or two getting a little bit annoyed with me but thankfully all that seems to be behind me. I'm getting good vibes from them now."

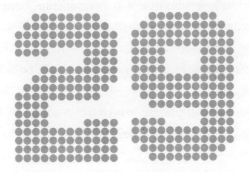

James Blond

For the national press, David James was the gift that kept giving – he was a terrific athlete, a fine keeper and undeserving of the public beatings he continually got...

D avid James is in no doubt as to where his home is these days. After an appalling savaging by the national press, which resulted in him being dropped for the Poland game, James returned to Manchester no doubt feeling as though he hadn't a friend in the world outside his City team-mates and England colleagues.

But the fans of Manchester City – mistrustful of the national media at the best of times – showed exactly what they thought of the man who arrived last January from West Ham United. Sustained applause rang out for the England goalkeeper when his name was read out prior to the clash with Everton, and took James' breath away. It was, of course, quite typical of the Blues faithful who were determined to show their No.1 what they think really counts.

"They were awesome," said James. "I was assured by people in the club that the fans would be behind me, but I never expected that level of support. Their response was magnificent, better than when I actually signed and I played my first game.

"It was a big game for me but my view on what happened with England and the way it has been reported might be a bit different to those reporting on it."

Sensitive types football players – take the reaction of his fellow City players as they attempted to 'ease' the pain James had suffered the previous few days.

"I caught the first shot in training on Friday and all the lads started clapping," said James, no doubt eager to repay the favour in the coming months.

"That was a good response to make," he smiled.

His performance after the ovation he received was his best as a City player and should have sent the correct message to the England boss that he is not about to let the error against Austria keep him down.

"It was a good and bad day for me, but overriding it all is the fact that it is a team game."

Referring to the Austria game, he was, as ever, philosophical about the events of 10 days ago.

"These are the things that make or break you and I will emerge from it a stronger person," he said. All I wanted to do after the Austria game was play again.

"I didn't get the opportunity the following Wednesday, so it was good to get out there against Everton. I am not a bad goalkeeper and to question the way I do my job would be too dramatic.

"Unfortunately, I have experience of going through a similar thing to this before. It is not something I would wish on anyone but you have to accept it goes with the territory.

"If a centre-forward misses 10 open goals, he can get away with it; if a goalkeeper makes a mistake, he is the worst in the world."

Now James will be aiming to prove that he is, as the City fans sing long and loud, England's No.1, even though Paul Robinson is likely to take over the gloves for the next game following the 2-1 win over Poland.

He may even step aside for tonight's clash with Barnsley to allow Ronald Waterreus a much-needed taste of first team action. But in both instances, he'll be back – make no mistake about that.

5:30

Silva has a shout for a penalty when being brought down in the box after a couple of one-twos with Tevez – the referee waves appeals away...

Are You Watching Nottingham?

More than six years after being released by Nottingham Forest for being 'too small', Shaun Wright-Phillips took exactly 19 minutes and seven seconds of his England debut to show why size really doesn't matter. Already a big crowd favourite at City, this was the first of many interviews with Wrighty...

There was a time, not so long ago – last month, in fact – when City fans feared that Shaun Wright-Phillips might be about to leave the Blues and head either 30 miles west to Merseyside, or to North London.

Of course, when Tottenham and Liverpool reportedly showed interest, the national press was convinced the 22-year-old would jump at the chance to join either of these two – obviously bigger – fish (yeah, right!).

One broadsheet went as far as actually naming SWP in a 'probable' opening day Liverpool line-up!

Media excitement hit fever pitch when Kevin Keegan publicly stated his desire to tie the midfielder down to a new, improved contract, but negotiations allegedly 'broke down'. This appeared to open he door for any possible suitors with price tags varying from the laughable (£2m) to the humorous (£10m).

The truth was the club never had any intention of selling the player and he never had any intention of leaving, but even the threat of exactly that happening caused a furore not seen at City for many years.

City and Wright-Phillips reached an agreement in the days leading up to the Fulham game and he signed shortly after the match. The Blues had done right by the player and supporters, and Keegan's statement that a City team without Shaun Wright-Phillips was 'unthinkable' was spot-on.

In the last couple of years, the kid who began life as 'Ian Wright's adopted son' simply became, well, Shauny Wright, Wright, Wright – an excellent young footballer in his own right.

And what perfect timing by the Blues! Days after signing a new deal, and with the ink barely dry, he goes out and scores a cracker on his England debut and adds another nought or two to his value.

The papers and television were full of it the next day and despite encouraging performances by fellow youngsters Glen Johnson and Jermain Defoe, there was only one name on everyone's lips.

So what does the man himself make of it all? Will all the attention change him from the lad nobody has a bad word about? Would the sudden clamour for an interview mean even City Magazine would struggle to have a chat with him?

Of course it didn't. He's the same lad he's always been – down-to-earth, modest and generous – and he was only too happy to speak to us about the events of the past month. But something has changed. There is an aura around him now that has him earmarked for greatness.

His manager watched him set two goals up and score a stunning fourth himself in the 4-0 win over Charlton and then say: 'There's no stopping him. He's on his way to the top'. Of course, he's right.

So, discussing the uncertainty of a contract a few weeks back, was there a chance he was about to leave the Blues?

"I never wanted to leave City," said Shaun. "It was just a matter of agreeing terms both parties were happy with and it finally happened. There was a lot of speculation but generally I don't read the papers.

"If someone tells me there's a story about me, I'll usually go and get the paper and see what it says, but it is never more than just speculation. I just get on with my job, play my game and try and do the best I can for City."

So what of the claims that the Blues had slapped a price tag on his head? Was that a story he heard and, if so, did it have any basis in truth?

"I saw the billboards with that story," he admitted. "I was out with Bradley that day and I then went and bought the paper to see what it was all about. I didn't really like what was being said in the paper so I phoned up and found out it was nothing to do with the club, so it didn't really bother me, but initially I wasn't too happy."

As stated earlier, the reaction from City fans was one of anger when they read the same story. Shaun admits their reaction and constant support since he first broke through into the team were the main reasons he committed himself to Eastlands for another four years.

"It meant a lot," he revealed. "Along with the players and the people around me, the fans are the reason that kept me here and they are another reason why I enjoy and play so well for City. They keep my confidence high, and for them to react the way they did, I now know that they're behind me all the time.

"I met some of the supporters on the street in that time and they were just asking me to stay and I told them I didn't want to go anywhere anyway."

The reception the 22-year-old received before the Fulham game, when City fans had no idea if he'd be signing the new deal or not, must have sent shivers down his spine. He knew he was about to reaffirm his loyalty, but the 43,000 increasingly desperate Blues fans didn't − does he wish he could have let them in on the news prior to the game?

"I would have liked them to have known, yeah," he agreed. "But even though I knew I was signing, I just wanted to concentrate on the game and sort the business side of things out later. It was nice to finally get it all sorted − a relief, in fact."

To make his day complete, he was then called into the England squad for only the second time to face the Ukraine. A badly timed knee injury cost him a run-out in the final warm-up to Euro 2004 in Sweden and also put paid to any lingering hopes he might have had of playing in the tournament.

"It wasn't meant to be. It just wasn't my time," he said philosophically. "I just watched England and learned as much as I could and I think I've come back from the summer break a more confident and better player."

If that wasn't his time, then now most certainly is and he was determined to make his mark when his time came to climb off the bench and make his England debut. Was there any City fan out there that didn't feel more than a tingle of pride as he stood on the touchline waiting to come on?

"He (Sven-Goran Eriksson) didn't tell me I was coming on at any point," revealed Shaun. "He put a few subs on and then I started to wonder whether I was going to get on or not. I thought to myself that if I got on, I was just going to play the way I do at City and show what I could really do. I came on and everything turned out exactly the way I wanted it to, really.

"I was really excited as I waited to get on," he continued. "I wasn't nervous at all. The other players had really welcomed me, which gave me more confidence and you know that they will give you the ball wherever you are and that helps, too, because you know they believe in you.

"They always want the ball, too, so you don't always have to try and beat someone. It all made me feel relaxed and at ease to play my normal game. Then I intercepted the ball and my first thought was to look for a pass. Defoe was marked up ahead and there was nothing else on so I pushed the ball forward until I was in a one-on-one situation and just tried to give myself two yards."

That two yards was enough to give him room to unleash a powerful shot across the box and into the far corner of the net – a goal he's scored several times for City and a move that he's familiar with for good reason.

"We practice that shot in training," he revealed. "It worked well there so I just try to bring it into my game whenever the opportunity arises. When it went in, I must admit it was a big relief because I'd scored on my debut for England. It was a big moment in my life."

Not only in Shaun's – the BBC cameras had one especially assigned to his dad who was watching in the stand. His reaction was every bit as excited as his son's and worthy of an Ian Wright special for Arsenal.

"I saw my dad celebrating on TV afterwards," grinned Shaun. "It made me feel good. It's the sort of thing we both wanted and the same with my mum as well as other family and friends. It's just nice to make them all happy.

"I spoke to my mum straight after the game. She was over the moon for me. She was crying, my Nan was – everyone! It was good."

With a three-year-old son and a daughter who has not long since turned one, there was even more pride in the Wright-Phillips family.

"My son realises I play and watches me on television," he said. "But my little girl is too young and she doesn't really watch the box at all at the moment. My boy says 'That's my daddy' when he sees me on TV and he sings songs about Man City, but he reckons any football team he sees is City!"

The coverage following the England debut must have taken him aback a little?

"I didn't read too much about what happened," he revealed. "To be honest, the next day I was just back to normal and was preparing myself for the trip to Liverpool. That's the way I kind of do things because it will always be a special memory and have a place in my heart, but I just have to move on to the next game. I have to get on with things and get back down to earth.

"There have been a few requests for interviews, but to be honest the press have been quite good, they haven't hounded the club or anything like that. I'm still the same person as I was before, so nothing like this would ever change how I am. I like me, so I would never change the way I am."

There was special praise for City's No.29 after that stunning debut from skipper David Beckham and Sven himself, comparing many of Shaun's attributes to Diego Maradona, no less – something Shaun wasn't aware of.

"He said that? I hadn't heard of that," he said. "I'm overwhelmed to be honest with you. It's a really nice compliment. As for Becks, he's a top man anyway and he looked after me and all the other young players. In the five-a-sides, he always has a laugh and it helps break the ice.

"It helped us relax and have the craic with each other, which was important. It's good to know people like that and play with them because you get to learn off them, too."

How long ago must the rejection by Nottingham Forest seem now? They couldn't see past Shaun's lack of inches when judging his merits as a footballer and now they must cringe every time they hear the name Shaun Wright-Phillips and his latest achievements.

"Forest basically just said that I was too small," said the man with the biggest heart in the City team. "They said I wasn't good enough and, to be blunt, I just wasn't what they wanted. They released me, but I'm the kind of person that if I get a setback, I like to keep trying. I don't like losing – I'm not a loser, although sometimes you don't have a choice – I always try to achieve the goal I've set out to achieve, no matter how long it takes me. Because it's doing something I enjoy, I'm willing to learn all the time off lots of different people. I just keep going."

Kieran Rafferty may not be a familiar name to City fans, but perhaps it should be. He is the man who reckoned City was the right club for the then club-less youngster. The club certainly owes Mr Rafferty a pint or two!

"He was the scout at Forest," revealed Shaun. "But then he left and was scouting for clubs in general and he just told me to come to City because I'd have a good chance of being taken on – which happened!"

Now there is a Wright-Phillips dynasty at City as Bradley hovers around the fringes of the first team, much to the delight of his proud big brother, and the pair also managed to realise their mum's dream during the pre-season.

"Yeah, we played together in a first team match for City," he said. "It was wicked actually – it was my mum's dream that we would play together, and it happened. We really enjoyed it, too. He's progressing really well and the fact that he's training with us (the first team) a lot more gives him the chance to work on the stuff he needs to work on. Hopefully, soon he'll get his chance."

Mr Motivator

Was Kevin Keegan's enthusiasm waning? With the coffers seemingly empty at City, his frustration was evident at times during quite a frank interview in 2004...

The hair may be a little greyer and a line or two might have appeared that weren't visible a couple of years ago, but the eyes still sparkle and the enthusiasm is as great as ever.

There really is only one Kevin Keegan and he is more determined than ever to bring success to City this season, especially after the last campaign, which left everyone connected with the club more than a little drained.

There hasn't been a tremendous amount of transfer activity this summer but there have been several arrivals and departures, both in the playing squad and in the backroom staff. Lessons have been learned and everyone at the club is geared up and raring to go out and prove that the 2003/04 campaign was no more than a hiccup – an anomaly on what had been a smooth transition from Division One hopefuls to a Premiership force under Keegan's tutelage.

Tanned from a holiday in the States and fresh from a productive morning's training session with his squad, the City manager settled into his seat ready for the interview. Had he enjoyed the summer break, I enquired?

"Yeah, it's been a good summer," he said glancing into the Carrington car park as Nicolas Anelka's borrowed Lamborghini gingerly crept over the speed bumps. "I spent quality time with my family. We had a holiday in America and then spent some of the time helping one of my daughters move down south. It's been good."

The close season was not without disappointment for the manager, though, and one of the biggest blows was the departure of reserve team striker Stephen Elliott who decided to pursue his career with Sunderland instead of force his way into first team reckoning at Eastlands.

It was a transfer that hit Keegan hard and left many fans wondering exactly why such a potential talent had been allowed to leave. It seems there wasn't a great deal that could be done to stop him going.

"I was very disappointed that Stephen left and I hope we get decent money for him at the tribunal because we spent a lot of time working on him and he was right on the fringe of the first team," admitted the Blues boss. "This close season would have been his chance to work with first team players and show us what he could do.

"But, you know, I think the Irish connection won him over because his agent is Irish, Stephen is from Ireland and Mick McCarthy played for the Republic and managed them, too. There were also other people at Sunderland involved with the Ireland set-up and I think that was a definite pull.

"They also offered him first team football which I couldn't do, and more money than I was prepared to pay him at this stage of his career. It's one of those things and I just hope we get the money we deserve because that's what the system is supposed to ensure. If someone takes one of your younger players, you should get adequate compensation – I think we'll get quite a bit.

"So yes, I was very disappointed and it leaves me with a bit of a problem because I'm looking for a young forward when I had one here already. That's football and you're never going to leave somewhere unless you are offered more money, but they offered him first team football, too. I could have done that to get him to sign a contract, but with the forwards I've got here, I would have been lying to him. It's a disappointment, but not the end of the world."

In other transfer activity, the prolonged saga of Daniel van Buyten ended with the towering Belgian signing – ironically – for Keegan's old club Hamburg. The manager had, on several occasions, stated his desire to bring van Buyten in permanently, but despite the player clearly enjoying his time with the Blues, a deal, ultimately, couldn't be arranged – much to the frustration of all connected with City – especially the manager.

"I was disappointed we couldn't get Daniel back," he said. "I knew from the day we loaned him that we couldn't afford him. That was made clear by the board, due to our current finances. I told Daniel's agent a long time ago – I was very upfront about the situation – and explained we didn't have the money.

"It wasn't a lot of money, but we just didn't have it. It wasn't unexpected when he didn't sign, and to be fair, he hung on a long time – perhaps too long – to see if we could raise the cash, but in the end, Hamburg told him that if he didn't sign the contract, they would have to look elsewhere because they needed to prepare for the new season.

"Daniel couldn't have given Manchester City any more time than he did, but the only way we could have bought him would have been if we'd sold a player, and that's what we were hoping would maybe happen, but it didn't. It just wasn't meant to be."

"He had some terrific games and linked up well with Shaun Wright-Phillips, and some games he was as good as you'd ever want him to be. But we got caught out defensively once or twice and I put it down to language problems."

One thing that Keegan felt did not need to be changed was the club captaincy. Sylvain Distin was confirmed recently as skipper for the new campaign and the manager feels he will have benefited from such a tough first year in the role.

"Yes, Sylvain is the captain," he said. "We had a long chat about it and he wanted to remain as captain, which was the most important thing. I didn't want to change the captaincy and I think he'll get a lot more help this year from the likes of Danny Mills.

"I think he will also benefit from the fact that he's a had a tough year as skipper, there's no doubt about that, because the club had a tough year. He's worked hard and I think he'll make a terrific captain. You know, you don't just become a great captain overnight – you learn to be good at the job, especially at Sylvain's age – 25."

With the new season ready to kick-off, Nicolas Anelka commented recently that the manager's rallying speech made him feel good and positive for the battles ahead. So what exactly was said?

"It wasn't so much a rallying speech," said Keegan. "I just said 'Hey, come on guys, we're all better than we showed last year. You know it, I know it, but we've got to prove it to people.' The expectation level now at this club is not the same as it was last year because we've lowered it with our performances, but we shouldn't lower our own expectations.

"We're not going to come out and set major targets this year, but I expect a much better season. People said our first season in the new stadium would be tough – I hoped it would be a plus for us, but we did struggle. I think that's the one thing we've got to turn around.

"Towards the end of last season, it felt like home, and we won our last two Premiership home games as well, which hadn't happened before, so that was quite good. Let's hope this season will be a lot better than the last one…I'm sure it will be."

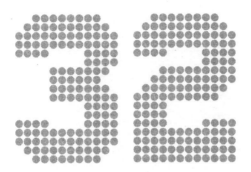

Saint Nic?

The last interview with Nicolas Anelka before he set off on his travels again was revealing and open – it was a surprise he was starting his third season with the Blues given his nomadic reputation. The signs were, however, City were no longer matching his ambition…

It seems that Nicolas Anelka had anything but a quiet break this summer, with his name constantly in the headlines for one reason or another. Throughout, the French star has reaffirmed his commitment to Manchester City, but it seems some factions of the national press refuse to let that get in the way of a sensational headline. Anelka, who received a rapturous welcome from the City fans last week against Lazio, is looking sharp and fit despite a foot injury hampering his pre-season build-up, and he is again likely to feature in the Premiership scoring charts this season.

The club have been at pains to stress the 25-year-old is not for sale and, despite a controversial story linking him with Monaco last week, Anelka insisted he is happy with the Blues and is looking forward to starting the new Premiership campaign.

If anything, the constant media speculation seems to have strengthened the bond between player and supporters, and after scoring 24 goals last season, he is once again on the fringes of the national team – now under the stewardship of a new coach following Jacques Santini's switch to Tottenham earlier this summer.

Last capped against Russia in April 2002, Anelka has already been singled out by former Under-21 coach Raymond Domenech, who has put the striker on stand-by for France's friendly with Bosnia-Herzegovina on August 18. Now, 'Nico' is hoping to force his way back into the squad by scoring goals for City this term.

"When I was injured, I missed playing football," said Anelka, who should be leading the line against Fulham this afternoon.

"I want to play every game. I think the Premiership will be the same as it always is. It is a difficult league to score goals in, but I will try my best. Even if you have new faces in different teams, it will still be the same.

"The Premiership is all about pace and fight, so I am expecting things to be difficult. I would love to play for France again, but I must first do my best for Manchester City. If I do that, maybe I will get back in.

"It doesn't matter who I play alongside for City. I like playing alongside Jon (Macken), Robbie (Fowler) and Paulo (Wanchope). The manager decides who plays here, and if he changes things around, we accept it."

"I am looking forward to playing more games for City," he continued.

"I like to score and make assists. It was nice to see the fans again at Reading. They gave me a nice reception as always."

That was again the case against Lazio, where for the second season running, Nico became the first player to score at the City of Manchester Stadium – taking just 38 seconds – as the Blues coasted home 3-1. It was also the fastest recorded goal at the stadium.

The standing ovation he received from the 23,000-plus crowd endorsed the feeling towards the striker many believe is the Blues' greatest asset.

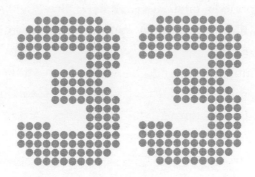

Blues Brother

Bradley Wright-Phillips was scoring goals for the second string and had a major advantage over his peers — he was Shaun's younger brother...

It's the season that just keeps getting better for Bradley Wright-Phillips. Top scorer for the reserves, the 19-year old has made his first team debut, scored a goal, and last month earned his first England Under-20 cap. Not bad for the kid brother of Shaun, and he is definitely making his own strides towards becoming the second crowd favourite in the family.

But now the affable Londoner wants to push on and win a run in the starting line-up, and the signs are that might happen before the season is over. He is a regular on the bench and has made nine appearances in total this campaign, but is yet to make his full Premiership bow. After agreeing a new deal last autumn, he has time on his hands, but he is eager for the opportunity to show the City fans what he can do.

"I know that I have to keep trying to impress every day in training and cannot afford to let up," said Wright-Phillips, who Nottingham Forest were reportedly interested in loaning recently. "I want to show the manager what I have to offer and the only place to do that is on the training ground.

"I am constantly listening and know that I have a lot to learn, but feel that I am progressing. Having said that, I take nothing for granted and know that I am fortunate to have my brother Shaun to talk things over with.

"The two of us are always discussing football — in fact, we don't talk about anything else. I am an out-and-out poacher and I just love scoring goals. There are 10 games to go this season in the Premiership and I have targeted another goal.

"It would be great to achieve that and I will be doing everything to get that goal if my chance comes along. I'm happy with my progress so far this year. It's good for me at the moment and the younger players are getting on the bench."

The Academy starlet has impressed his manager who paid tribute to his poaching instincts.

"He makes things out of nothing and scores goals when you don't expect him to score goals from impossible positions," said Kevin Keegan. "He has only been with us since the summer, but he has impressed us with his attitude.

"There are still things that he has got to learn, but he is willing to learn and he will strengthen up. He is a real predator, a natural goalscorer, and he reminds me of his dad."

High praise, indeed!

15:34 City build up the play yet again but struggle to penetrate with Nasri overplaying a five-yard pass before it runs out for a goal-kick...

A Class Of His Own

Nedum Onuoha was a graduate in more ways than one – educated, and a success of the Blues' Academy, he was just making his way in the game, and with little or no money to spend, he also represented the immediate future of the club – youth...

City's talented defender Nedum Onuoha believes furthering his education will pay dividends for his football career, after flying through his exams last year. He will undertake a part-time degree in the near future, and after achieving A-grades in his chosen subjects, he is keen to continue to learn while he is playing. His father Martin is a teacher and it's clear his – and his mother's –

influences have ensured that he has another career when his days as a professional footballer are over.

"Alex Gibson at the Academy always told us to set ourselves targets as it is something to aim at," said the articulate 18-year-old. "When you reach that target, then create a new one – something that is bigger and better for you to achieve.

"I also learned in my business studies that when you create an objective, you must know it is possible to achieve it. But at the same time, it must not be something that you achieve quickly in a second or two, you must have something of a hurdle so that you can grow."

Onuoha, who has doubled as the Under-18s skipper this term, has made nine appearances in a City shirt in his first year as a professional, and he believes his studies have helped him to think about the game more.

"I suppose my studies are helping in my game or in the approach to my football at least," he added. "I think my studying has made me less rash as you have to think about things more carefully.

"In business studies, you have to think things out stage by stage and look at what if this or what if that happens. That can work on the football pitch as well, though, it is also a question of time on the pitch.

"The pace of the game can mean that you don't get time to make decisions, but there is no doubt that education can help. But at the same time, I know that a player may not be bright academically but can perform as a genius on the pitch. So there is a football brain as well."

He may be the thinking man's footballer, but the boyhood City fan is also keen to push for a regular place in the starting line-up. But as with everything, he is philosophical about his chances and also knows he has time on his side.

"I would love to get more experience at Premiership level. That has been my aim from the start of the season," he said. "I have just kept plugging away throughout this term. I don't think it is a case of sharpening my focus now on the Premiership as we are coming towards the end of it. I don't believe that is right. I have been focusing on it all season.

"If I get more games, I will be delighted because that is what I have been looking for all year. At the moment, I would say that the players who are in the side are playing better than me.

"When the time is right, and I am playing better than them, then I believe I will deserve my chance, and in football, you do get what you deserve.

"A lot has happened for me this season. I signed my first professional contract, made my Premiership debut and scored on my international debut for the England Under-20s.

"Now I just wonder what will happen next season for me, who knows? Things always seem to happen around my birthday, for some reason.

"Two years ago I made my debut for the reserves and last season I scored for the reserves. It was the winning goal in the closing minutes of the game.

"This year I made my debut in the City squad and was on the bench for the win over Chelsea. So who knows what will happen next year?"

15:35 Yaya Toure appears to be struggling with an injury and he hobbles off to receive treatment from the physio who begins to assess his hamstring...

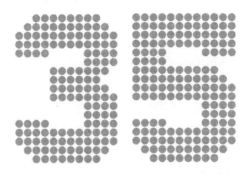

The Wright Stuff

I spoke with Shaun again as a preview of a match against Middlesbrough for the Manchester Evening News – he had become the darling of the City fans but as his worth increased, the chances of the Blues cashing in increased, too...

Shaun Wright-Phillips is aiming to add another spectacular goal to his already sizeable collection of wonder strikes when he takes to the field against Middlesbrough this afternoon.

The 23-year-old England international scored perhaps his best goal of the season against Aston Villa last Saturday to signal his return to form after a rusty first few matches following his knee operation. The young attacking midfielder missed six weeks' worth of action but is gathering momentum as the season draws to a close and he is focused on making Boro his latest victims – and duly propel his side into Europe at the same time.

"I don't know whether people expected too much of me when I came back from the operation – I expect a lot of myself – but it takes time to get back to full fitness," said Shaun.

"I am feeling strong and relatively fresh, though perhaps not quite as strong as I want to be, but I am working on that. It was important that I didn't rush back and I was a little bit cautious because I didn't want to do any more damage, but now I am feeling sharp again and we cannot wait for the clash with Middlesbrough.

"The spirit in this side is incredible, as good as I have known it at the club, and we want to use that to our advantage. We were without two of our best players in Robbie Fowler and Richard Dunne at Villa, but we managed to overcome that and the players who came in did fantastically well. That is a great signal of the mood the squad is in. We haven't lost for a long time and we like the winning feeling."

Better still is Shaun's reiteration that, despite the continued (and annoying) media speculation linking him with a move away from the Blues this summer, he wants to not only stay for next season, but also remain a Blue at least until his new contract runs out in 2008.

"I signed a four-year contract last August and when I signed that, it was with the intention to stay at the club," he insisted. "That's where I want to be, and until my contract runs out, I'm not thinking of moving.

"It's my home. The fans have really taken to me and I think that is because I have come through the ranks. I came here when I was 16 and went from the youth team to the first team and the fans supported me all the way. I'm settled here."

Proof, if it were needed, that Shaun's career can achieve all it deserves playing for City, has come over what has been an amazing last 12 months. Various awards and an ever growing fan club around the country have made the young Londoner take the odd reality check every now and then to take everything in.

"It's kind of strange when I look back at the season," said City's joint-top scorer. "It's like something you dream about, but it has happened in real life.

"I was pinching myself at the start, but as it's gone on, I've realised what has been happening. Being voted runner-up in the Young Player of the Year award was great and it's nice to know that so many people believe in me.

"To get so many votes was a great compliment to me and gives me a lot of confidence to try and go on and do even better next year. It's been a great season, but it's something I've got to build on again.

"I need to keep up my consistency levels to make sure it keeps happening. That's the hardest part, really – to build on what you have achieved so that you can achieve even more in the future."

Home James

David James wasn't your average footballer – there was much more to the England keeper than met the eye and he had an air of confidence about him that set him apart from his team-mates…

After spells at several top clubs, England goalkeeper David James finally seems to have found his spiritual home. In many ways, James and Manchester City were destined to come together at some point and both parties are equally glad that in January 2004, it finally became a reality.

But James' career began in far less auspicious surrounds than the City of Manchester Stadium. Born one of eight children – though most of his siblings lived in Jamaica when he was a child – baby David arrived on August 1, 1970, in Welwyn Garden City, but his family settled in Hatfield, London.

He then attended Ride Primary School before moving to Welwyn to live where he then started life at Applecroft Primary. Naturally athletic, James had no real interest in football until fate played a hand in his future, pardon the pun.

While he'd play in schoolyard knockabouts, he aspired to get more involved, but the games offered little opportunity to have a real taste of playing competitively. Never one to let the initiative slip, James decided he'd see some action one way or another and decided to start keeping goal.

"I think I made the choice to keep goal myself rather than being shoved in there," he recalled. "I couldn't play out and during a PE football lesson, I decided to give it a go. The kid who was already the 'keeper was letting loads of goals in and I'd just been standing around like a spare part with the ball going past me all the time, so I thought, 'I can do a better job than the guy in goal'. I gave it a go and loved it."

Things began to develop from thereon in. From little acorns and all that…

"I then played for my school and there were some kids I used to go to cub scouts with, and I'd played a game the day previous and the other kids were saying things like 'Wow! Did you see that save he made yesterday?'."

It wasn't just his peers who were beginning to notice what David was capable of and he soon found himself making his way to Tottenham for a trial, but things didn't quite according to plan.

"I went to Spurs for a year, played one game and we lost 6-2 against Watford. I thought that was the end of it. Then my mate Jason Solomon, who I used to play with at Spurs, told me Watford wanted me to join them. I may have been beaten six times when I'd played them, but obviously Watford saw something that day that they liked.

In truth, they could have won by 20 during that game."

The young teenager signed up for Watford and remained at Vicarage Road until he was 21, progressing through their youth and reserve set-up to the first team.

James was also showing talent at both the high jump and javelin at school while with Watford. In fact, there were those who believed that with a little application, he could go onto great things in other avenues of sport.

"I jumped 1.85 metres at a meeting, which is nothing, really," David recalled. "My coach turned round and told me the England high jump coach was there watching me and that he reckoned I could do 2.35 metres and break the English record within the next three or four years. If I was interested, the England coach was willing to back me.

"I thought, 'this is good' and was interested. Football was going through a bit of a decline and there was a lot of crowd trouble and it was just stupid. Even at Luton you could be sat there and nearby there was someone getting beat up. I thought that if there was a chance I could do something in athletics, especially as my schoolwork wasn't going the right way, then I'd do it.

"I asked what I'd have to do and was told I'd just train; if things went well, the best performers get paid. I didn't want to be a superstar, just earn a living, but with only those at the very top making reasonable money, if I didn't excel, I would have to pretty much make my own way, and I couldn't do it.

"I had a choice of pursuing the high jump career or staying on my YTS deal at Watford on £27.30 a week, and the latter won, plain and simple."

The rest, as they say, is history. After playing a major role in Watford's FA Youth Cup final victory over City in 1989, aged 20, David made his full league debut for Watford against Millwall. Ironically, City played a big part in David's elevation from reserve to first team, as he explained:

"Our first choice goalkeeper, Tony Coton, had signed for City and Mel Rees was the reserve. I'd had a terrible year in the reserves the previous year because I had no particular goal in football.

"I arrived for pre-season believing Mel would be the new No.1 now Tony had moved on, but even though I didn't even have a particularly good pre-season, the gaffer tells me I'm in for the first game.

"I just said, okay, and that was that. I later learned they'd tried to sign just about every goalkeeper in the country and nobody fancied it! The first few games were a bit tough. I ended up playing all 46 games."

James then missed just three games the following season and with his reputation growing, Liverpool signed him for £1.3million as the then joint-most expensive shot-stopper ever.

He remained at Anfield for seven seasons, clocking up 214 league appearances in the process, and his time with the Reds was something of a rollercoaster, with plenty of ups and downs.

"I went straight into the first team for the first game of the new season," recalled David. "I literally peaked after about three games and things went downhill after that because I didn't know what I was doing.

"It was awesome to play in front of the Kop, and on my debut against Sheffield United, the Kop started roaring and I just stood there thinking 'Wow! What's going on?'

"It was a superb feeling, but my early form wasn't good and I didn't keep a clean sheet in my first 12 games, which was worrying. I didn't play again for the next four or five months."

Things got much better for him, though, and away from football, his good looks won him a modelling job with fashion giants Armani. He also made his full England debut in March, 1997, keeping a clean sheet in a 2-0 win over Mexico.

He left Merseyside for Aston Villa in 1999 and after two seasons he moved south to join West Ham United, enjoying his stay at Upton

Park. But the Hammers' relegation cast a doubt over his future with England, and when Kevin Keegan lodged a bid of £2m, the England No.1 severed his ties with the East End and became a Manchester City player.

"I'd heard that there was interest from City in the summer of 2004," he admitted. "It was logical that there was some truth in the rumour because Kevin Keegan was the man who brought me back into the England squad."

James made his debut in a 1-1 draw with Blackburn in January of last year and has been virtually ever-present since that game. He may have temporarily lost his England place, but the signs are good that one of – if not the – Premiership's most consistent club performers will still be on the plane to Germany as part of the 2006 World Cup squad next summer.

If he does get to add to his 33 international caps, it will be no more than he deserves – and it'll be a poke in the eye to his detractors in the media who seem to rejoice in any error he makes. Fortunately, where Manchester City is concerned, they've never had the opportunity.

Aguero wriggles past a couple of defenders before floating a cross into the box which clears everyone, including Nasri at the back post…

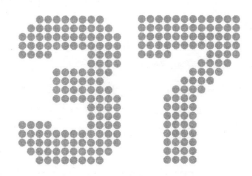

Learning To Fly

After an initial interview, Nedum Onuoha would become someone I'd enjoy talking with over the years. Hhe was also a boyhood City fan, musician and was thinking about moving into law – not your average footballer…

There have been many success stories so far this season, with the young talent literally flooding into the Blues' first team squad. Willo Flood, Stephen Jordan and Bradley Wright-Phillips have all made inroads into the senior eleven and will be expected to push on again in 2005/06.

There are many others, too, staking their own claim, and players such as Paddy McCarthy and Lee Croft may well get their chance before the end of the current campaign. All have impressed the City fans, who love nothing better than home-grown stars in the side.

But it is perhaps Nedum Onuoha that has impressed the most, coming into the team earlier this season for the Coca-Cola Cup clash with Arsenal and looking like a seasoned regular from day one.

Such is Kevin Keegan's faith in the articulate youngster, he gave him his full Premiership debut at Highbury last January with the simple mandate of marking Thierry Henry! That the ace Frenchman was kept quiet for most of the game is testament to Onuoha's ability – and he only turned 18 last November.

Now the Academy Under-18 skipper is knocking hard for a regular place in Keegan's starting eleven and may well be given an extended run before the current campaign is over, though he is happy to wait for his chances.

Now the fruits of his hard work are paying off, Nedum is quick to pay tribute to his mum, Anthonia, who has become a well-known figure among the hardy souls who follow the Academy and reserve teams home and away over the years.

She is a also good friend of Academy chief, Jim Cassell, who recently claimed Mrs Onuoha was "a magnificent ambassador for parental support of their children."

"I think when I first started playing for the Academy, my mum always took me wherever I needed to go," said Nedum. "She watched all the games when I played for the Under-11s and most of the games since.

"She comes along to the games – even if I'm not playing – and has been to every away game this season. She pays for it all out of her own pocket and does it because I'm involved – that's the key thing with her.

"She is a City fan, but me just travelling with the first team is enough for her to travel to places like Portsmouth and Norwich. My mum's backed me from the moment I really began to take an interest in football.

"I can't remember the first time I kicked a ball, but there is a photograph at home. When I first started playing for my school and then local team, initially the input was coming from my teacher who selected me for the school team and then gave me phone numbers of local league sides.

"I spoke to my mum and she said if that's what I wanted, she'd support me as best she could from thereon in."

Nedum went to Miles Platting Primary School, just a few miles from what would become the metropolis that is SportCity. Little could the youngster have known that he would one day be realising his dreams of playing for the Blues on what was then a patch of wasteground near the huge gas tanks.

The school he attended has since changed its name – he's not sure what to, and was close to his old family home. The Onuoha family moved to Harpurhey eight years ago and have remained there ever since. In leaving Miles Platting, they left behind an area not without problems.

"I wouldn't say it was a rough neighbourhood," said Nedum, "but at the time, there was a lot of crime in the area. Some of the lawlessness was serious enough to convince my family to move away and there have been no real problems in the area we moved to."

With a new home and a more settled environment, Nedum's mother, a civil servant; and father, a school teacher, may have been wholly behind their son's football ambitions, but when it came to education, they were even more intent on helping him achieve goals other than those on a football pitch.

"It's been exactly the same in education as it has with the football," he said. "My parents' support has encouraged me maybe even more when it comes to education, and the courses I'm doing now are down to them wanting to get the best out of me.

"My dad, Martin, used to be a footballer in Nigeria, but he picked up a serious injury and now he's doing well for himself. He didn't play for a major side, but the fact that he did play and had to finish through injury, has convinced him that I need something to fall back on should a similar fate befall me."

Nedum received straight A's in his exams last summer and will undertake a part-time degree before long, so he clearly will have something to fall back on when he hangs his boots up.

But that will, hopefully, not be for a very long time and he is already being tipped as a star of the future. He has pace, strength and can pass the ball intelligently and well.

Physically, he can already hold his own with the very best, as he proved when marking Henry, but he isn't 19 until November and still has some growing to do, and if all goes well, he should be a permanent member of the Blues' defence for many years to come.

In fact, may City fans are eager to see him given an extended run this season, but Nedum knows time is on his side and is respectful of the players ahead of him for selection.

So when he sees Champions League clashes on TV involving the likes of Real Madrid, Barcelona and Milan, does he, too, imagine playing on a similar stage one day?

"I'm not to sure what I imagine in the future," said Nedum, who has three City-supporting sisters. "But it would be more like a dream to play against those types of teams.

"But if I don't ever face those types of clubs, it wouldn't bother me at all, just as long as I'm playing, especially for this club because I've supported them since as long as I can remember.

"I was saying to somebody just recently, I've been here so long I can't imagine being anywhere else."

So how does he feel about the fans' eagerness, expressed on various web polls, to see him given a run in the side? Like everything else, it seems, Nedum looks at the bigger picture and is more than happy with the way things have gone for him this season.

"A lot of people don't see the whole picture," he said. "They'll see the game on the Saturday but not what happens the week before. For example, if someone plays badly at the weekend, it could be going against the whole training regimes that have been done in the week.

"Some players might have been magnificent during the week but then have a bad game on the Saturday, so there's a lot to consider. Playing for the first team and being involved as much as I have so far, was far more than I could have hoped for and I'm very happy at the way things have gone.

"Not many people will ever get to mark the likes of Henry at Highbury, so I know how fortunate I am. I often ask myself how many of the lads I used to play with in junior sides are doing other things now, so I have plenty of patience.

"At the moment, I would say that the players who are in the side are playing better than me. When the time is right and I am playing better than them, then I believe I will deserve my chance, and in football you do get what you deserve."

So what exactly was it like marking arguably the greatest striker in the world? Nedum admits he was kept very busy for 90 minutes.

"Thierry Henry is an amazing player and I have even greater respect for him after playing against him than I did before," he said. "It's different watching someone on telly because you can't see everything they do during a game, but he is so hard to keep track of and rapid, too. His movement is fantastic."

Under FIFA rules, Nedum still qualifies to play for the birth nation of his parents, Nigeria, and admits he would consider playing for the Super Eagles in the future, if he hasn't won a full cap for England in the meantime, of course.

"Right now I just want to concentrate on progressing and playing for City," he said. "If Nigeria asked me, I'd maybe have to say no for the time being as I have a lot of learning to do with my club.

"Stuart Pearce has told me to watch other players who play in my position and I think I'm going to watch John Terry play soon, as Stuart says he is someone I can learn a lot from."

That may well be the case, with Terry one of the best defenders in the country of late, but it's a fair bet that it will be Nedum doing the teaching in future years, perhaps both on and off the pitch. England better move quickly!

Foul by Zamora on Silva – free-kick awarded. Taken
by Vincent Kompany as City again begin to probe
the QPR defence...

15:38

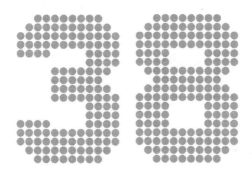

One More Hero

*Of all the interviews I've done over the years, this remains
my favourite – Stuart Pearce arranged to meet me at the
hotel he was staying at in Mere, Cheshire. I'd said half
an hour, but ended spending three hours in his company
– the question was, with Kevin Keegan quitting, could he
guide the Blues to glory with little or no money?*

Managers in the Premiership these days tend, by and large,
to be School of Science types; some bespectacled, others
looking like they've just stepped out of Burton's shop
window. The tracksuit boss of yesteryear is a much rarer beast these
days, at least in the nation's top division.

155

But there are some notable exceptions. Martin Jol at Spurs and David Moyes at Everton are definitely old school when it comes to simple touchline coaching, and looking like the fans believe a manager should.

And now add the name Stuart Pearce, who was finally confirmed as manager of Manchester City by the Blues' board last month as reward for a (slightly more than) impressive start to his tenure in what was generally regarded throughout the game as a 'caretaker' role.

Pearce is your archetypal tracksuit manager and he just wouldn't look right in a Jose Mourinho coat or sporting those Specsaver specials a host of lower league bosses now wear in an attempt to make them seem more intellectual. With Stuart Pearce, what you see is definitely what you get.

He is a leader of men and a dying breed in the English game, but his drive and belief may just be about to catapult City back towards the top again – if the last nine games of the 2004/05 season are anything to go by.

The Blues, meandering in mid-table under the weakening influence of Kevin Keegan, handed Pearce the job until the summer when Keegan left the club with a quarter of the campaign to go.

The transformation of the team could hardly have been more dramatic, and despite losing his first game at Spurs, Pearce seemed to send an electrical charge through his team and the re-born Blues came within a whisker of claiming the final UEFA Cup spot on the last day of the season.

Pearce likened the form that saw City win four and draw four of their last eight to that of a "cup run", and he was right. The atmosphere within the City of Manchester Stadium became vibrant and expectant for each match, and the groundswell of support for Pearce was undeniable.

With one game to go, he was given the contract he deserved, and now, after being given the job permanently, a position he says is a "fantastic honour", the City fans are hoping his passion and determination can take the club back to the glory days again.

And while Pearce may be old school in his attire on match days and his values as a man, he's a modern manager in every other sense and is employing the latest technology alongside his own ideas – plus tips he learned while playing under the likes of Brian Clough, Kenny Dalglish and Harry Redknapp.

In fact, there aren't many managers anywhere who would have the initiative – or balls – to put his goalkeeper upfront as an attacker for the last few minutes of a must-win game as Pearce did against Middlesbrough.

Football fans relate to him as a man, too. He started out on the bottom rung of the football ladder playing non-league football and trained as an electrician, so he knows all about working for a living. When he missed a penalty for England in the semi-final of the World Cup in 1990, he had the guts to take one again in Euro '96 against Spain – and scored.

People don't forget these things, nor should they.

I don't think the values I have are old values, just a necessity," says Pearce. "I believe what is right is right, believe in hard work, honesty and loyalty. They are values my parents instilled in me and I think they are values everyone else should adhere to as well.

"Yes, I am a so-called 'modern manager'; I am very open-minded and I don't have my mentality and views set in the past and I never had them as a player, either. When the rules changed and you couldn't tackle from behind anymore, everyone was saying I was going to get sent off every week.

"It didn't happen and it didn't happen because I'm not stupid. It's the same with modern-day football now – I'm a realist about it and I know what makes certain people tick and I know what I would enjoy.

"I've had players coming to Carrington looking forward to training and I will put expectations on those players. If anyone steps out of line, they can't expect me as an ally. If they work their nuts off, they will, and it's as simple as that.

"I'm very open-minded as a manager and I'm open to new ideas. I'm not a dinosaur by any means and if I think an addition to the training staff will help the squad in any shape or form, I'm very open-minded to that and always have been."

Pearce will turn his thoughts to a more permanent residence in the city in the coming weeks after four years of life spent between a Cheshire hotel and the family home in Wiltshire where his wife Elizabeth and their two children Chelsea, six, and Harley, one, live.

I'll probably find myself an apartment up here, now," he says. "But I won't be moving my family to the North West. As much as I like Manchester, it's nice to get in the car on a Saturday night and drive away from the city and freshen my mind up.

"I wake up on a Sunday morning, put my little boy in the pram and take him for a walk through the village. Nobody really cares about football there and it's fantastic for me.

"When I'm back in Manchester, I have nothing else to think about apart from football. I don't have to watch the clock and think about picking my children up or what time I'm meeting my wife – I've got none of that.

"Football is all that I'm here for and it works brilliantly for me and has done so for four years and I think it will as long as my wife and family is content with that, because obviously they come first. They'll be there for me long after football has gone and I'm lucky to have a very understanding wife in that respect."

Pearce admits that he sees little of Manchester itself because he rarely has chance to visit the city in between work and home life.

"I travel up from Wiltshire on a Monday morning and arrive at the training ground at about 7.15am, and if I'm not rushing off to see a game, I'll leave when it's dark and then I find a bed somewhere – that's my life.

"I wouldn't say I get out a great deal. I must have been into town for a meal about three times in four years and that's it. But I do go to concerts all over the place, that's probably my one passion and my one love.

"I jump in the car in the evening, grab the NME and see what's on and go somewhere and see something – that won't change."

Pearce's love of music, particularly punk, is legendary, and while Sir Alex Ferguson may have been wined and dined by some of the biggest corporate names on the circuit, Stuart Pearce is the only Premiership manager to have introduced the Sex Pistols on stage. Which has more credibility with the man on the street? Hmm, tough one. He's seen more live gigs than he can remember and has seen The Stranglers perhaps 50 times to date.

"I saw Stiff Little Fingers recently and saw them a few times on the tour they were just on," he says. "They're very good. I saw Spear of Destiny at The Band on the Wall and have seen Stereophonics, Green Day and Marilyn Manson – he was good showman – up at the MEN Arena, too.

"I think it's a good catchment area around here, with so many good, decent Manchester bands – I went to see the Drop Kick Murphy's at the Liverpool Academy recently – they were very good.

"I travel up to Stoke, Crewe, and Blackburn to see gigs. It's good because within an hour you can get quite a way to see either football matches or bands."

So what reaction is there when Stuart Pearce mingles with the crowd? Is he able to come and go as freely as the other punters or is it not as straightforward as that?

"I think they are used to seeing me now," says Pearce. "Everyone knows and because it's a fairly close-knit community, you do tend to see some familiar faces at certain gigs.

"Quite often I go on my own and if the band is on at 9.30pm, I'll get there about 9.25pm and the lights are down and I'm gone at the end, unless I know a couple of members in the band and then I will pop in and have a quick drink with them and shoot off afterwards.

"There's no big song and dance about me being there – no 'Elvis is in the building' sort of thing.

"I went to see The Stranglers at an all-dayer at the Birmingham Academy not so long ago. SLF, The Buzzcocks, The Beat and various others were on, but it was a longish day and I must admit I was feeling my age at the end. I wouldn't have liked to have cleaned up after the gig, that's for sure."

Music plays a big part of Pearce's life away from football, but it would be naive to think it didn't play at least some part of his motivational thinking for the City team. In fact, the dressing room is a totally different place under the new Blues manager.

"We have music in the dressing room all the time," he revealed. "I was the instigator of music in the dressing room at Nottingham Forest and also Newcastle United – I just think it relaxes the players.

"I'm a great believer that the sights and sounds influence your moods. We turn it off about ten minutes before kick-off when we are really trying to key into a game, and then it's bang! Time to get you mind on other things, but I love music in the dressing room.

"The music the team runs out to is important to me, but tradition dictates at times at football clubs, but we've tried different things since I've been in charge. For instance, the walls of the changing room were a bit bland, so we've put motivational things on the walls, team orientated stuff from some great coaches from other professions.

"To be honest, it used to be like walking into a bloody doctor's surgery, so from day one we went in there and I said, right, from the first home game, I want a picture of every player on their individual locker, motivational slogans on the wall; stuff that gives us some identity.

"To walk into a dressing room and walk out again and not have a clue which team play at this football club is wrong. I went on a course at Twickenham a while back and I went in the dressing room and you knew exactly who owned each locker and who played there because it had so much identity and I think that is of key importance, I really do.

"If you walk along and you hear music or you see walls with messages and information on, you digest it subconsciously."

One gets the feeling that with Pearce in charge, the players and the fans are now all singing from the same hymn sheet. Let the chorus begin again this August.

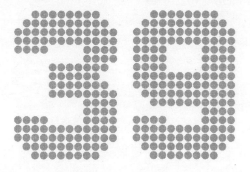

> **GOAL!** Silva picks the ball up at the edge of the area before sliding a pass through to Toure. Toure flicks the ball on to the on-running Zabaleta who stabs the ball at goal where Kenny can only push the ball upwards and it loops over his head and in off the post to put City 1-0 up...

15:39

School Of Hard Knocks

Ben Thatcher was a decent player and a good bloke – but his signing failed to capture the imagination of City fans who were becoming concerned at the lack of star names coming into the club...

Ben Thatcher already looks like part of the furniture at Carrington and has settled into life at City like a hand into a glove. He's lean, quick and plays like a good old-fashioned left-back should – totally committed, while taking no prisoners.

Already his hard but fair tackling has impressed the Blues' support, and whether he likes it or not, he certainly puts you in mind of the footballer who perhaps influenced him more than any other – joint-first team coach Stuart Pearce.

Along with Danny Mills, it's fair to say that City's defence has taken on a much sharper edge, with neither full-back ever likely to give opposing forwards anything but a tough 90-minute workout every time they play.

Thatcher began life at Millwall's Academy, attending the Lilleshall School of Excellence where he continued his soccer education with other talented youngsters. It was while he was there that the Swindon-born player studied Kenny Sansom, and due to the location, he was able to go and watch Pearce play for Nottingham Forest and see how the best left-back in the country plied his trade.

After impressing at the New Den, where he made 90 starts in four years, he was off to join what was still The Crazy Gang at Wimbledon, who paid in excess of £2m for his services. A former youth international, he won the first of three England Under-21 caps with the now extinct Dons before George Graham signalled him out as his number one target.

The then-Spurs boss shelled out more than £5m for Thatcher, but far from being his dream move, the defender picked up an injury that severely limited his appearances for the White Hart Lane side. In his absence, Glenn Hoddle arrived as manager and that was the beginning of the end for the player.

Thatcher recovered from an operation that had kept him out for more than six months, but Hoddle had signed Christian Ziege to play in his position. The relationship between Thatcher and Hoddle, who played Thatcher only in fits and starts, deteriorated rapidly and a move away was the best for all concerned.

Mickey Adams needed a solid defender to strengthen his newly-promoted Leicester City side and Thatcher fitted the bill perfectly. The deal was agreed and the player couldn't wait to make a fresh start with the Foxes.

Thatcher proved to be one of the most popular players at The Walkers Stadium last season but relegation from the Premiership was not something he needed after battling his way back to his best form. He'd also won his first Welsh caps after a loophole in the rules allowed him to switch from England to the birth nation of his grandmother.

Though he would have been happy to remain a Leicester player had nobody come in, Portsmouth and City emerged in a tug-of-war for his services and he chose the Manchester Blues ahead of Harry Redknapp's side. Now he's raring to go and is already enjoying life at his new club.

"I was disappointed to miss the first two pre-season games with a dead leg," said Thatcher. "Other than that, we've had a 100 per cent record in the other games and we've scored a few goals along the way, too. It's been a good pre-season and I think it helps that we played at Hull, Wolves and Reading, who all have decent grounds.

"I think it's better when you don't go away on those long tours because you can spend more time with your family. So it's all gone well so far."

Having played for three London clubs and a Midlands side, the early impressions of being part of the City squad have all been very positive.

"This is a massive club in its own right, no doubt about it" he declared. "Leicester have a great stadium and the training facilities are all really good, but things at City are all a notch up. Everything is very professional and yet very friendly as well.

"For instance, the kit man, Chappy (Les Chapman), is different class. Anything I've needed from anyone has been taken care of, which is really good.

"As for home life, we're buying a house in Cheshire at the minute and hopefully all the paperwork will be sorted out shortly and we can get all the family up in time for school in September.

"The children are only young – my daughter is three and my son is two – but once they are all settled in, and my wife is settled and happy, it will all make my life a lot easier.

"I'm living in a hotel at present, which is the only downside of things, but we should be moving into the house in the next couple of weeks. Another plus concerning the move to City is that my parents live in North Wales and my brother lives in Blackburn, so I'm a lot closer to my family now and I'll be seeing much more of them."

It's still a case of 'getting to know you' for both player and the supporters in the early weeks of the new season, but the travelling Blue Army have already left an impression on the 28-year-old, who spends as much of his free time with his young family and his dog as possible.

"I went to watch the lads at Bury and during the second half, there were still City fans streaming in. I think there was about 9,000 for the first away game, and while Tottenham are supposedly a big club, they couldn't get anywhere near that kind of following.

"It just makes you wonder what might happen if this club can really get going – it could be absolutely frightening."

Mission Impossible?

As Joey Barton's star began to rise, his off-field problems intensified. I always enjoyed Joey's company. He was an intelligent and articulate lad, but whether he continued to press self-destruct remained to be seen...

If there is one man on a mission this season, it's Joey Barton. The talented midfielder's well-publicised problems could even have seen the club turn its back on him this summer, but instead, manager Stuart Pearce imposed an eight-week fine and ordered Joey to attend Tony Adams' Sporting Chance clinic in Hampshire to undergo lifestyle coaching.

Pearce has already noticed a big difference in the former England

Under-21 star on and off the pitch and Joey has been a major reason the Blues go into today's match with Portsmouth as one of the leading pack.

Now wearing the fabled No.8 jersey, he aims to repay his boss, the chairman and the supporters by showing his debt of gratitude in the shirt, though he has never given any less than his all when he has played in the past.

"Stuart Pearce did not have to do what he did after Thailand," said Joey. "I have great admiration for him, not just as a manager, but also as a man.

"Hopefully I can repay him with performances of a high standard. I am so glad to be part of it and glad the club stuck by me through bad times.

"Everyone knows what kind of summer I have had because it has been well-documented in the media. My release is getting out on that pitch. You get people having a go and saying stupid things, but that's opposition football fans, they see a chink of light and they go for it.

"When I get on the pitch, all the things in my personal life are finished. It is all about beating my opponent on the day and me playing for my football club."

With City aiming to equal an 18-year record today by remaining unbeaten for a twelfth successive game, Joey was also keen to pay tribute to the fans that have given him amazing backing in the first few weeks of the campaign.

The ovation the player received, firstly against Olympiacos and then West Bromwich Albion, is something he will never forget and is determined to repay. Though his popularity has never been in doubt, he has been moved by the vocal backing and messages of support in the past month.

"The fans have been different class," he said. "I knew they would be because I know what they are like when you pull on that shirt.

"Andy Cole might not have been flavour of the month before he got here, but once you pull on that City shirt and have that badge on your chest, you are one of them, and as long as you perform and give everything that you have got, then they will accept you. You cannot ask for more than that.

"The lads have got to be humble by the way the supporters turn out every week for us and get behind us – I know that I am. Who knows what we can achieve together.

"There is a great level of professionalism and will to win within this squad. We are 11 games unbeaten now and only Chelsea can top that. It was just unfortunate that last season ended when it did.

"No one wanted to play us at the end of last term because they knew that everyone in our team was fired up, everyone was fighting for the same cause and we have carried that over into this season. We have still got a lot of work to do, but it is exciting times."

Fast And Not So Furious

*Darius Vassell was a quiet, almost shy person. He signed
for City for about £1.5m − and proved to be well worth
that fee in a productive spell with the Blues...*

D arius Vassell recalls with a shudder the first time he came
within touching distance of Stuart Pearce. He was a young
striker with Aston Villa, desperately trying to make a name
for himself. Pearce, on the other hand, was in the twilight of his career
playing for Newcastle, but still had a formidable reputation.

While Vassell was going through his warm-up in the changing rooms,
waiting anxiously to make his second appearance for his boyhood
club, he kept hearing from the older heads in the Villa team the kind
of treatment he could expect from an gnarly old pro like Pearce.

Jogging out onto the pitch, Vassell was mulling over a couple of things, mainly how he could get himself some space during the game, when the unmistakable hulking frame of Pearce loomed into view. It was then that Vassell made his decision.

"I would definitely say that the gaffer was the type of player you stayed away from!" says Vassell, bursting into laughter as he sits in the plush new video lounge of City's Carrington training retreat.

"I made sure during that game I stayed on the other wing to the one he was on! You certainly didn't want to be on the end of one his tackles back then and even now I'm sure he could still give as good as he gets!"

Happily for City fans, that first impression didn't scare Vassell too much as late last month he was only too happy to accept Pearce's offer to leave Villa Park for a different challenge in the North West.

For what could prove to be the bargain price of £1.5m, Pearce has signed an England international with lightning pace, who knows how to find the target and – given that he is still only 25 – whose best years are still ahead of him.

The move took Vassell by surprise as he had been preparing for the new campaign with Villa in Sweden, anxious to make up for the disappointment of last season, most of which he spent trying to recuperate from a broken ankle.

But when the call from Pearce arrived, Vassell knew the time was right to bring an end his long association with Villa – he had come through the ranks to become a Holte End favourite – and embark on a new adventure.

"Stuart was a great player who has achieved a lot in the game," continues Vassell. "The players have got a lot of respect for him, which is important, and hopefully that can all work together to make us a better team.

"Moving came as a big surprise. I had been at Aston Villa for a long time and the thought of leaving had never really crossed my mind. But I had reached a period in my career where the approach from City came as a massive boost for me.

"My last season at Villa was a bit of a non-event and certainly didn't go as well as I would have hoped. The injury was a big disappointment, but I am fit now and raring to go and a fresh start is what I need having played for Villa for so long.

"This is a good opportunity to take a step forward and further my career. I think a lot of people at Aston Villa felt it was a decision I should make, too. In fairness to them, they have pushed me and done their best for me and that's a really nice feeling."

Villa boss David O'Leary quipped that Vassell's car could probably have arrived at the club training ground on autopilot, given how long the 25-year-old had spent there, so it would have been understandable if he had any nerves over his first move.

Not so. After being escorted around Carrington and then taken on a tour of the stadium by Chief Executive, Alistair Mackintosh, Birmingham-born Vassell couldn't wait to dot the i's and cross the t's on a four-year deal.

"It didn't take me too long to make the decision," he enthuses. "This is the place to be and I can't wait to get started. The training ground was the first place that I came to and I could immediately see the differences of what I had been used to.

"It's really exciting. Obviously, being a Villa lad and a supporter as a kid, they were the best thing in the world for me at one point, so if I did have a move, I wanted it to be to a club of a similar stature, if not bigger.

"It's certainly not a step down coming to Manchester City. It's a step up and I'm looking forward to some success here. For another manager to come out and buy me is very flattering because it is not something that I had been used to.

"I have been around for a long time and played a lot of Premiership football, but this is the first time I have had a move, so it's taking a bit of getting used to. But I'm not a 17-year-old kid any more. I'm a 25-year-old man.

"I know the sacrifices that have to be made to get the best out of your career. Moving house is a minor thing and I'm looking forward to starting a new life in Manchester and creating a good impression on the Manchester City fans.

"I'm the sort of person who likes to keep himself to himself and I'm just looking forward to getting settled in Manchester because it seems like a great place. Both sets of supporters have been helpful to me from day one, which is very encouraging."

There is little doubt that moving will have a galvanising effect on Vassell, and if he can recapture his best form, then surely he will come into Sven-Goran Eriksson's thinking for next summer's World Cup in Germany.

Eriksson, after all, handed Vassell his international debut against Holland three years ago and was rewarded with a spectacular goal. He has since gone on to win another 21 caps as well as keeping up an impressive scoring ratio with more goals.

However, Vassell has had little involvement with the England team since missing a penalty in the Euro 2004 quarter-final shoot-out defeat against Portugal, mainly due to the injury that limited him to just 17 appearances for Villa last season.

But anyone who believes he has moved to City simply to boost his chances of getting on the plane to Germany are mistaken. First and foremost, 'Vas' wants to prove himself to everyone at City, and if rewards come after that, so be it.

"Every season is a big one," he says, matter-of-factly. "Last season it was highlighted that I was out with injury and that was disappointing. But it doesn't make this season any bigger because I still want to achieve the same things and I have the same ambitions. It's just for a different set of people now and I can't wait to do that."

As he can't wait to get going – nor can City supporters wait to see him in action. The prospect of him, Robbie Fowler and Andy Cole all hitting top form through the season is something to savour.

More Local Produce

Stephen Jordan was another Academy graduate to break into the first team – could he make the left-back position his own?

A long with everyone else connected with the club, Stephen Jordan was pleased the Blues managed to keep their excellent home form going with a sixth successive victory against Sunderland a week last Sunday.

Jordan, 24 last week, is enjoying his longest spell yet in the first team and admitted that the basement club caused one or two problems in what turned out to be Mick McCarthy's last game in charge.

"We'd scored two goals in the first ten minutes and then let them back in it and it was backs-to-the-wall stuff at certain times," he said.

"But to get the win was the main thing and that was pleasing."

What wasn't so pleasing was the 'soft' goal conceded midway through the first half that allowed the Wearsiders a lifeline after looking dead and buried at 2-0 down.

"Defensively I thought we did really well to keep them out after giving them the goal," he said. "You are always disappointed as a defender, because as part of a unit, you want to keep clean sheets," he added. "And to let one in the way we did was a bit sloppy. But we got the three points and that's all that matters."

It was the first time City have managed to win four consecutive home victories in the Premiership, and if the Blues are to push for one of the UEFA Cup places, they must continue that kind of form home and away.

Jordan, a boyhood City fan, confirmed European football is the main focus for the team with just a couple of months left before the end of the season. He said: "We can definitely get into that sixth or seventh spot needed for a European place. So it's just a case of keep pushing on and getting there."

While he has been pleased with his own progress this season, Jordan admits his sending off at Everton last month left him feeling flat and angry with himself, but he intends to learn from what was his first early bath since his teens.

"I don't think the first yellow card at Goodison Park was a booking because I think I got the ball, but the second booking was deserved," he admitted. "Arteta elbowed me on the nose prior to the second yellow and I just lost it for a few seconds and dived into the next tackle.

"I hadn't been sent off since I played for the youth team, so it was weird running off at that point because we still had a few minutes to get back in the game. When I got in the dressing room, though, I realised what I had done was a mistake and I was fuming with myself.

"The gaffer told me afterwards to try and play with my head and not my heart, and he was right because I'd lost control for a few seconds."

That apart, Jordan has been one of the most consistent performers for the Blues this season and if he can top last year's appearances total, he'll be pleased overall with the way things are going

"I played 21 times last season, so my aim is to better that, and hopefully by the time the Aston Villa FA Cup tie comes around, I will have achieved that in all competitions," he said.

"I signed a two-year contract last summer, so I've got the rest of this season and all next season to work hard, and it goes without saying that I'd like to stay here for as long as the club want me to."

French Lessons

*Antoine Sibierski never quite won the City fans over
– partly because he replaced Eyal Berkovic in the team.
Not his fault, but true all the same...*

After two seasons of being a regular first team member, Antoine Sibierski has had to fight harder than ever this term for a place in Stuart Pearce's starting line-up. The French attacking midfielder clearly has a big part to play in Pearce's plans after recently penning a new one-year extension to his current deal, but the form of the central midfielders, plus the strikers, has reduced the former Lens man's starts so far.

But after his match-winning display against Birmingham City in the last home game, the manager may find it difficult to leave him out if he continues the same level of performance each time he plays.

Even so, the 31-year-old realises he will not walk back into the team – competition for places is fierce and he accepts he may have to bide his time and wait for his chance in order to re-establish himself in the side.

After making his first start since the October visit to Highbury, he managed to get his name on the scoresheet – his first of the season – and made two more in the 4-1 drubbing of Birmingham City – his most productive display in a City shirt.

"It was a good victory, and we had to win after the poor game we had against West Brom," said Antoine, who is not far off reaching 100 appearances for the Blues. "For me it was important to get into the game because I have not played a lot this season, and Darius and Andy are two very good players.

"It's not been easy for me to play this season, but when the manager needs me, I have to give my best to show he can trust me when he needs me. That's what happened against Birmingham and I'm very happy.

"We had a respect for Birmingham, but we had a high tempo from the first minute, scored twice in the first quarter of an hour and that's why we won. I knew on Friday I would play, but I did not feel too much pressure because if you think too much about it, it will affect your game."

Whether Antoine will start today's game against the Premiership champions or not, is yet to be decided. The result and team performance against Wigan Athletic will no doubt play a major part, but he is, as always, philosophical about the dilemma.

"Maybe I will play – I don't know, it is up to the manager to decide," he said with a customary smile. "But if he needs me, I'm ready. Even if I know that I'm not going to play every game because Andy and Darius are his first choice, I am here if he needs me."

And that's exactly the attitude that convinced Stuart Pearce that this is a player he doesn't want to lose in a hurry.

The ball reaches Aguero who drops a shoulder and takes a shot which Kenny saves comfortably to his right-hand side...

15:44

Dreadlock Holiday

Kiki Musampa was typical of the signings Stuart Pearce made during his time as City boss – steady, experienced and either free, on loan or in the bargain basket. He wasn't a bad player, Kiki, but it was ultimately a brief stay...

Kiki Musampa hasn't given up hope of joining the Holland squad for next summer's World Cup and knows top-notch performances in a Manchester City shirt will be his only ticket into Marco van Basten's squad.

The naturalized Dutch midfielder was part of a training camp for Holland last summer in recognition to his impressive end-of-season

178

form with the Blues, which included several sizzling goals along the way, and he his eager for more involvement.

He knows being content with his off-field life is crucial to showing his best form, and in that respect, he couldn't be happier. Whether van Basten deems his performances for City good enough to join a squad that indirectly enabled England to guarantee qualification for Germany 2006, remains to be seen.

Kiki, formerly of Ajax, Bordeaux and Malaga, will be giving it his best shot and is relieved he is still in Manchester after a brief period of uncertainty following Kevin Keegan's departure.

"I was happy I made the choice to come to City and experience English life," said Kiki. "Even if my loan hadn't been extended in the summer, I thought, no matter what happened, I was glad I came.

"It wasn't up to me what happened as regards to me staying here, so I just had to wait, but Stuart Pearce had a conversation with me just before I left for the summer break and he made things quite clear to me.

"After that, there was no doubt in my mind that I'd be returning to play for City this season. I am enjoying my football and life in Manchester, so staying with City was always my first choice.

"I must say I'm very happy here both as a player and living in England. Everything about the club is great and I've had great support from the crowd, which is very important. But as for my future beyond this season, I'm just going to have to wait and see what the club wants to do.

"I feel better and better each week and if this loan move becomes permanent in the future, I'd be even happier."

Toure fails to continue and comes off, receiving a standing ovation from the City fans. He is replaced by Nigel de Jong. Three minutes of added time result in any meaningful action and the whistle goes for half-time: City 1 QPR 0.

15:45
15:46
15:47
15:48

No Man Is An Ireland

Stephen Ireland – gifted and a popular figure among City fans – his ability and talent would mean this was the first of several interviews with the quiet Irishman...

Stephen Ireland has burst into the first team this season with all the confidence of a seasoned pro. The Cork-born playmaker made a big impression during pre-season, with boss Stuart Pearce impressed with the way the youngster adapted to the senior squad with such aplomb.

Now, following impressive cameos against Bolton and Newcastle,

180

plus his full debut against Doncaster, Ireland is set to up the ante and challenge for a regular spot in the team.

The good news for City is that the 19-year-old is love with the Blues and would like nothing better than to end his career with the club he's been with since he was 14. He is also father to a toddler and certainly is a level-headed young man who knows where he wants to go and what he wants to achieve.

"To succeed in football, a lot of it has to be up in your head," he said. "I want to progress, and having had a taste of first team football, I'm hungry for more of the same. I just have to be patient and make sure that I continue a steady development.

"I speak to Willo (Flood) and Nedum (Onuoha) about their experience at first team level. I asked Nedum what it was like when he played at Highbury last season and stood next to Patrick Vieira in the tunnel.

"He said, of course it was natural for your heart to be racing and butterflies in your stomach. But when you are on the pitch, you have to play to the best of your ability. There is nothing else you can do.

"You can't hide in big games like that. When the fans are screaming at you, they expect a lot. I always wondered how I'd feel in that situation and whether my nerves would take over.

"I don't suppose it's bad to be nervous, though. Nerves show you've got desire."

Stephen arrived in Manchester five years ago and was signed from Roy Keane's former club, Cobh Ramblers. His girlfriend lived in Ireland up to last year, but they are all together now and that's helping him settle down even more.

"Jennifer and Joshua moved over here almost a year ago and I couldn't be happier," he said. "Some people reckoned it would halt my career when my son was born when I was just 17, but Joshua is brilliant and it hasn't wrecked my career at all.

"It just changes your life. It's up to you how you change it. My son has been a massive inspiration to me and that's why I'm more determined than ever to succeed."

Judging by his performances so far, succeeding with City has already begun and not since the departures of Eyal Berkovic and Ali Benarbia has the club had such a natural playmaker. He has already become something of a crowd favourite and international recognition can't be far away, either, if he continues to impress. But City are first in his thoughts, as he explains: "I don't want to rush into anything with internationals. I have seen people go away from their clubs for two weeks to play friendlies, come back, play a reserve game and then go away for another three weeks. I don't want that.

"I want to stay with my club and keep progressing. I want the manager to see what I can do for him. He's not going to say: 'Stephen's had a great game for his country, so let's put him in.' Having a great game for the reserves is more important.

"If I have a long a successful career here, it wouldn't bother me if I never played for my country. I'm in love with this club and want to do everything I can to keep my place in the future."

City start with intent. Clichy puts in a dangerous cross which Aguero meets at the front post before his effort is directed wide by Kenny out for a corner. The corner is cleared at the near post. De Jong then wins a free-kick around 30 yards from goal...

Clever Trevor

This brief interview with Trevor Sinclair was a preview for an upcoming match during a barren spell in terms of goals...

While only Chelsea, Arsenal and Manchester United can equal City's record of six clean sheets this season, the Blues' well-publicised lack of goals is among the worst in the country.

Chances have come and gone for Stuart Pearce's side, but just four home goals this season is a concern for a team that is still looking to spark into life on the road, too. It's a problem the players are working hard to solve and Trevor Sinclair believes it is just a matter of time before the goals start to flow again.

"We know that scoring has been a problem for us and we are working hard to put it right," said Sinclair, himself yet to get off the mark this season.

"It's not for lack of effort that we are not scoring – that's for sure. We have put in extra training on our finishing to the point that the manager has to drag us in because he doesn't want us to have heavy legs.

"We have kept plenty of clean sheets and there is no doubt that we now need to concentrate on scoring goals. Everyone, including the manager, has been putting in the hours on the training ground to make sure that we put it right."

Those extra sessions will hopefully bear fruit this afternoon against Chris Coleman's Fulham, though the Cottagers have proved a tough nut to crack on the road since their 5-1 opening day mauling by Manchester United.

If chances are at a premium, set-pieces will become even more important in the effort to end the goal drought – and today's clash with Fulham is the ideal time to start, with the West London side having completed the league double over the Blues last season.

"The manager has introduced new ideas on set-pieces and they have helped us create more openings at Charlton and against Newcastle, and we've been really unlucky that they've not paid off so far," said Sinclair.

"We have to keep battering away and hope that something drops for us. When it does, I think we will start scoring more regularly.

"We've kept quite a few clean sheets and we need to do that more away from home and that will help us. At home we've not conceded a goal as yet and we need to concentrate now on finding the back of the net.

"We're all working together and pulling in the same direction, but we'll keep battling away and we just need something to drop for us and start scoring."

Nasri bends the free-kick towards the top corner but it clears the crossbar and QPR survive again...

Oh, Danny Boy

Daniel Sturridge always got a bit of a rough deal as far as I could see. A young lad, could anyone really blame him for accepting a better offer at Chelsea? The truth is, he never really wanted to leave in the first place. We travelled to his home in Cheshire for this interview and spoke as we walked around a local lake – all long before his move south...

Rarely, if ever, has there been such intense media speculation about a young player at Manchester City as there has Danny Sturridge over the past couple of years. The teenage prodigy has been happily banging goals in for club and country in recent seasons, and as he neared this 16th birthday, national tabloids confidently predicted Chelsea or Arsenal would whisk him away to the capital.

In fact, it was as good as over if you read certain red tops, and the Blues would have little say in the matter. The London giants would wave their magic wands and that'd be that. Of course, the reality was something, as Monty Python used to say, completely different.

The ill-founded press reports didn't take into account (or rather ignored) the fact that City were determined to hang on to their talented youngster, and more importantly, young Sturridge had no intentions of moving south to further his career.

While the interest from other clubs is almost certainly true, City always felt confident that Sturridge would realise the best opportunity of being fast-tracked into first team football, depending on progress, was with them.

It was with some degree of relief, then, when Sturridge put pen to paper on a three-year contract last month and committed his immediate future to the club. Now the quietly spoken England Under-17 star can concentrate on impressing Stuart Pearce in the coming weeks and months as he continues his football education.

Football is in Danny's blood, hailing from something close to a football dynasty. The Sturridge family has now spawned four professional players and including Danny and his father, Michael, there are his uncles, Simon and Dean, who have both enjoyed distinguished careers in English football.

It's clear to see that he is being brought up to be a fine young man with no airs or graces about him and a solid family alongside him all the way. He doesn't have an agent; when he needs advice, his father – a former pro at Birmingham City – and his older brother, Leon, are always there for him to help guide him down the right path.

Intelligent and respectful and undoubtedly destined to be something of a pin-up boy, Danny arrived in the world at the same baby unit another young City star was delivered slightly over a year before.

"Yeah, I was born in City Hospital, Birmingham – the same hospital as Micah Richards, actually," smiled Danny. Perhaps City should station a scout permanently on that particular maternity ward?

"I first played for the school team as a seven-year-old, but I was on the bench because most of the boys were older than me. Some of them have also gone on to do well. Two of the lads are at Coventry City and one plays for Villa – it was a good side to play in.

"I think I ended up playing as a striker because I was quite small. I used to play with my brother Leon and his mates who were all a lot older than me and I used to get knocked about a bit.

"Leon would always look out for me and he set me up as often as he could with tap-ins. Along with my dad, my brother's taught me everything I know. I also played for Cadbury's Athletic from the age of seven and their home pitch is actually on the site of the chocolate factory grounds.

"I reckon it's still one of the best playing surfaces I've ever played on. I was with them for a year, but being naturally left-footed, I hardly ever used my right, so my dad drilled me for around five years straight until I'd improved sufficiently – it's been a huge help in my development.

"It was while I was at Cadbury's that I was scouted for Aston Villa, but because I was seven, I was too young to sign for them. I'd go along and train with their Under-9s, but it wasn't until I was nine that I actually signed forms of any kind. I think because I've always played with older kids, it really helped my development because physically I learned to handle myself and adapt my game.

"My uncles, Simon and Dean, were always around when I was small. I've always been around football, whether it was playing with my brother, my dad training me or watching games with my uncles involved. I can't remember a time when I didn't have a ball with me.

"I watched uncle Dean whenever I could when he was at Derby County and used to go along to Pride Park and the Baseball Ground before that with my dad. The team I supported was Newcastle United, though, because that's who my brother supported and I generally followed and did as he did.

"Kevin Keegan was manager at the time, too, which is ironic because he was manager at City when I signed five years ago.

"The reasons I came here are simple, really. I played for Coventry against Manchester City in an academy game and Frankie Bunn got chatting with my dad. I was about 11 by this time and it wasn't long after that game that I first met City's recruitment officer, Barry Poynton.

"He paved the way for me to join City and talked at length to my dad about what the club had to offer. My dad asked if I'd like to move up to Manchester and added he felt that moving out of Birmingham would be good for me.

"It was another change of environment – more so this time because it was a new city away from my friends and some of my family – but I thought 'why not?' I liked the area and was impressed by the facilities at City, but Barry is the main reason I moved here and I've him to thank for the way things have gone since.

"I did get to speak to Kevin Keegan as well, and it was good to meet him, if not a little weird having been a fan of Newcastle when I was a kid. City had some great players and he said he thought coming to City would be the right step to take at that stage of my career, and I agreed.

"The City fans have been great with me, especially in the FA Youth Cup final where they got behind us hugely. They've stuck behind the first team when things haven't been going well and, for me, they are the best supporters in the country."

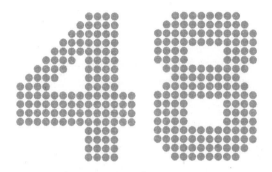

Brief Encounter

Bernardo Corradi — the truth is nobody had really heard of him. He would have limited impact during a short spell before he was packed off on loan...

Bernardo Corradi, City's new Italian striker, is a cert to become a favourite, not only with his team-mates, but also the Blues' ever-growing female following.

At 30, Corradi has reached a level of maturity that allows him to take moving to a new country in his long and powerful stride.

He has already sampled a working life in Spain, but it is England that has tugged at his wanderlust ever since he was a boy kicking around a ball in the streets of that wonderful Tuscan idyll, Siena.

As you would expect from the son of two bank employees, Bernardo took no risks when it was suggested he might be talented enough to become a professional footballer.

Instead of dashing off to a glamorous club where he might have just been another face; another hopeful kid mortgaging his future without a squad number, he decided to take his parents' advice; invest in his education and become a rounded individual rather than a teenager institutionalised in the sport.

The fact he lived in an area known throughout the world for its natural beauty hardly helped propel him at warp factor nine towards the industrialised big city, but he nevertheless slowly but surely made his way from his local club to becoming an Italian international.

Just as important as the fame and fortune, Bernardo achieved his lifestyle aims at the same time as keeping the friends he made as a boy.

"I didn't start travelling around until I was 19 or 20, and though I might have lost some years playing in Serie A, I enjoyed a normal life with my family and friends in the place I love," he refreshingly declared without the merest hint that he felt he had missed out on anything important.

"The way I think is that you can't have everything, and those boys who joined clubs in their early teens missed out on so much. They miss their family and they lose their childhood friends because they are always travelling somewhere with the club.

"I know who my friends are, which is important, because when you are a footballer with fame, a lot of people stay around you because of what you are.

"It was a conscious decision by me to build my career up slowly. First from the third division, to the second, to the first and then the Premier league, step-by-step, which was nice.

"I started with my hometown team, Siena, for a couple of years and then moved to a team nearby. I had to finish my schooling before my parents would allow me to play football, so in some ways I suppose I am something of a late starter."

Despite his self-imposed tardiness at trying to get his name in lights, Corradi did have a bit of a head start given that his dad also played in the Italian lower leagues – part-time – for a decade and a half.

City's new centre-forward not only inherited some of the natural family ability, but also the family values.

"My father played from the age of 20 until he was 36 and he still always tells me he was better than me," chortled the striker with an oh so Italian shrug of the shoulders followed by a dismissive waving of the hands and a huge grin.

"When he played, it wasn't like it is today where a footballer can make a lot of money – he had just finished his studies at a very good school and was offered a position in the bank, which he took. He decided that would be his career, and though he continued to play football, it was only at third division level. He could have played at a higher level, but that would have meant leaving his job and moving from Siena, and he wasn't prepared to do that.

"He played for a team where the owner was a very wealthy man who put a lot of money into the club. The owner paid good wages and the team behaved and were treated like professionals. They didn't need to wash their kits as it was all done for them – unheard of at that level – and he enjoyed his time with them. Unfortunately I never got to see him play because by the time I had the opportunity, he had stopped playing."

Despite his laid-back approach to life off the pitch, Corradi knows what he wants from life now and in a few years time when he retires. He will head back to the Tuscan hills about which he never tires of talking.

"Siena is about 60km from Florence and I think it's one of the most beautiful places in the world because you have good weather, good wine, good food and we are surrounded by natural beauty. Everywhere is so green – it's an amazing place," he gushes.

191

"There are a lot of hills and on one is the historic city centre with an ancient wall running around the perimeter, which was used for protection many years ago.

"The streets are up and down, small and winding and the town is full of historic places and museums. It's a wonderful place and when I've finished playing football, I will return to live there. It's where I've always had a base and where my family and friends have always been. We have the countryside, mountains and sea – we are very lucky!"

So what of his dramatic debut and red card at Stamford Bridge? He smiles at the mention of it.

"I'm so sorry about my debut at Chelsea! Getting sent off was not what I intended, but I felt the second yellow card was a bit harsh.

"I'm not sure what Essien was trying to do when he grabbed my hair – maybe he likes it, so I will cut off a lock for him when we play Chelsea at home! I may even give him the address of my stylist!

"I had to take something from the red card, so I looked at it that I had a few extra days to prepare for my home debut against Arsenal! Things went much better in that game, I think!

"I'm looking forward to my friends and family coming to see me play for City – they are all very excited at the thought of coming to Manchester. Things are so different because in Italy we don't have a restaurant inside the stadium, and before a game we'd all stay in a hotel, even for home games.

"Here, I can stay at home until three hours before a home game, then travel to the stadium with my parents and friends if I want to. I've already found a lot of nice places to eat in Manchester, and if I'm alone, I'll eat out because it's boring cooking for yourself.

"If my family are over, we'll eat in because I'm not a bad cook. I'm enjoying myself in England and I'm feeling at home already. One of my dreams from being a teenager was to play in the Premiership in England and now I aim to make the most of it."

Kevin Keegan

Mario Balotelli

Claudio Reyna

Joleon Lescott

Yaya Toure

Ali Benarbia   Gerard Wiekens   Paulo Wanchope

Sylvain Distin   Kevin Horlock   Nicolas Anelka

Peter Schmeichel   Darren Huckerby   Jihai Sun

Marc Vivien Foe   Eyal Berkovic   David Seaman

Michael Tarnat

Jerome Boateng

Christian Negouai

Arni Arason

Paul Bosvelt

Robbie Fowler

Shaun Wright-Phillips

Bradley Wright-Phillips

Nedum Onuoha

Stuart Pearce

Kevin Stuhr-Ellegaard

Ben Thatcher

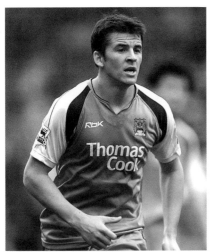

Joey Barton

David Silva

David James

Carlos Tevez

Craig Bellamy

Pablo Zabaleta

Aleksandar Kolarov

Kolo Toure

James Milner

Nigel de Jong

Samir Nasri

Micah Richards

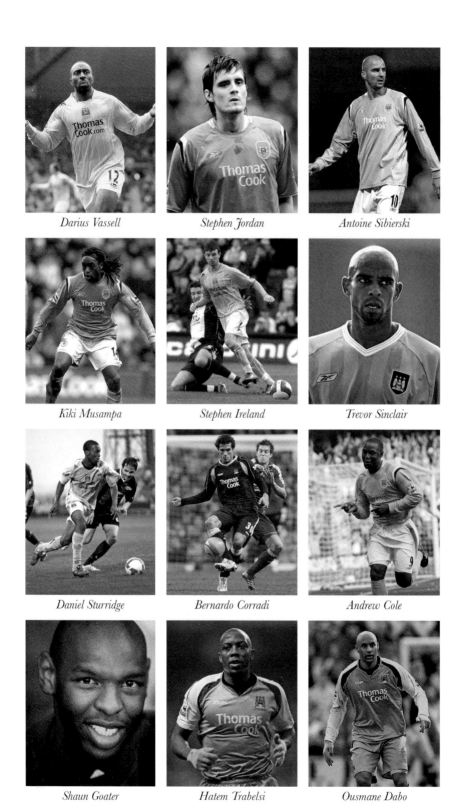

Darius Vassell   Stephen Jordan   Antoine Sibierski

Kiki Musampa   Stephen Ireland   Trevor Sinclair

Daniel Sturridge   Bernardo Corradi   Andrew Cole

Shaun Goater   Hatem Trabelsi   Ousmane Dabo

DaMarcus Beasley   Georgios Samaras   Sven-Goran Eriksson

Rolando Bianchi   Valeri Bojinov   Nicky Weaver

Elano   Geovanni   Richard Dunne

Mark Hughes   Tal Ben-Haim   Robinho

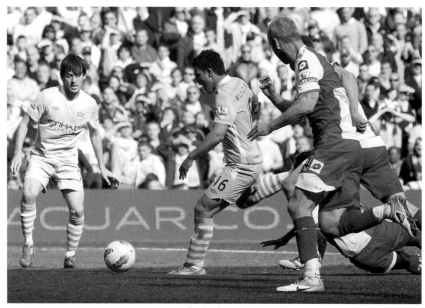

Sergio Aguero

Joe Hart

Vincent Kompany

Roberto Mancini

Steve McManaman

16:06

There are wild celebrations from the visiting fans and players which last almost a minute before City kick off again...

Cole Mining

Who'd have thought United favourite Andy Cole would ever end up in City colours? He was welcomed nonetheless, and proved he still had what it took to score at the top level, but it would be his last season as a professional. We met at Carrington and he was a nice guy, though very quiet...

Andy Cole has started his City career pretty much the same way he has done at each club he's played for – by finding the net regularly. With just three appearances to date for the Blues, he's already bagged two goals and set up another couple for good measure.

Any concerns over his links 'across the road' were banished when he received a standing ovation as he ran off after being substituted against Greek champions Olympiacos last Saturday.

Now the prolific striker is hoping to carry that fine start into the Premiership, starting with today's match with West Bromwich Albion, and prove his blood runs blue these days.

At 33, he is second only to Alan Shearer and one place ahead of Robbie Folwer in the all-time Premiership scoring lists, and he is hoping to add to his 268 goals from 504 starts in all competitions this season.

"The move came out of the blue but the opportunity was too good to turn down," said Andy, who isn't sure why such a big thing has been made of calling him 'Andrew' in recent years. The truth is he's fine with either version and suspects it was a little mischief in the press that started it in the first place.

He is also acutely aware of the tradition and size of the club he has joined and was delighted when Stuart Pearce came in for him.

"I have been fortunate to play for some big clubs and this is another big club that I am going to play for," he said. "I've played against the gaffer a few times and know him reasonably well.

"When he said that he wanted me to come to the club, that was very important, and I knew that I couldn't turn him down."

Just as was the case with Peter Schmeichel and Terry Cooke in recent years, the City fans have welcomed Andy into the fold with enthusiasm, and his predatory instincts are likely to earn him an even bigger fan club as the season progresses.

He is aware there is work to be done, but that doesn't frighten the former England striker at all.

He said: "I am a player who has always liked a challenge and this is definitely another challenge. I am not the first player to have played for both teams in Manchester and it's not as if I have come straight from Manchester United to City.

"I have had two clubs in between – Blackburn and Fulham – and I can't see it being a problem. Whatever club I have been at, I have given 110 per cent, and that will certainly be the case here.

"When I play football, I play to win. If anything changed in me, I would stop playing the game. I give my all and that's what I am about. Also, I never left the Manchester area and this is our family home.

"We've been here 11 years now and my wife is a Londoner, but this is where we love and want to live. It's a beautiful part of the world and there's no way we'd uproot now," added the Nottingham-born forward.

"I'm really happy to be a City player and this club has amazing support. The problem City has had in the recent past has been stability – they'd come up, go back down again and so on – and the fans have suffered a lot of heartache along the way.

"For them to come out in the numbers they did in Division Two and Division One takes some doing. They've shown amazing loyalty and I look forward to playing in front of them."

50
Catching Up With The Goat

After ghosting Shaun Goater's autobiography, I was lucky enough to meet up with Shaun again in Bermuda on holiday — we did the interview at a soccer school he was hosting, sat in the bleachers under a red-hot sun...

Anyone looking for the perfect example of a modern-day cult hero need look no further than Bermudian striker Leonardo Shaun Goater, a man who refused to give up on a dream and despite not being blessed with the skills of his boyhood heroes Zico and John Barnes, he possessed the heart of a lion and immense courage and determination in his quest to follow his dream.

His is a story that borders on a modern-day fairytale and is a perfect example to anybody who refuses to give up on their dream. But to achieve his status as City's favourite modern-day player, he had to embark on a journey of self-discovery with an apprenticeship that would have seen off many a hardened pro to win over a set of supporters who, in football terms, were more often than not on the verge of a nervous breakdown.

Goater's tale began in the anything-but-ethereal surrounds of Court Street in Hamilton, capital of Bermuda. Born into a large, close-knit family, he was, for most of his younger years, the only child, with his father – in typical style of one of the ghetto areas of the picturesque island – little more than a puzzle; a shadowy figure in the background and someone he would know nothing of until he was in his late teens.

"I didn't need my daddy," says the eloquent Shaun. "I had my momma, aunts, cousins and the rock of the Goater family, my grandmother, Dorothy Dillon. We got along just fine and I had a happy childhood."

Civil unrest – caused by the assassination of the island's Governor – meant that a four-year-old Shaun was living, and playing, in the middle of rioting youths and looters, but the Goater family reputation for strong-minded independent women, several of whom lived at Shaun's grandmother's house on Court Street, meant that any local hoodlums or drug pushers ensured the naive kid was kept out of harm's way. Better that than feel the unbridled wrath of Dorothy Dillon or her daughters.

"We didn't have much money but my mom would always make sure I had everything I needed," recalls Shaun. "She worked hard as a housemaid in the local hotels, often having two jobs to make sure we had food on the table and clothes on our back. It was a good grounding for me because it ensured I always counted my blessings and appreciated everything I had."

He soon earned the reputation as a promising young footballer, often urged on by his mother ("pass the ball to my son – he'll score the goals!") and by his teens he was playing for one of the island's best sides, North Village.

It was his prowess as a footballer that would earn him a scholarship in the USA, but a strange twist of fate was about to turn his world upside down and present an opportunity that would – controversially – offer him a path to one of the most famous clubs in the world.

"I was doing okay in my schooling but was missing home and playing football," recalls Shaun. "I returned to Bermuda during the Thanksgiving break and discovered Manchester United had taken a short mid-winter break to the island."

An alleged incident in a local nightclub led to Manchester United star Clayton Blackmore being arrested and accused of a serious assault. Though no charges were brought and the case being dropped, Shaun has always felt that the political wheels didn't just begin to turn following this event, but rather spin furiously and he found himself the centre of attention when, following an exhibition match showcasing Bermuda's best young talents, Manchester United invited him to England for a trial.

"I did okay in the match," he says. "It was a kind of pre-match entertainment before United played the national team, and I was considered one of the best young players in Bermuda, but the offer of a trial seemed almost too good to be true.

"I have always believed there were politics involved in the offer – a kind of headline diverting move by United and possibly officials in Bermuda, too. The stigma attached to the accusations was damaging to Manchester United and the future of such clubs visiting Bermuda in the future – not that I was complaining. It's just a gut-feeling I have backed with no solid evidence that I was being used as a pawn."

The offer of a trip to England and the chance of following his dreams of becoming a professional footballer were in conflict with his schooling, but everybody he knew and cared about agreed this was a chance too good to turn down. He simply had to make the trip and see where it took him.

He travelled to Manchester, met Alex Ferguson and did his best during his brief stay before flying home to begin an alternative career as a junior in a surveyor's office. He was playing for North Village again and also blossoming for the national team, and it was on one such jaunt overseas that the news he'd dreamed of, and hoped for, was announced.

"Several months had passed since my trial," he recalls. "I'd pretty much given up on the idea of being signed by United and then the national coach, during a team briefing blurts out 'and congratulations to Shaun Goater who has been offered a two-year deal by Manchester United' – I was like 'say what?'."

He said his goodbyes to his family and high school sweetheart and travelled to England to begin his professional career, and though the money was poor (he could earn more back home packing groceries for wealthy American tourists), he began to learn his trade.

But his suspicion of the motives behind his move to Old Trafford was always at the back of his mind, and though he did well for the youth team and reserves, when injury and suspension offered the possibility of a first team chance, he was overlooked on several different occasions.

"I watched my team-mates Lee Sharpe and Mark Robins progress, but I felt that even if I saw my two years out at United, I'd never get anywhere. In truth, I was no better than lads who were already at United and had travelled from around the UK as opposed to being invited over from a country several thousand miles away, all of which further aroused my suspicions of why I was there in the first place. So when Rotherham United came in for me, initially requesting a loan deal, I thought 'why not?'

"The fans at Rotherham didn't take any crap and they'd let you know if they thought you weren't pulling your weight," he says. "I remember this guy waiting by the tunnel for me as I came off at Millmoor and he was about 16 stone and covered in tattoos. 'You're ripping us off Goater' he shouted at me and I just thought 'At £400 a week, you're ripping me off!' – though self-preservation ensured I kept my observations to myself."

Financial incentives didn't exist at Rotherham and despite his goalscoring record, they weren't prepared to up his wages and he felt he wasn't appreciated by the club. When Bristol City offered an escape route, he took it willingly and he and his wife Anita moved to a place they reckoned was as near to life in Bermuda as possible in England.

"The sun shone more, you could smell the sea and there were seagulls everywhere," he says. "We walked around town and knew it was the right place to move to. I felt happy and recharged and I think it showed in my play."

Goater became a popular figure at Ashton Gate, finishing top scorer in his first season and he was flying in his second campaign and headed for Division One as Bristol steamrollered their way to promotion.

But in the league above, Manchester City were fighting to keep out of the relegation zone and with seven games to go, they still had a chance to crawl away. Manager Joe Royle had remembered Goater from his days as Oldham's manager – when the young striker had scored against his reserve team – and followed his career ever since.

He lodged a bid of £400,000 with Bristol, which was reluctantly accepted, and with just minutes of the transfer deadline left, Shaun's dream move hung in the balance, as he explains: "I loved my time at Ashton Gate, but when I was told Manchester City were interested in signing me, I knew this was the move I'd been waiting for. I had a series of forms to sign by fax, but with time running out, my bloody temperamental fax machine at home broke.

"My wife Anita ushered me away and said she'd sort it, but the deadline passed without me knowing if the forms had reached City in time or even at all. I was a nervous wreck!"

The forms had reached Maine Road and Shaun was now a City player. He still hadn't actually spoken to Joe Royle up to that point, but he didn't care. It had taken nine years of hard graft to get to a club this big and this was the stage he'd been hoping for.

Nothing would stand in his way from here on in.

He made his debut at Bradford City and his new team were soon 1-0 up, and though he almost scored with a clever lob, his neat flicks and touches were ultimately in vain as the hosts fought back to win 2-1.

He managed to score on his home debut against Stockport, but City were a club with numerous problems. The fans were tired of their underachieving players and Shaun had walked into the eye of a storm. Even at the training sessions at Platt Lane, the players were subjected to hecklers and confidence was low among the squad.

"There was this guy who was having go at everyone, including me, saying that we were rubbish and a waste of money," smiles Shaun. "All the self-belief and verve I'd arrived with from Bristol with sapped away within a few weeks and I was soon as edgy as the other lads were.

"I felt the crowd were waiting for us to make mistakes, especially at home, and it was an awkward situation to be in."

The inevitable final day drama City have often found themselves over the years meant that even if City won at Stoke, if the three teams above them all won, the Blues would be relegated to the third tier of English football for the first time in the club's proud history.

The fans were also suspicious of Goater's talents and whether this journeyman striker was worthy of leading their team's fight against the drop. His record to that point of one goal in six games was, in their eyes, not good enough and his name synonymous with lower league successes, not the grandeur of a club like Manchester City who had seen the likes of Francis Lee, Mike Summerbee, Dennis Tueart, Trevor Francis and Niall Quinn lead the front line – who was Shaun Goater anyway?

City battled away at Stoke and, frustratingly, looked a class apart at times. Shaun scored twice in a 5-2 win – but it wasn't enough. The dreaded scenario of winning being merely academic had actually happened and the Blues were relegated to what was then Division Two. Ironically, one of the teams replacing them in Division One was Bristol City!

"Some of my former team-mates called me and invited me to their promotion party in Bristol," says Shaun. "I went along and despite them ribbing me, saying I should have stayed where I was, I still thought City had great potential and I wanted to make my mark and show a few thousand people what I was capable of."

The next season began with a 3-0 win over Blackpool and Shaun opened his account that day, too. But though he was finding the net regularly, he didn't feel the fans appreciated his efforts, and as the team faltered in the autumn, he found himself the target of the disgruntled support.

"The goals were still going in, but if I missed one, I could feel that the fans just weren't with me," he remembers. "I knew our situation wasn't good and that the fans expected us to be running away with the league, but we were finding it hard.

"We were everybody's cup final and by Christmas there was a very real danger that we'd be spending another season at this level, which was totally unacceptable to everyone."

But things were about to get at least a little better. Shaun had been on the bench as Stoke took a 1-0 lead into half-time at Maine Road. The large Boxing Day crowd had watched their team outplayed and outfought for much of the game and were baying for blood.

"I can't say I was relishing the prospect of being part of a side that was potentially about to blow their promotion chances," he smiles, "but I never shirked from my responsibilities, so when Joe said I was going on, I knew that here was a chance to play a part in something positive.

"We wanted to get in among it and turn this game around – and that's exactly what happened."

Shaun played a part in the equalising goal and the entire City team were flying around the pitch like men possessed – Paul Dickov and Tony Vaughan in particular just managed to stay within the laws of the game with several ferocious challenges.

City won 2-1 and the game sparked a run to the play-off final, with Shaun's winner against Wigan in the semi-final raising his stock a little, and he played a part in Paul Dickov's last-gasp leveller against Gillingham that eventually led to promotion via a penalty shoot-out. The man who had volunteered to take the fifth penalty? Shaun Goater. What might have happened had he actually been required to take that spot-kick would have either hastened his rise in popularity or potentially been his death knell at Maine Road – as it was, City's fourth spot-kick put them in an unassailable position.

City took Division One by storm and Goater was scoring for fun, yet he still felt the fans weren't totally convinced. Dickov, however, scored less than half the amount of goals, yet the fans adored him and it was when Shaun suddenly clicked as to why that was, that his path towards Cult Hero status was finally cleared.

"I began to study Dicky's game," he says. "I wanted to know why he couldn't put a foot wrong with the supporters and it soon became clear that I needed to take the aspects of his game that were missing from mine and see if that did the trick.

"Dicky was all about aggression, all-out effort and never giving up on a seemingly lost cause. I began to chase down defenders, put myself about a bit, giving my all for the shirt. I had been doing what I felt was best for the team and what benefited my game prior to that, but with the added 'Dickov factor', things began to turn around."

And how.

For all his limitations as a player, Shaun Goater possessed bucket loads of courage and his subtle change in style would see one of the most dramatic turnabouts in popularity ever seen at City. By the end of his second full season at Maine Road, he was a popular member of the Blues' first team and though injury ruined his first ever campaign in the Premiership, he still finished top scorer and had proved that he could score at any level of the game.

City were relegated back to Division One in 2001 and that cost Goater's biggest fan, manager Joe Royle – who had stuck by his signing through thin and thinner – his job. His replacement, Kevin Keegan, decided one of his first tasks would be to off-load Goater to Wolves and the deal very nearly came off. That it didn't, meant that both player and manager would never be entirely at ease with each other, with Shaun distrustful of a man he'd admired as a player and there were even suggestions that the City board had refused to sanction the deal, such was the regard for the man everyone knew simply as 'The Goat'.

Keegan brought in players with creative flair who helped Goat's goal tally rocket to almost 20 before Christmas. Players such as Eyal Berkovic and Ali Benarbia. And that season, the song 'Feed the Goat' was born, becoming perhaps one of the most popular modern-day terrace chants in Britain and making Shaun Goater a household name.

"I didn't know what they were singing at first," he smiles. "Then the lads said 'did you hear that, Goat? They were singing about you.' I thought, yeah, I'm having that!"

It would be the first of many songs as his popularity soared and the goals continued to fly in. He became the first City player in 30 years to top 30 goals in a season as the Blues stormed to the Division One championship, but the best was still yet to come.

Goater, occasionally partnered by £13m new signing Nicolas Anelka, found his place under threat, but the final Manchester derby at Maine Road was to be the day he reached the status of deity. On 99 goals for the Blues, the fairytale scenario and final chapter in his City career was waiting to be written, and Goat didn't disappoint.

His hundredth goal for the club, with the scores at 1-1, arrived when his endeavour and belief that every ball was worth chasing was rewarded ten-fold. He followed a wayward Marc Vivien Foe pass towards the byline where Gary Neville was attempting to shepherd it out.

When Neville realised it wasn't going to happen, he dithered, Goat stole the ball away and headed in towards Fabien Barthez. From an acute angle, he expertly slotted home the ball into the back of the net to put City 2-1 up.

One hundred goals in the bag in the last ever derby at Maine Road. His celebration was muted and he looked focused: "I'd seen other teams go ahead against United, over-celebrate and then end up losing. I didn't want any of that. I wanted to win and make sure I didn't lose sight of the bigger picture."

Shortly after the break, he made it 101 with a deft chip over Barthez, and City won this most historic game 3-1. There was more to come, but it never really got any better than that. He scored an equaliser at Old Trafford in the return match just eight seconds after coming on as a sub, and had a second disallowed in injury-time, but Keegan gradually phased him out of the team, just as he'd planned to do all along.

He wanted multi-million pound signings leading the line in his team and Shaun Goater just didn't fit the bill. He brought in the ineffective, half-fit Robbie Fowler and made it clear that Goat's future lay elsewhere. At least he had the decency to make him captain for the last game at Maine Road, but, in truth, there would have been riots if he hadn't.

On the last day he ever played a competitive game for City, a clue to why the Bermudian striker became so popular could be seen in the 400 or so City fans who waited patiently out in the pouring rain after the game for their hero to emerge.

Goat signed each and every item he was asked to and didn't leave until everyone was happy. It seems, years later, that everyone has a story about Shaun Goater the man – a popular, generous and warm fella who made time for everybody.

The City supporters love nothing more than a trier and they recognised the effort this man had put in to win them over and ultimately help the club restore itself as an established Premiership side. He scored goals off his shin, hip, chest and knee and his short-comings eventually endeared him even more to the fans.

He refused to give up on his dream and that he had to win over the fans to get to where he was headed, and he reaped the rewards in the form of love and adulation. He is quite possibly a one-off in the modern game.

Nasri bursts past the full-back before firing in a dangerous cross which Hill clears over his own crossbar. Corner for City...

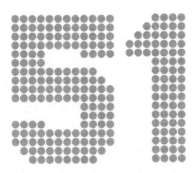

Another Loan Ranger

The succession of loaned foreign stars with their best days behind them continued as Pearce's City became a shadow of the exciting side Kevin Keegan had shaped in the first two years of his reign. Hatem Trabelsi was just another ageing player who briefly stopped by...

If his performance against Newcastle United is anything to go by, Hatem Trabelsi is set for a terrific season with City and could yet prove to be the creative influence needed in the Blues' midfield.

The Tunisian skipper seems to have shaken off his early season injury niggles and looked sharp last Saturday and appeared to revel even more when moved to a more central role for the latter stages of the game.

He has shown exciting flashes of his ability in his handful of starts so far and his crossing is excellent – and now he feels he is ready to show the Blues faithful what he is capable of.

The versatile 29-year-old, who has come close to opening his scoring account on several occasions already, said: "I feel good. I had some problems at the start; I came here a bit late and the football is a little bit different to what I was used to in Holland. New players need time, you need a few weeks to adapt, but I feel much better about everything now and I hope I can continue this way."

The former Ajax and Sfaxien star knew English football was played at a high octane pace, but he feels he is adapting well and is now hoping he can remain injury-free for the rest of the campaign.

"The game is more physical here; in Holland it's a bit more technical," said Hatem. "You need time to adapt, you need to train hard, you need pre-season and maybe it takes a couple of months to get used to it.

"I needed time to play in the way I know I can, and now I feel better than I did a few weeks ago. I don't think I've given 100 per cent to the team as yet, but that's why I am starting to get better in the games now.

"I have only played for 20 or 30 minutes so far, but when I feel I am at 100 per cent, I will be able to give the team everything."

The veteran of three World Cups and an African Cup of Nations winner, Hatem believes City haven't been having the rub of the green of late and is hoping that the fine home form will yield goals and three points against Fulham this afternoon.

"We have been unlucky and we have played well," he said. "We have created plenty of chances, but you also need a bit of luck sometimes.

"We have to concentrate for the next game because we are not in a good position in the table and we need a win for our supporters. We have some great players and we should do better.

"When you work hard, the luck will come. In the last game we created six or seven chances, but we missed them."

The corner-kick falls to Zabaleta around 25 yards from goal. He strikes it first time, the ball falls into Aguero's path but he fails to divert the strike on target…

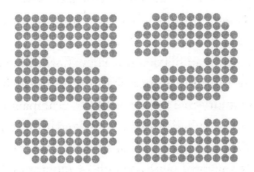

More Of The Same

Ousmane Dabo was never going to be the answer to City's midfield problems and, like a dozen others before him, he would have little impact at City, other than to be the unfortunate victim of a Joey Barton beating…

French holding midfielder Ousmane Dabo can't wait to resume his place in the first team after almost two months on the sidelines. The former Lazio star has endured a stop-start beginning to life at the City of Manchester Stadium, but he has recovered well from a minor knee operation and is now concentrating on building up his fitness in anticipation of a return to action within the next few weeks.

And that's great news for City's No.5 who, by his own admission, is a rotten spectator.

"I find it very hard to watch matches," admitted Ousmane. "Since I arrived, I have played just three times, then I received a three-match ban and then I needed an operation on my knee to remove part of the meniscus, and have had to wait until that settled before I could train again.

"Now I am steadily regaining full fitness. I'm not sure if I'll be playing a few reserve matches or not – I'll just wait and see how the gaffer wants to play it."

Ousmane could have added more games before the op but for the controversial red card he received in the 1-0 defeat at Reading.

He was ordered off when it appeared Steve Sidwell jumped into his arm as the pair went up for a header. The Reading midfielder – believed to have been a summer target for Stuart Pearce – crumpled in a heap and made the referee's decision easier, something which angered Ousmane.

"That kind of thing has never happened to me before," said the former French international. "I am a very fair player and would never intentionally hurt another player.

"I jumped with my arms down and Sidwell caught my arm and went down. I was very angry with him because, in my view, it wasn't a bad challenge, but I think he made the most of it. I was disappointed."

While he has convalesced, Ousmane admits he has been as perplexed as anybody at the Jekyll and Hyde nature of the Blues' early performances, but reckons City will soon start to climb the table.

"Our home form is excellent, but away it's been difficult and I don't really understand why," he said. "It's something we need to correct, but we are proud of our performances at the City of Manchester Stadium and I think we are a good side.

"I'm looking forward to challenging for a place again soon, but I need to regain my fitness. I just need a few games under my belt and I'll be ready for when the boss needs me."

Aguero attempts to twist and turn inside the QPR box but he's challenged in the end and the ball is cleared, but only as far as Lescott who starts another attack...

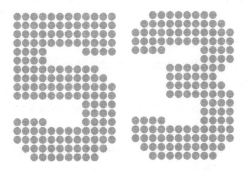

Stevie Wonder

This was the second chat with the upcoming Irish youngster who liked to do his own thing off the pitch...

Manchester City fans have been weaned on a diet of skilful midfielders over the past few years. Rewind just over a decade and you could include the likes of Maurizio Gaudino, Georgi Kinkladze, Ian Bishop, Ali Benarbia and Eyal Berkovic. Visionaries, flair players, call them what you will, but all great footballers who had an innate ability of making a team tick.

Add to that list, Stephen Ireland.

It seems Ireland has always been destined for the first team and international honours. There can't be an Academy player of his generation that hasn't cited him as their 'best player played with' and, only last month, Micah Richards mentioned him in the same breath as Diego Maradona! High praise, indeed.

Only time will tell whether he emulates the little Argentina legend, but whether he does or he doesn't, he certainly possesses the ability to become a world class midfielder and has already made his mark for his country in recent months.

The Cork-born playmaker is one of the game's deep thinkers and is committed to being the best player he can possibly be, but he is also aware he's just taking the first steps on what he hopes is a long and successful career.

But how many 20-year-olds can also claim to be a committed family man and a father-of-two? Not many, but Stephen joined that select band last summer with the birth of his first daughter – and is already the apple of her daddy's eye.

"Her name is Jessica, she's eight months old now and she's beautiful," he smiled. "Having a second child has been fantastic and I've actually found it's been easier second time around. My son, Joshua, is two now, but obviously the first baby represents a steep learning curve for any new parent. It seems far more natural this time and you can take things much more in your stride.

"Having such a young family at my age makes you focus harder and gives you even more determination to be a success because I have to look after them and secure their futures, too. There are no more on the way at the moment, not for a while, anyway, but I do want a big family in the future. I've only just turned 20, so two will do for now."

As ever, behind every successful man there's a strong woman, and Stephen's partner is his rock and also someone who is completely in tune with his uniqueness of his day job and the solitude that Stephen sometimes needs.

"I have a wonderful girlfriend who takes a lot of stress off my back and I owe a lot of credit to her," he said. "Of course, I do my bit and always want to be with the kids, but she understands that the day before a match, I need to focus and concentrate, so she takes the little ones elsewhere so I can have the house to myself.

"I need a lot of time to prepare myself and it's vital there are no distractions. Even when we play away and stay over somewhere, I like to be alone to think, so I can be mentally right.

"I turn my phone off and need peace and quiet and that includes not having team-mates around, either. I have what might be perceived as strange preparation rituals, but I have to do it to get myself focused.

"After a game, if things haven't gone well, I won't be able to sleep and I'll know it will have been because something went wrong during my preparations leading up to the match, and I strongly believe in that."

In a fascinating insight into what a footballer needs to do to ready themselves for battle, Stephen reveals his habits and thought-process are so vital to his pre-match routine: "What do I think about? It's hard to say, but I like to unwind and chill out as best I can.

"I might watch a bit of TV and think about what I need to do during a game. I try not to think too much about particular situations and what I will do with the ball when in possession. It's more along the lines of work rate, how much running I'll need to do, my positioning and stuff like that.

"If I look too far into the game and immerse myself in it, it can work the other way and be more of a hindrance to me. It's something I've always done since being a young boy.

"I used to get quite nervous before games and, to be honest, I still do up to this day, but it is knowing how to utilise that nervous energy in a positive manner and use it to my advantage. It keeps me on my toes."

The summer arrivals of Ousmane Dabo, DaMarcus Beasley and Didi Hamann seemingly put Ireland's first team claims back a peg or two, despite pretty much establishing himself as a regular during 2005/06.

In fact, with just one start going into December and five appearances from the bench, the talented Irishman was beginning to wonder if his break would ever come. It would be an injury to Claudio Reyna, and the American's subsequent surprise departure, that would favourably alter the course of the campaign for Stephen.

"It was a frustrating first half of the season for me," he admitted. "I speak a lot with Richard Dunne and he told me the second season is always the hardest and that I had to ease off the gas a little in training.

"I watched as new midfielders came in and the gaffer looked at different options before looking towards me. Different combinations were used and swapped around, but I kept working hard and forcing my way into the reckoning as best I could. Eventually, I got my chance before Christmas when I came on as a substitute for Claudio at Old Trafford. I knew that this was the perfect chance for me to hold down a place in the side and I've been in the team pretty much ever since.

"Now it's up to me to keep the shirt or down to me if I lose it, which is as much as I could ask for. It was hard work and determination that won me a place back and I need to maintain those levels of industry."

RED CARD! The assistant referee spots that Tevez has gone down under a challenge from Barton on the edge of the City area. Mike Dean consults with his colleague before sending Barton off for an elbow...

16:11

American Flyer

DaMarcus Beasley followed the familiar path to City of journeyman footballers from overseas. A bright, likeable guy, you could sense he didn't feel his long-term future lay with the Blues...

DaMarcus Beasley knows he's going to have adapt quickly after his first appearance in a City shirt ended in defeat at Blackburn. The USA international could solve the left midfield problem for manager Stuart Pearce, who has used several members of his squad in the role in the opening weeks of the campaign.

It's never easy arriving from slightly less hectic leagues, such as the Dutch Eredivisie, and perhaps unfair to expect foreign players to slot in seamlessly – but that's pretty much what Beasley will have to do in the coming weeks as City attempt to haul themselves up the table, starting with a victory over West Ham this afternoon.

Beasley, on a season-long loan deal, arrives having made a name for himself as a speedy wide man for the USA and a crowd favourite at Dutch giants PSV Eindhoven, for whom he made 56 appearances, scoring 10 goals.

He joined City on deadline day last month and should make his home debut against the Hammers, and with more than 50 caps for the national team, he is keen to show the Blues fans exactly what he's capable of.

"I heard before I even came that City had one of the best fan bases in England and I'm excited to be here," Beasley declared. "I want to gain their respect quickly in the first couple of games that I play.

"If they get behind me, that will encourage me and hopefully I can give them the work ethic that they will be looking for from me."

Born in Fort Wayne, Indiana, Beasley excelled for his country at youth level, winning the Silver Ball for being voted Second Best Player at the Under-17s World Cup in New Zealand in 1999.

He has at least one familiar face at City in former USA skipper Claudio Reyna, but he's quickly settling into life in Manchester and is looking forward to showing his manager and team-mates he's worth a permanent deal in the future.

"Stuart Pearce is a coach that you go to talk to if you have a problem," said the man nicknamed 'Jitterbug'. "He's open and he's always out there on the training pitch, he really knows his football, so I'm happy to play under him.

"I've been here two weeks now and I'm settling in pretty well. The guys in the team have been good with me, and the manager and coaching team have as well. I'm enjoying the way it's going here so far."

Beasley began his career in Major League Soccer with Los Angeles Galaxy and then moved on to Chicago Fire, winning his first cap for the USA against China in 2001.

He played in the 2002 World Cup before moving on to PSV as a replacement for Arjen Robben in 2004, and he was also one of America's most productive players during last summer's World Cup in Germany, assisting their only goal and having another harshly chalked off against Italy, though the tournament was something of a disappointment for the USA.

"I'm ambitious to win, I want to win and I want to help Manchester City win within my capabilities," said the 61-times capped midfielder. "If my number's called, I want to show the fans that this is a club where I want to be."

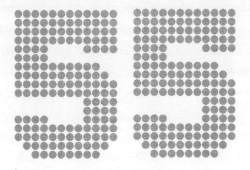

Greece Is The Word?

At £6m, Stuart Pearce blew virtually his entire transfer budget on a YouTube striker – the problem was, he looked better on video than in the flesh and was not really cut out for the Premier League…

A year on from his big move from Holland to England, Georgios Samaras insists he has no regrets about joining City. It has not been an easy 12 months for the 21-year-old, whose relative inexperience is sometimes lost in the rhetoric over his £5m-plus transfer fee from Heerenveen.

In and out of the team, on and off the substitutes bench, the subject of intense media scrutiny in his homeland while getting to grips with life in yet another foreign country, it has been a hectic year in the life of the Greek international.

He has attracted a huge female following and critics in equal measure, although the figures – the ones the football statisticians dissect, not the ones that cause hearts to miss a beat – are not as bad as some people might imagine.

Samaras' first 28 games yielded no fewer than 11 goals at a ratio of one every 2.4 games. It's not prolific, but just for comparison at the same stage of the 2006/07 campaign, Wayne Rooney was also taking more than two matches for each goal and £30m Andriy Shevchenko has one goal in every five Premiership starts.

There is little doubt that Samaras, the Blues' second most expensive player ever and the costliest of Stuart Pearce's reign by some distance, has been burdened with a significant weight of expectation. He hasn't been helped either by the other forwards proving so goal-shy and thrusting the spotlight back in his direction.

It is to his lasting credit that he has not let the criticism or perceived lack of success in England change his optimistic outlook on life, or made even the slightest dent in the mannerly and professional approach he takes to his job.

"It has been a really interesting year and I have learned a lot of things," he ventured, flicking his trademark long hair out of the way so as to make better and more polite eye contact. His English has certainly flourished.

"I have never had a problem with my life or the game. I feel physically and mentally stronger than I have ever been in my life. I know I have a strong character that will enable me to succeed and I am 100 per cent sure that coming to Manchester City was the right move for me to make.

"When you leave your own country at the age of 16, you get used to looking after yourself, and having a supportive family is a really important part of that, but really my life is just geared to help me improve my football."

After just five minutes talking to the willowy, languid striker, it is clear that the so called 'Baby Bentley' set of nightclubbing, fast-talking, fast-spending, young footballers who would rather have a fleet of Ferraris than a cabinet full of medals and international caps, are far removed from Georgios Samaras.

While admitting he is not a social hermit, there is a strict code by which Samaras lives his life during the season that has presumably been handed down by his dad, who was once a Greek international who felt the full force of Pearce's studs in a competitive match.

"In a sense, it doesn't matter where you live, be it in Holland, Spain or England, what is more important is how you live your life," he stressed, leaning forward as if to emphasise the point.

"Players must put everything they have into their training and their work and then go home and rest the body and mind as much as possible. I like nothing better than to go home and relax by watching television or DVDs, reading books or listening to music.

"It is important also to eat well and to sleep a lot before going back to train the next day. There really isn't a lot of room for much going out, except maybe to eat because I am not a great cook!

"Manchester is great for that, especially now I know my way around the city centre and the roads. I have found some really good places where I like to eat and know which parts of the city to avoid, but there really hasn't been all that much time to discover the areas around Manchester or other parts of England. Whenever we get time off, I am either resting or travelling for international duty."

Samaras is driven only by improving all aspects of his game, and the laid-back approach that often seems all too apparent from the stands, hides a burning desire to succeed in his job and realise his full potential – the one on which Pearce gambled so much of the Blues' money and his own reputation as a talent spotter.

"I am still hungry for football and learning about the game, and I don't think that will ever stop," said Samaras.

"Every day is an opportunity for me to get better, to listen and to learn new aspects that I can bring into my game. That is how I approach football and life."

Mark Hughes shakes his head as calm is gradually restored. Aguero is okay and City regroup to try and take advantage of the situation...

16:13

Project Manager

Sven-Goran Eriksson — a truly international manager if ever there was one — was he the man to turn the Blues' fortunes around? With the backing of a Thai multi-millionaire, he couldn't fail, could he?

When Sven-Goran Eriksson talks about his 'project' and smiles studiously from behind his owlish, almost professorial glasses, it is not hard to picture him as a master in a posh educational establishment.

At first glance, he doesn't always appear the most likely candidate to be working in the hardest football school of all – the Premiership – let alone the right man at the right time to teach City fans how to love their club again after three seasons of standing still.

It was England international Trevor Sinclair, on departing from the Blues at the end of his contract, who summed up 59-year-old Eriksson perfectly in just three words. 'A football scholar' reckoned the midfielder, and it is easy to see what Sinclair was getting at.

What you see with Eriksson is clearly not what you get. There are no histrionics, no balling and shouting, not even – at first glance – much interaction with his players.

Instead, there is a studious, analytical brain watching and weighing up individual ability and character while exuding a calm exterior and maintaining a polite and professional relationship with all those under his managerial wing.

In the furore that surrounded Eriksson's arrival as Thaksin Shinawatra's personal choice to lead the Blues out of the doldrums and into the Promised Land, he has seemingly been the calmest man of all.

Put up as, at best, a 20-1 shot by the bookies to succeed the sacked Stuart Pearce, Eriksson confounded many with his decision to step back into the day-to-day footballing cauldron that is the Premiership.

After the vilification and lampooning he received at the hands of the English press in the wake of his perceived failure with the national team – though the statistics suggested otherwise – it took a man with a thick skin, huge inner-belief and a forgiving, phlegmatic nature to make City his first job after being unemployed for a year.

He has met some of his media tormentors already in the first month of his tenure and has greeted them with a smile and a handshake. If Eriksson bears grudges, then no one would be able to detect the fact.

There is no doubt that the promise of Shinawatra's millions is the reason that Eriksson is now flat hunting in central Manchester. If there had been no money to reshape City, then there would have been no Sven – or Svennis as he is known in his home land.

That isn't being mercenary on his part, just sensible. He knows that given time and resources, he can do for the Blues what he did for Benfica and Lazio. Without cash, he would have been left to battle the odds like Stuart Pearce before him.

Fortunately, Eriksson has the happy knack of being able to take clubs forward and then win trophies, and anyone who manages that after 32 barren years at City, will be an instant hero.

"My first job is to make sure that the team is better than it was last year and that results are better, too," he said very precisely after confirming that Richard Dunne would stay as captain and that he felt Pearce had done a good job bringing on the young players..

"I don't feel as if I have anything to prove. The more pressure there is on me to succeed, the better I like it.

"It is bad to work at a club where there is no pressure because that would mean you are beaten or resigned to your position before you start. It will not be like that at Manchester City.

"I know the new owner wants to make City bigger in every way; raising the club's profile all over the world and improving its results. It cannot be done in one night.

"I am here because I am convinced this club wants to be more successful and I am convinced that it can be. It is a big challenge.

"City fans can be assured I am not here for the money. They can be quite sure that I still have the same hunger for the job that I have always possessed, especially when I have lived one year without football. That year out of the game was the most stressful time I have had in my life.

"All managers want to be at big clubs and this is a big club. This is an extremely good job. I have never worked in the Premier League before so I don't know if I have to prove myself or not, but I know what I have done in the past and I am looking forward to an exciting job and an exciting season.

"Every time you are a coach, you have pressure, whatever team it is. I hope I will have a big pressure as that means I am at a big football club in the best league in the world.

"I had some offers in the past – in a year out of football, some offers were bound to come in – but I am happy I didn't accept them. I couldn't care less if I was second, third or fourth choice, I am here and the job is mine."

By the time Eriksson was emphasising his mission statement and explaining why the Premiership is such an attraction, he had already asked for, and received, a £250,000 revamp of the club's impressive training facilities at Carrington.

As this article was being penned, Eriksson had just sealed the arrival of former Bulgarian player of the season Martin Petrov from Atletico Madrid and Brazilian international Geovanni. Two flying wingers charged with bringing style and panache back to City's play.

They took the manager's spending to £17million and let everyone know that the Blues, with Shinawatra writing the cheques and Eriksson finding the players, mean serious business.

"Football today is such that you have to shop all over the world, and that is what we have done and will continue to do," declared the manager. "If you want to be competitive, you have to open your eyes to every possibility."

Rolando Bianchi has been bought to bolster an attack that hasn't scored a home goal in its last eight league games, stretching back to New Year's Day, and the £9m man will not be the last forward to arrive this summer.

Eriksson, for all his reputation of playing safety first football, particularly with England, is determined that there will be a style and a swagger about his City creation.

"Thaksin Shinawatra is showing with his backing that he was serious when he said he wanted City to be challenging close to the top and not near the bottom of the Premiership," declared the boss.

"Petrov, Geovanni and Bianchi are players all well known to me. They give us goals, width, pace and lots of international experience.

"They also give us a touch of class, and in the Premier League, that is what you need. I am confident that the supporters will take to all of them and that they will each be a big success.

"There is one thing for sure, our forwards will not be short of balls coming into the penalty area this season. Whether it signals a certain style of play or not you, will have to wait and see, but wingers have never been out of fashion in football and I want City to play attractive football."

Sven will be hoping things go better for him than they did for Kevin Keegan who also headed for City after the Three Lions and also had £50m to spend; and better too than Graham Taylor and Glenn Hoddle, who never really tasted domestic success after leaving the employ of the Football Association.

"I'm sure that in the future we will see Manchester City higher in the table," he grinned. "I think I'll do a good job. Thaksin Shinawatra has already shown he means business by allowing me to spend what I have spent, and there will be more to come. This is an exciting project for us both and we want City to succeed."

All over Sweden during the recent tour, the newspapers referred to their Premiership visitors not as Manchester City, but 'Svennis City', a sure sign that they have a high profile boss, though Eriksson is adamant that the club has more to offer than him as manager.

"It is not the case that I am bigger than the club," he insisted. "No one is ever that. I am only famous because I was England manager. If my reputation attracts players here, then good, but those players and the fans are the important ones, not me."

All the way through his truncated pre-season, Eriksson has refused to set targets for his charges until he knows the exact make up of his squad when the transfer window closes at the end of this month.

Top half, two good cup runs and some entertainment would be enough to satisfy most fans in his first season and Eriksson emphasises that he will need some time to change things around.

"We know we are not going to win the Premier League this season," he reiterated. "I cannot set targets until I know our strength at the end of the window. What I can promise is that we intend to go the right way this season in small steps and one day be playing in the Champions League.

"I want the fans to have that dream and dreams are never impossible. The new owner has the same dream for the club to be bigger and better and he is ready to invest his money to do that. He wants us to eventually be competing in Europe and then the Champions League.

"He knows that will not happen this season and that we will not be in the top four today or tomorrow, but we are determined to be there one day."

Italian Lessons

Like Corradi and Samaras before him, Rolando Bianchi arrived in Manchester as a relatively unknown quantity. He would remain just that after an unsuccessful stint with the Blues…

Rolando Bianchi arrived in Manchester, ready to disbelieve the 'Rainy City' tag and enjoy some summer sunshine before the new season kicks off this month. Cue the wettest summer on record.

Not that it's dampened the 24-year-old's enthusiasm in any way, and now, with grey clouds lifting and the country drying out again, he is champing at the bit to begin his City career in earnest.

Bianchi, whose 18 goals put him fourth on the list of Serie A top scorers last season, became Sven-Goran Eriksson's first signing when he paid Italian side Reggina approximately £8.8m last month.

The former Atalanta and Cagliari forward is one of the most highly-regarded upcoming talents in Italian football and will wear the coveted No.10 shirt.

Bianchi reckons he can become a big hit with the City fans in his first year and will be doing everything he can to ensure that happens. He said: "I know that it will take time and hard work for me to adapt to playing in England, but that will not be a problem.

"Having fellow Italians Bernardo Corradi and fitness coach Stefano Marrone here means I am able to settle down in England much quicker. Plus the manager can speak fluent Italian as well, so there won't be any major communication problems early on.

"They have all been a great help in helping me to get to know Manchester and English life in general. I like Manchester very much – apart from the rain! It's a very nice city and I'm already feeling at home here.

"The first thing I did on arriving was buy an Italian-English dictionary and then an adapter to charge my phone and use my PC. I have to admit I struggled the first few days with English breakfast! Instead of a croissant and cappuccino, I had eggs and bacon, which I'd never even seen before, but it wasn't exactly the end of the world!

"I am taking English lessons and looking for a new house in or around the city, so I will be very busy in my spare time for the first few months. We have a magnificent stadium and I have already been able to feel the passion of the supporters and I can't wait to be playing in front of our fans in a packed stadium for the first time. I have dreamed of games such as the Manchester derby, and the club wants to make serious inroads on United, which I am very happy to be part of.

"I hope I can do the club, myself and the supporters proud in the coming weeks and months. As for celebrations when I score, I don't think I could compete with Bernardo's, which are very special – I saw him Knight Joey Barton last season and thought it was excellent.

"When I score, it will be a spontaneous celebration of joy – I don't have anything in particular planned, but it will be a special moment whatever happens. My main aim is to work very hard and play well for City and hopefully catch the eye of the national team coach Donadoni as well in the coming months."

Defensive substitution for QPR who bring on Armand Traore for the goalscorer Cisse as the visitors look to defend for the remaining half an hour or so...

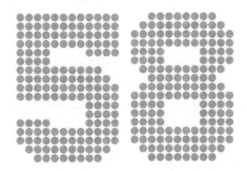

Promise Unfulfilled

Valeri Bojinov's time with City was ruined by injury –
two lengthy lay-offs meant we never really saw what the
talented Bulgarian was capable of...

The worst injuries in football are often the most innocuous looking ones, as City's new £6m striker Valeri Bojinov will attest to. The 21-year-old Bulgarian international was just six minutes into his full debut against Manchester United when he jumped with Patrice Evra and landed awkwardly on his knee.

He knew something had gone badly wrong as soon as he hit the ground. He tried to stand up, but immediately had to slump to the ground again. His season was over.

A friendly and likeable character, Bojinov will still get to know his team-mates and Manchester during that time, as well as being kept busy at home where he will be celebrating the birth of his first child at some point this month.

"I had no doubts this was the right club for me," he smiled. "I only had to speak with Pavel Nedved at Juventus who said, 'Don't give joining Manchester City a second thought. I worked under Sven-Goran Eriksson at Lazio and he is a great manager and he will make you a better player. It will be a great move for you.'

"I've always admired English football because it's always been the most popular league to follow for people around the world. The stadiums are always full, so naturally it draws players from everywhere because you want to play in that type of atmosphere every week. I enjoyed my time in Italy, but after eight years or so, it was the right time to move on."

Tevez takes a short corner to De Jong and receives the ball back before firing a strike on goal which Kenny saves before it falls to Aguero whose shot almost crosses the line – but Kenny claws it back...

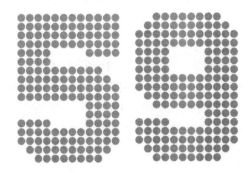

Dream Weaver

Nicky Weaver had spent almost a decade at City and was one of the nicest guys you could meet. The hero of the 1999 play-off final was nearing the end of his time with the Blues, for whom he had been a magnificent servant...

It's almost been like winding back the hands of time and reliving a past life for born-again hero Nicky Weaver. The Blues' keeper is idolised by the City fans who have watched him rise from raw teenage talent to one of the best young goalies in the country, then seen him on the brink of injury-enforced retirement, right back up to being a surprise omission from recent England squads.

It's been a rollercoaster career for the 27-year-old Sheffield lad and, giving City's history over the past 25 years, it's a marriage made in heaven. At last, Nicky's fortunes have taken a sharp upturn and there can't be a single football supporter in England who wouldn't applaud his amazing fight back and wish him well for the future – though the fact he is a boyhood Wednesday fan might stick in the craw of today's visiting supporters' throats, somewhat!

'Weaves' was at his best again when the Blues drew 1-1 at Everton and he will start his ninth consecutive game this afternoon, all being well – a run he didn't even dare dream of during his three-year injury nightmare.

Now he has thrown down the gauntlet to new signings Andreas Isaksson and Joe Hart, and it should prove quite a challenge for both keepers in the coming months.

"I have a philosophy of taking every day and every game as it comes along," said Nicky. "I just give my best and that's whether people are injured or not injured, and it's up to the manager whether to pick me or not to pick me.

"Hopefully Andreas will come back sooner rather than later because having gone through what I have, I don't like to see anyone on the treatment table for a length of time.

"I am enjoying my run in the first team because six months ago I wouldn't believe this was happening. It is eight games now and we are not leaking many goals.

"I will never get complacent or think that the shirt belongs to me, I have just got to work as hard as I can. I am enjoying the football and, touch wood, the injuries are all behind me now."

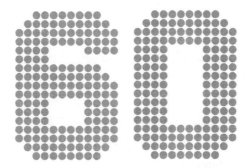

Life's A Beach

Elano arrived at City as one of the first signings since Thaksin Shinawatra's takeover pumped much-needed funds into the Blues' empty bank account. With Sven-Goran Eriksson installed as the new boss, suddenly the club had a fresh injection of optimism. Elano was a gifted player and, at last, the supporters had someone to idolise again...

That boy Elano — what can you say about a player with the kind of talent he is blessed with? Not much, except 'thanks' to the people who brought him here, and we all know who they are. People often ask what players are really like away from the pitch and out of the public eye, and the answer is, well, they are mostly just like everybody else. In Elano's case, it's unlikely you could meet a

235

more humble and friendly character – always smiling, courteous and generous.

It's always a pleasure to be in his company and let's hope he's a City player for many years to come. Launching the new Nike Brazil shirt at Pau Brasil – Manchester's only Brazilian restaurant (and highly recommended) – Elano attracted the attention of the 'nationals', journalists from papers such as the Times and The Independent as well as a plethora of TV stations including Sky and the BBC.

He must have conducted in the region of a dozen interviews over a four-hour period – a gruelling test of anyone's patience – but he was still smiling by the time the tape recorders were finally turned off and the cameras replaced in their various bags and cases.

He is learning English, but for obvious reasons spoke through a Portuguese interpreter for most of the afternoon. Some of the questions he was asked left this particular writer a little bemused, but perhaps it is of interest if he plans to wear gloves ("maybe, but not if it's raining") or when he bought his first car ("when I was 20 – I paid for it in five instalments and it had no air conditioning – not good in Santos where the temperature is 35 degrees!").

Surely most City fans would be more interested in how he is settling in Manchester and his thoughts of the season played so far? Well, that was my angle and the answers will make sweet music to the ears of Blues everywhere.

"I'm very happy to be here," he began with a customary smile. "Things have gone so well for me so far. I arrived here as an unknown and I thank the supporters for the way they have treated me, but it is a team effort and no more. I'm sure if we can carry on the way we are, the whole team will get the appreciation it deserves.

"I think the way we have started has surprised everybody, especially when you take into account that the club brought in so many new players and had a new manager. It is down to the competence of the manager and players that we have started so well and we are doing a very good job considering the Premier League is such a tough league."

Elano arrived unable to speak English, though he didn't let that stop him trying to get to know his team-mates, as he explained: "Even though I don't speak the language very well, I tried to communicate with my team-mates when we were still getting to know each other and made jokes with everybody to keep their spirits up.

"I might not speak English yet, but I have a lot of friends now in England and I would like it to carry on that way and keep the positive atmosphere going – besides, I don't want to upset any of them as they are all bigger and stronger than I am!

"I'm having English lessons two or three times a week. I've never felt alone in England because the warmth and welcome from the other players, staff and supporters has been amazing. Even in training, the other players are trying to teach me how to say different things that will help. When I first arrive at training, I just speak to everyone and try and make them laugh with little jokes."

Elano also admits he thought the Blues played in front of gates half the size of the average at the City of Manchester Stadium! The packed crowd and happy atmosphere quickly filtered through to the players, hence the incredible start the Blues have made on their own soil.

"It was a massive surprise to me because I was told before I came here that City's attendances averaged somewhere between 15,000 and 20,000!" laughed Elano. "Of course, it's actually more than 40,000 each week and it's great to have so many fans behind us every time we play at home – and away – it makes us feel good to know that many people want to support us and I hope they keep turning up in numbers for a long time."

So how far can City go this season? Top ten? Top six? Top four…?

"We are hoping to win a trophy this season and I'm sure the supporters would be very happy with that," he reasoned. "One of our main objectives this season is to qualify for the UEFA Cup or Champions League. We know it is very difficult to win the title because there are at least four sides with a lot of quality. If we qualify for Europe, we will be very proud."

Finally, what does Elano make of the adulation he's received since signing for City, and bearing in mind he's had to settle in a new country, adapt to a new style of football and learn a new language, is there more to come from the Brazilian maestro?

"It's very difficult to talk about myself," he says, modestly. "However, I do believe I can give even more than I have so far, but I like to do my talking on the pitch – that's where I can show the City fans what I can do.

"They have been fantastic towards me and, of course, it makes me very happy, especially when they sing my name – it makes me do even better because I want to please them even more. I've only been in England for six months, but I am already talking about staying here for 10 years or so."

Kenny clears the ball upfield after ushering his team forward...

16:18

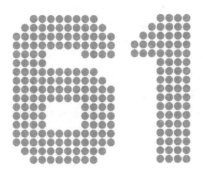

City Of God

You wait for one Brazilian to arrive and then another comes along straight after – Geovanni became an instant crowd favourite with the City fans who were getting a taste for exciting new talent...

'Geo', as the City fans have already nicknamed Geovanni, looks lean and confident as he settles down to talk. He seems relaxed that he can speak at length in his native tongue, rather than communicate in broken Portuguese or Spanish with certain members of the Blues' backroom staff.

Carrington and Manchester must seem a long way from the small town of Acaiaca in Brazil, Geo's home and his place of birth on January 11, 1980. His path to stardom wasn't easy, as he explains: "My mother was a housewife and my father worked on the railways. I am the youngest of eight children and my parents always called me their 'little miracle' – I shall explain why in a moment.

"Of my siblings, my eldest brother, who is now 57, almost got to be a professional footballer, but he was as close as anyone to making it in the family up to that point. My parents had seven children and it had been 12 years since their last child – then I came along! My mother was 49 and my father 54, so you can understand why they call me a miracle – because of their ages. They told me I was a complete joy because it is so rare that people can have a baby so late in life."

It hasn't taken City fans long to buy into the Geovanni miracle, either. His winner against Manchester United sent his popularity – already high – soaring to new heights.

Geo has four full caps for his country – so how does it feel to pull on the yellow shirt of Brazil and represent the most successful footballing nation on the planet?

"I was 17 the first time I pulled on the yellow shirt," recalled Geo. "That was for the Under-17s and I later played for the Under-20s and went to the Sydney Olympics in 2000.

"In 2001, I played for Brazil in the Copa America and it was then I first met the national coach Luiz Felipe Scolari, who would become like a second father to me. He was another inspirational figure in my life but he was very demanding of me, which I needed because it brought my game on to new heights.

"To play for my country at senior level was the proudest moment of my career and I think playing for Brazil is the greatest dream any footballer can have."

That dream just kept getting better with the move to the Nou Camp that same year and he made his debut against Atletico Bilbao to great acclaim, winning the man of the match award in the process. It was fairytale stuff, but the hefty transfer fee weighed heavy on his shoulders, with expectations of him unrealistically high from the demanding Barca supporters.

"I was just 21 and, in truth, it was difficult for me initially," he admitted. "It was a dream come true to play for one of the biggest clubs in the world. All Brazilian kids want to be successful and play in Europe, but there was definitely pressure to perform.

"I took a lot from my two years with Barca, however. I learned a lot and I was still reasonably happy, but it took time. It was my grounding in European football – albeit on a massive stage – and I believe I reaped the benefit in later years, first with Benfica and now with Manchester City, playing in the best league in the world.

"There wasn't just the fact Barca had spent a lot of money on me, there was the fact I was still quite young, had left my country for the first time, and had only recently married my wife, Roberta. I had to adapt to all these things in order to play my best football, and it did take a little time."

After two years in Spain, Geo moved to Portugal – destination for countless Brazilians over the years – attracted by the mother language and the temperate climate. Benfica spent £11m on bringing the precocious midfielder to the Stadium of Light (the real one, not Sunderland's) and he soon had the supporters eating out of his hand.

In 2005, he first came to the attention of City fans after his diving header dumped Manchester United out of the Champions League. It was a momentous moment for Geo and Benfica, who moved on to the latter stages of the competition as a result of the victory.

"That goal was very important for me and my team," he smiled. "It helped Benfica progress to a stage they'd never reached before and it was obviously a very high profile goal to score.

"I didn't know how important it was at the time, but have realised since. Many City fans seem to remember it very well!"

The Geo jinx struck the Reds again in the first Manchester derby of this season, with his 25-yard effort just evading the fingertips of Edwin van der Sar for the winning goal against United. It was a dream come true for the 27-year-old Brazilian, and the rest of the City of Manchester Stadium that afternoon, bar a couple of thousand from down south!

It had Geo running to his latest adoring public with his hand to his ear – his trademark celebration and exactly the same manner in which he celebrated his goal for Benfica. Forgive our Red cousins if he isn't exactly flavour of the month at Old Trafford!

"The celebration of putting my hand behind my ear is because I want to hear the supporters cheering to their maximum. It's an indescribable feeling having forty or fifty thousand people celebrating something you've just been part of.

"I have a one-year contract and, regardless of what happens in the future, Manchester City are part of my history and in my heart," said Geo. "I feel a lot of respect and affection towards me from the City supporters and I thank God for everything.

"This club is made from the loyalty and passion of its supporters and I find it amazing they are shouting my name already. They are chanting my name even when I make a good pass or do a trick – I couldn't ask for better backing after such a short time at a new club. It's been a long time since I have had that kind of adoration and I'm really happy with the way things are going. I haven't been with City long, but I already feel I've achieved a lot."

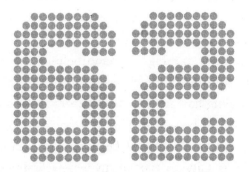

The Boy Dunne Good

A modern-day City legend, Richard Dunne was an unassuming, laid-back guy who had won the hearts of the supporters with his no-nonsense committed style...

It's been many years since City have had a young player that has matured into such an inspirational leader as Richard Dunne, and the fact he has just been crowned the Blues' Player of the Year for a historic third successive year speaks volumes of how the supporters view the 27-year-old Dubliner.

With seven seasons under his belt, and 262 appearances for the Blues, he is already assured of going down in the club's history as one of the all-time greats. Next season he should move into the top

20 appearances list for City, and with several years still to run on his current deal, there's every chance he might one day make the top 10.

With the word loyalty almost considered a pariah in the modern game, Dunne is happy to fight the tide of club-jumping mercenaries and can't see the point of swapping clubs simply to bolster his bank account. He knows things haven't gone well this season, but he can see how things could be next year and in future years with a little fine tuning.

"Things didn't quite come together as a whole unit for us this year, and while we have to be pleased from a defensive point of view and kept 14 clean sheets, we've had too many nils at the other end and struggled to find the net too often," said Dunne.

"Looking at the positive side, our defensive record gives us a solid base to build on and if we can keep hold of Sylvain for next season, we should have the same back four again.

"Michael Ball has come in and done really well and together we've hopefully given the manager a good base to build his team around. The gaffer's said he knows the areas he wants to strengthen and I'm sure he'll bring in the right players."

Dunne has been City's Mr Reliable for many years now, but the 2006/07 campaign saw him raise his own lofty standards yet higher with consistently excellent displays from the start to finish.

With 28 caps under his belt for Ireland, he's deservedly recognised as one of the best defenders, not only in the Premiership, but Europe, too. He admits he's been satisfied with his performances this season, though believes there is always room for improvement.

"I'm pleased with the way things have gone but I always think I can do better," he said. "I find it difficult to talk about myself, but as a defensive unit, we've done well, and I base my performances on how many cleans sheets we've kept and how many goals we've conceded. On that basis, yes, we've done a decent job overall."

It's hard to imagine Dunne not being captain, so adept has his leadership been, but it's a role he's had to grow into and learn as he's gone along. "It's a case of having to do things, really," he says. "There are different situations where people look to you to be told how to do certain things and it's my job to get that right. I've had to say things at times that I didn't really want to say but just felt needed saying, and as the season has progressed, I think that's something I've got better at.

"I'm not the most vocal person on the pitch, so I just say what I think needs saying and that's enough – I try and lead more by example than anything else. I'm a quiet lad in some ways, but I've never had a problem expressing an opinion or telling somebody something I think will benefit them and the team as a whole.

"I don't intend to criticise and I'm happy to accept advice from my team-mates to help me improve – we're in it together and if I do have a go at someone during a game, it doesn't mean I don't like them – it's all about taking advice the right way, in a constructive manner."

Dunne is always quick to cite his defensive partnership with Sylvain Distin as one of the reasons his own form has been so impressive. With Distin's future the subject of intense speculation all year, Dunne confesses to being uncertain as to who will be partnering him in the back four next August.

"I enjoy playing alongside Sylvain," he said. This was our fifth campaign together and I feel it was also our best. We've gradually got better as each seasons has gone by and that's why it's important the club does all it can to persuade Sylvain to agree a new contract.

"With the possibility of new investors coming into the club, there are a lot of things that could change, and so far he's not said that he wouldn't sign, so there's still a chance he will put pen to paper.

"If I were in his position, I'd want to stay because, in football, you have to be comfortable with the players you're playing with and it takes time to build up understandings and being a centre-half is one of the most important jobs in the team.

"You have to be the rock of the side and hopefully Sylvain will realise that and remain a City player. If he doesn't and leaves for another club, it's worth noting that there is a lot of chopping and changing at other clubs with regards to central defence and it's difficult to get a settled partnership like the one he has here."

If he does go, is there a ready-made replacement already at the club? Dunne reckons there probably is. "I definitely think there is," he says. "If the manager has money to spend, he may want to buy another centre-half, but I think Micah and Nedum have both played in that role this season and both done brilliantly.

"That's also their natural position, but they are young and it takes a little time to settle into the role. It's harder than playing full-back, but the best way for them to learn is to play there and learn from your mistakes. There are definitely options already available for the manager."

Though City have threatened to go on decent runs during the season, and reached the quarter-finals of the FA Cup, there have been too many games when the team have come off thinking what might have been. The chronic lack of goals hasn't helped. So how does the skipper switch off after the team has not delivered the goods?

"It's difficult, really," he admits. "You just have to hang around the dressing room until everyone's gone and then get off home as quickly as you can. Sometimes it's a case of locking the windows and doors, avoiding Match of the Day and not reading the Sunday papers.

"But I can't afford to get too down because I'm expected to lift others, just as the manager has to with everyone at the club, it's my job to do the same out on the pitch. I can't let it affect me for too long – it's just a case of it's over, done, move on and improve next week.

"Besides, my daughter Lyla doesn't allow me to dwell on things for too long and after a few minutes of being back home with her, you just think 'it's not that bad'."

In his role as skipper, Dunne caused a bit of a stir in the tabloids with his comments about foreign players not settling in well at the club prior to the FA Cup tie with Blackburn – except that wasn't what he'd said.

His quotes were taken out of all context and he never singled out any group or individuals when he spoke to the press.

"What I actually said was some of the manager's new signings had come in and not settled – I never mentioned whether that meant foreign players or otherwise. Obviously, a number of the signings have been foreign and that's been the popular interpretation of my comments and maybe some people took it the wrong way, but in the eight games after the Blackburn match, we lost just twice, so whether anyone was upset with me or not, we haven't had many bad performances since.

"The season was just drifting once we went out of the Cup and I felt at the time there just wasn't enough passion within the team. Since then, I don't think anyone could really fault the efforts of the team and I think everyone's given everything and done really well."

The PFA awards passed again without the name of Richard Dunne among any of the nominees. It was the same old, same old, despite his consistency and, to be frank, it's an insult to keep wheeling the same players out for the Player of the Year award and the Premiership Team of the Year and ignoring the just claims of the rock of City's defence. Does he get fed up with the continued snub from his peers?

"It's always the same people," he said, echoing the thoughts of the supporters. "It's the same for clubs like Reading, where Nicky Shorey, statistically, is among the best defenders in the country, but he was nowhere to be seen among the nominees.

"I didn't vote for him, either, because I hardly ever see him play and you tend to vote for players from the top four clubs because you are most familiar with them. You see them on the TV all the time, whether it be Premiership or Champions League, and you base your vote on that – it's just the way it is.

"To be truly successful, you have to be part of a team that's successful and we've not been that this season. I think Cristiano Ronaldo was a worthy winner this season and the players he was up against deserved to be in there, too.

"I don't really think about it, to be honest, but at least Micah was nominated for the Young Player of the Year award and deservedly so, but playing for England and being touted at a value of £20m has certainly made people sit up and notice."

Talking of huge price tags, how come Dunney isn't linked with mega money moves as most other players of his calibre often are, even if it is no more than paper talk?

"I'm sure if I asked my agent to go and tell the newspapers that I wanted to move for £20m, they'd run the story, but I've always been very happy here and I'm enjoying my life, so why would I want to go anywhere else?"

While he may not receive the plaudits he deserves from the PFA, when it comes to the Manchester City fans, it's another story entirely. In May he picked up his third Player of the Year award in a row – the first time that has ever happened and only club legend Joe Corrigan can match winning the coveted prize three times during his 17-year career with the Blues – so what does it mean to be voted the best by the supporters?

"When I first won it three years ago, I thought 'brilliant', but when I picked it up for the third time last month, it really hit me as to what an achievement it actually is. Looking at the names who have won it previously, and then seeing that none of them had won it three times in succession, is really special. Back in Ireland, everyone is over the moon and my phone never stopped ringing in the days after.

"It's a great personal achievement and while I may not have won recognition from the PFA, being voted Player of the Year by our own fans, who watch us every week, is what really counts for me rather than players I play against twice a season. As long as I'm doing right by our fans, that's good enough for me."

16:20 Aguero tries to bring the ball forward and his attempted pass through to Tevez is cleared by Hill for a City throw-in...

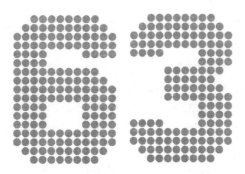

Hughes The Man

With Sven gone after just one season, Mark Hughes was selected as the man to take City back to the glory days. It wasn't too long before his employer, Thaksin Shinawatra, was also gone – it was a dizzying period in the club's history, but an exciting one, nonetheless...

It's true Mark Hughes played around half his competitive games in the shirt of City's neighbours, but the last of those was 13 long years ago and his thoughts these days do not stray to Old Trafford. The Blues' new boss is acutely aware some supporters will forever link him with United, even though his impressive CV boasts numerous other teams such as Bayern Munich, Barcelona and Chelsea.

"I did play for other clubs, by the way," was his smiling reply to the first of a barrage of early questions about his past.

"Sometimes in football, appointments are made because maybe twenty or thirty years ago you played two games on loan for someone's reserve side! That's how it is. There are appointments that are not made on logic and the ability of the person to do the job, and I would like to think that I am here at City because so far I have made a good fist of what I am trying to do.

"Allegiance, affinity and empathy from fans for ex-players goes out of the window if your results and signings are not successful, and it works the other way around, too. Many high profile ex-players fall by the wayside when they come into management because it quickly becomes apparent, no matter what their allegiances playing-wise, that they are not ready for that step. They still think as a player does and not a manager.

"I'm a professional football manager; I don't wear the shirt anymore, I try to lead the people that do. I'm a manager that has been shaped by the experiences that I have had, that includes my playing career.

"I am now at a great club, with a great fan base who have been really positive in their reaction to my appointment, and I am pleased about that. Now it is a case of settling in quickly and moving this club forward.

"I am absolutely delighted to be at City, I have already had some great support from the fans and I'm pleased with the positive reaction to the appointment.

"The United connection doesn't bother me. Some kind of reaction was to be expected and part of what I am as a person and a manager is shaped by the past experiences I have had. I have been at a number of top level clubs and have gained from being at all of them; they have helped shape me as a manager. People will harp on about certain clubs, but it is not an issue to me.

"City fans have always impressed me. I have lived in the area now since 1988 and I know so many Blues that are neighbours and that I have come across over the years. I know what love they have for their club. All my experiences of City fans are based on experience and fact, and I am acutely aware of the passion they have for their club and the way they have loyally stuck by it.

"The really exciting thing for me in that respect is that I know if we can do well on the pitch and get things moving forward and keep that going, this is a huge club to be successful at. That's what we all want to be.

"As I said, I knew those questions about United would come but hopefully people view me as a professional football manager. I'd like to think the reason I was brought to City was that people think I am good at what I do."

It was a typically robust response from a player who brooked no nonsense on the pitch and now doesn't take any off it either.

Quietly spoken but clear in his football ideals and desires, the Wrexham-born 44-year-old is clearly as at home in both his tailored suit as his tracksuit.

Bubbling just beneath the surface is that aforementioned drive, determination and old fashioned work ethic that, for the thick end of two decades, set him apart from the majority of his contemporaries.

On first meeting, there is not the immediate sense of the instant joviality or razor sharp wit of Joe Royle, the impish sense of frenzy and busy excitement of Kevin Keegan or the rakish world wise charm of Sven-Goran Eriksson.

But there is, nevertheless, something indefinably special about the countenance of the latest City chief. He has a sense of presence.

Leslie Mark Hughes OBE, MBE, is clearly a man on a journey to the top of his profession and a man who wants to arrive there as quickly as possible. He has the quiet but confident aura of someone who knows he is exceptionally gifted at his trade, and while he is polite and courteous, there is always the sense that he will not suffer fools or their foolish questions for too long.

He admits that the quality of the playing staff that he has inherited from the popular Eriksson was another of the reasons he felt the move from East Lancashire was in his best interests.

He had nothing but praise for his predecessor, both as a coach and a man, and understands why City fans were so vehement in their defence of the Swede when it became clear that his job was under threat.

"Sven is one of those people who engenders that type of affection; that is the type of person he is," admitted the new City chief.

"I have a great deal of respect and admiration for Sven. Our paths crossed many times when we were just watching games or came up against each other competitively. He was always very gracious and a very humble man and I liked being in his company.

"Obviously, what happened here, I was on the outside looking in like everyone else. But when one door closes for one person, it opens for another, and on this occasion it was me. Sven left behind a talented squad of players.

"What we will do is try to provide the quality of coaching and preparation that allows the players to be the best that they can be. In the end, if they are not up to the mark, they will have to look at themselves. We will make sure they are the best prepared that they can be physically, tactically and technically.

"We expect, as a group, that the players have a drive and a purpose to their work and that they hold the view that they are going to get better. Within that, there will hopefully be an environment created by the players themselves that will see them create a certain amount of peer pressure, too. That way, any dissenting voices will soon realise that it is a waste of their time.

"I am not a stickler for rules and regulations and I'm not overly pedantic, but there has to be a structure in place where people know the boundaries of where they can go and where they cannot go.

"I am very clear on a day-to-day basis what the standards should be at the training ground, and there has to be intensity; that is what I am looking for. I am not looking for great quantities because the days of lapping the training ground have gone years ago. What I want is quality, and that is the same for all the coaches.

"We all sing from the same paper, and that way the message gets re-emphasised on a daily basis. Every hour, every minute is all about being better prepared and ready for the challenges ahead. That means a lot of work on the training ground, and a lot of work in the gym, so we have to ensure we have that base of fitness that enables you to perform at the highest level, which is what we have to do in the Premier League.

"The players and the supporters will know from experience that my teams work extremely hard and are committed, but I am an advocate of attacking football.

"Those that have played for me week-in, week-out, in the past are technical players that play the type of football that I want to be played. Hopefully, the fans will see that very quickly in the teams that I will produce.

"My passion, my drive and my ambition is there for all to see. If you see how my teams play, and the intensity that my players have, you will see that the work I do and my coaches do has a positive effect.

"In terms of targets, there is only one, and that is to be successful," he emphasised. "I have not been given a timescale of where we should be after three months, six months or nine months. It wasn't discussed in those terms.

"I have come here to be successful; that is why I left Blackburn where I am sure I could have stayed for a number of years and been very comfortable and secure in my position, but I wanted to move forward and test myself at the highest level and that means competing for what is on offer

"That is why I made up my mind very quickly to come to City. We met club officials in London and had a number of hours discussing where we wanted to take the club, and I was very excited by what I heard. There is a unity of purpose from the boardroom.

"I took great pride in the fact that they actually asked me to be part of where they want to take the club, and stressed that I was the man they wanted to help them do that.

"I enjoyed my time at Blackburn, but there was a limit to where we could go. I needed to move to a club that matched my ambitions and I have. I am really excited.

"The ambition of the whole club is to challenge at the top table – not only in this country, but in Europe. If we can get the right players in the right positions, it's more than realistic.

"There is always pressure, every Premier League manager is under pressure. It's a results-driven business and you are judged on results and the key decisions you take. It doesn't faze me – it's something you have to work with and you have to thrive on."

QPR drop deeper and deeper; showing no intention of going forward as Taiwo clears the ball downfield to Joe Hart who starts yet another attack...

Tal Stories

Mark Hughes' second signing raised one or two eyebrows. At around £5m, was Ben-Haim really the sort of player City needed to advance?

T al Ben-Haim is hoping to become as popular as the Blues' last Israeli.

The 26-year-old came to England in 2004 having already become a big name back home in Israel. Bolton, then managed by Sam Allardyce, took the plunge and brought him to the Premier League and he had a successful period at the Reebok.

He had been invited for a trial with Aston Villa where their then boss David O'Leary turned down the chance to sign him, but Allardyce was not so reticent as his Midlands counterpart and after a two-week trial with Wanderers in the summer of 2004, Ben Haim joined the Trotters on a three-year contract for a bargain fee of less than £200,000.

"It was a very big move for me," reflected the defender. "I was playing in Israel and then I came to the best league in the world. It took a lot of patience on my part. Sam Allardyce told me that I would have to wait for my chance. I did that and when it came, I played well and stayed in the team."

Although essentially purchased as 'one for the future', the no nonsense defender soon fought his way into the side and made 27 appearances in his first season. His versatility as either a central defender, or right or left-back, made him almost indispensable to Wanderers, but brought inevitable attention from other clubs, particularly those in London, headed by Chelsea and West Ham United.

It was the Stamford Bridge side who finally landed their man some 12 months after their initial enquiry, a move prompted by injuries to both John Terry and Ricardo Carvalho and the fact that Ben Haim was a free agent after 110 first team appearances for the Reebok side.

Although he played a full part in Chelsea's season of near misses under Jose Mourhino and Avram Grant, Ben Haim could not establish himself as a first choice regular at the Bridge, and when Luiz Felipe Scolari took over this summer, he decided that a fee of around £3million was a fair price and allowed the player to move to City.

Ben Haim jumped at the chance to move back to the North West and be part of Mark Hughes' reshaping of the squad following the departure of Sven-Goran Eriksson at the end of last season.

"Results are everything and I think we can achieve many things here, but people should not expect too much, too soon," he cautioned, after a mixed pre-season and then a far from fluent start to competitive action before the win over West Ham.

"This season is just the beginning of the story for us. Mark Hughes has only just arrived and is trying to build something new and bring in fresh players. So this is just the start and we are all looking forward to an exciting time. For me, it is not just about getting into the team, but also about my football and how I can improve and learn.

"I think City is a good club with great expectations and one that wants to go forward. We have fantastic fans who definitely deserve more than they have had in terms of success in the last 20 or 30 years. They want to see more wins, more attacking football, more aggression and more passion to the play of the team, and I hope we are going to give it to them so they can enjoy watching us."

City probe through Silva and Zabaleta but the ball is brought out of defence by substitute Traore who moves past Kompany down the right wing...

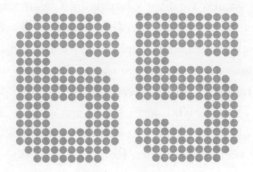

Kompany Man

Vincent Kompany cut an impressive figure from the moment he walked into Carrington. Focused yet calm and laid-back, he was the first of a new breed of player coming into the club...

Vincent Kompany joined the Blues towards the end of August from German club SV Hamburg, though he didn't take part in the recent friendly between the two clubs. Kompany can play either as a centre-back or in a midfield holding role, and he arrives with an outstanding pedigree.

Born in the Belgian town of Uccle on April 10, 1986, Kompany joined Anderlecht as a youngster and progressed through their youth system to the first team. He went on to make 73 appearances for 'the

258

Purple' and was regarded as one of Europe's hottest young talents and he was linked with numerous top clubs, including Chelsea and Real Madrid.

While with Anderlecht, he won several club and individual honours, including the Belgian Golden Shoe and the Belgian Ebony Shoe, twice. He also gained valuable Champions League experience and earned his first international cap for Belgium before leaving to play for Hamburg to replace former City player Daniel van Buyten after his fellow countryman had moved on to Bayern Munich.

A shoulder injury meant he only managed to start 28 games for the Bundesliga outfit, who were then reluctant to allow the fit-again 22-year-old to represent his county at the Beijing Olympics. A compromise was reached when Kompany agreed to play just two matches for Belgium, but he had a sending off in his first game against a Brazil team that included the soon-to-be club team-mate, Jo. A one-match ban muddied the waters and the player was at loggerheads with his club who had expected him home earlier, while Kompany understandably wanted to help his country win a medal of some kind. The matter was eventually settled and he returned to Germany, but was soon on his way to Manchester to embark on a new chapter in his career with City after agreeing a four-year deal.

GOAL! Traore whips in a deep cross which Mackie reaches with a diving header, directing the ball down and over Hart and the flailing attempts of Lescott on the line. City 1 QPR 2. The Blues must score twice to win the title...

16:23

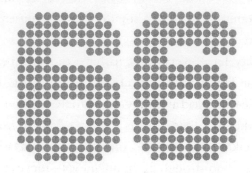

Glittering Prize

With Sheikh Mansour and the Abu Dhabi United Group taking over City so late in the transfer window, there was just enough time to give the Blues fans one new gift before the window closed. Robinho's signing was just the beginning and City fans knew that, at last, the right man now owned the club. The sky was the limit...

Pioneer, genius, superstar...call him what you will, but there is no doubting one thing – Robson de Souza is one hell of a footballer. The gifted Brazilian has already lit up numerous dull Mancunian afternoons with his samba skills and clinical finishing, and the chant the City fans serenade him with, "We've got Robinho!" is one largely borne out of disbelief that the slightly-built striker is actually here playing in sky blue.

From the moment he signed on deadline day at the start of September, it was love at first sight from the City fans, most of who were still on cloud nine from Shaun Wright-Phillips re-signing not so long before. As Sky Sports broke the news that he'd signed shortly before midnight, there were ecstatic scenes at the stadium and homes around Manchester – as well as a smattering of bemusement that our club had captured one of football's great natural talents.

Of course, City have every right to have the very best players at the club, but the fact is we're just not used to it – yet. The £32.5m capture from Real Madrid not only more than doubled the previous transfer fee paid by the Blues, it was a signal of intent from the club's new owner, Sheikh Mansour, and on a day when David Villa and Dimitar Berbatov had strongly been linked with moves to the City of Manchester Stadium, it was the news that Robinho was coming to the Rainy City that captured the imagination more than anything else.

As soon as City shirts with his name and squad number 10 started flying out from the City store the next day, it was clear the 'Robinho effect' had already kicked in and was not going to go away. The supporters had got the superstar they'd always craved – probably the first player who could genuinely live up to the title – and they are going to enjoy having him in their team and, it seems, he's enjoying playing in front of them every week.

From the moment he struck home the free-kick against Chelsea on his debut, Robinho joined that rare breed of footballer who becomes untouchable. You'll never hear him criticised, he'll be encouraged to do whatever he wants with a football and you can bet that on the rare occasion he misplaces a pass, it'll be the other guy's fault for not being on his wavelength! That's what hero worship is all about, but, as Stan Lee once wrote in Spider-Man, 'with great power comes great responsibility' and the 24-year-old, Sao Vincente-born star carries the hopes and dreams of the supporters every time he steps out to represent the Blues.

He wants to be the best and is on a journey to see his own dreams realised, though he is well-grounded, approachable and level-headed enough to not read too much into his own press. Speaking exclusively to the City mag, Robinho – 'little Robin' in literal translation, said: "To be honest, when I was nine or ten years old, I was never thinking about being one of the best players in the world. I was dreaming about being a good professional footballer and I think I've fulfilled that, but I don't think I should be compared to somebody like Pele because he's an incomparable footballer. Pele is Pele and Robinho is Robinho."

At Santos, he was a child protégé, taken under the wing of Pele who kept a close eye on this most precocious talent as he slowly rose through the ranks with the legendary Brazilian club side. Playing alongside Elano, he scored 44 goals in 104 starts for Santos, who had repeatedly resisted the overtures of numerous top European clubs.

He made his debut for Brazil in 2003, aged 19, and has since played a further 55 times for his country, scoring 17 goals. As his star continued to rise, Santos knew they could no longer hold on to their prized asset, and when Real Madrid offered around £17m, a clause in Robinho's contract was automatically activated and, after agreeing terms, he joined David Beckham and company at the Bernabeu, becoming a Madrid Galáctico in the process

In a team of superstars, Robinho quickly settled in, making his debut as a second-half substitute against Cadiz and showcasing his silky skills to the Spanish fans and quickly becoming a crowd favourite, though his reputation preceded him in many ways.

"In the beginning it was quite difficult, particularly at Real Madrid," he said. "Now I am more used to people expecting big things of me and it doesn't bother me at all. At every club I've played for, there were expectations of me and pressure to perform to a very high standard, but I'm completely used to that now.

"At Santos, there was pressure; for the national team, there was pressure; at Real Madrid, there was pressure and at Manchester City, there is pressure, too – you just get used to it and I can deal with it. There's no special place or a particular ritual I have for relaxing.

"I spend as much time as I can with my son and my family and keep myself calm, though just before the matches, I do feel the pressure building up – just not in-between."

"The expectations at a club like Real Madrid were huge and the supporters demand the best, but I had the support of my family and spent a lot of time in their company, so any external pressures I felt, I was able to deal with. But I feel that it is the same for any player who wants to be the best in the world – the pressure goes with the territory, so to speak."

However, a very public fall-out with Madrid president Ramon Calderon meant Robinho had to quit the club in order to progress with his career. It's doubtful Madrid's relentless pursuit of Cristiano Ronaldo did little but exacerbate the situation, with Robinho linked with being part of a package plus cash deal Madrid were allegedly willing to agree to in order to take the Manchester United winger to Spain.

Chelsea expressed strong interest in taking the Brazilian to Stamford Bridge and Robinho, no doubt desperate to leave a club who had made it clear they were looking to replace him, stated he wanted to come to England and play under his former national team boss Luiz Felipe Scolari.

As the transfer deadline loomed, it seemed only Chelsea could afford the £32.5m asking price, but the Pensioners baulked at the fee, offering less than Madrid's asking price. As the clock ticked, Robinho's prayers were answered, though it was the new kids on the financial clout block – Manchester City, not Chelsea – who matched Madrid's valuation.

Once he learned of the Blues' interest, a deal was quickly agreed and Robinho became a City player. But what would have happened had the deal not materialised?

"I would have carried on doing my job, which is playing football – that's what I would have had to do," he said. "I had scored three goals for Madrid already before I left, but it's more convenient for people to forget about things like that – that's the way in football.

"Of course, I did speak with Elano before I joined City and he was very happy that I was coming to Manchester. I already knew him very well from playing for Brazil and we were team-mates for four years at Santos, too. I consider him as my brother."

Away from the goldfish bowl of Spanish football, Robinho is quickly adjusting to life in the Premier League and has taken to English football like the proverbial duck to water, scoring eight goals for the Blues in his first dozen games. He looks happy, relaxed and is enjoying life – particularly relishing the role of being a father for the first time. Evidence, if needed, of the doting dad's dedication to his son can be found in the fact he'd rather watch Bear in the Big Blue House with his infant rather than Champions League matches on TV.

"I don't really watch much football when I'm at home," he confirmed. "I prefer to play with my son, watch movies and relax rather than watch other games on TV."

So what of Robinho junior? Is he showing signs – even now – of following in his father's footsteps? Robinho smiles at the suggestion. "He will have all the incentives he needs to do well in any sport, basketball or whatever, but if he chooses to play football, of course, he'll have my full support, help and advice.

"Becoming a father changed my life completely because nowadays I spend most of my time at home with my family, playing with my boy and enjoying their company.

"If I do ever go out, it's for a meal in a restaurant or maybe going to see a movie, just like anyone else, really. I love listening to Brazilian samba music and yes, I try and incorporate it into my game whenever I can!"

Lionel Messi, Kaka, Sergio Aguero and countless other superstars have all been linked with moves to City by various media organisations since the club became dubbed 'the richest club in the world' – and Robinho doesn't mind dreaming of who his possible team-mates might be in the coming months.

"Both Sergio Aguero or Kaka are fantastic players and Manchester City have a very exciting project developing – if either of those players came to the club, of course, it can only be good for our team and I'd be very happy," he smiled. "Aguero is an excellent footballer who is having a lot of success with Atletico Madrid. I hope I am the first of many stars to come to Manchester City."

And what of Manchester? Robinho was quoted as saying he feared Manchester would be some kind of wasteland prior to his arrival, but the reality was totally different and he was delighted to be proved completely wrong about his new home. He said: "It is a beautiful city and I'm adapting very well to life in Manchester. Every day I'm learning more about my new home and getting to know the city even better as I go along.

"People obviously recognise you when you are out and about, but I don't mind at all – this is the life I've chosen and it's never a problem. The Manchester City fans are very respectful of my privacy when I am out with my family. They always have very good manners and occasionally they might ask for a photo, but that's part of being a well-known figure."

Go to any park in Manchester on a Saturday or Sunday morning and you will see legions of kids copying their new idol. Where it was once Ronaldo and nothing else that Mancunian kids seemed to want to be, now it's Robinho, a genuine threat to the moody Portuguese star's crown as local kids' favourite footballer. Robinho is surprised his influence is already in the parks and streets of his new city – but delighted, nonetheless.

"I'm very happy that this is happening," he said. "If I can influence a generation of young kids, that is fantastic, especially if they play with the same happiness as I do. It will make me very proud and happy. I love playing football and enjoy doing my job immensely and love playing in front of the City fans.

"I get very motivated when I hear them singing my name – it inspires me even more and makes me try harder for them because the fans mean everything to me and they deserve the best.

"I have to admit, I was prepared to be liked by the Manchester City fans, but I never imagined they would like me as much as they do. But with hard work, good play and great goals, I hope they will like me even more in the coming months and years.

"I love to play for City and I think I have adapted quite quickly to English football. The manager allows me to play in a position I enjoy very much and I think I've done quite well so far because the game in England is very physical and very quick and I'm enjoying it very much. In fact, I think I've adapted a lot quicker than I thought I was going to. It's going to be fun."

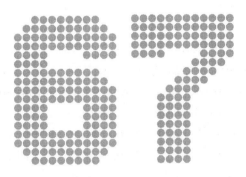

Warrior

Pablo Zabaleta is a modern-day warrior. It would have been so easy for him to slip under the radar, play a few games here and there and then move on. Not Zaba. Grit and determination have made him a first team regular for more than three years...

There are few more exciting places to visit in the Americas than Buenos Aires, capital city of Argentina. Home to more than three million people, the crowded metropolis was a far cry from the peaceful, semi-rural town of Arrecifes, some two hours away, where Pablo Zabaleta spent his early years.

Football and horse riding was the daily staple for the young Zaba, before an invitation to join Boca Juniors meant leaving home at the age of 12 and relocating in a club apartment in the centre of Buenos Aires.

It would be the first of three major cities Zaba would live in, with Barcelona and Manchester to follow for the future City defender.

"I grew up in Arrecifes," he began. "It is around 200km from Buenos Aires and is a typical small Argentinian town with a population of maybe 25,000 people. My family still live there, in fact.

"It was the first house for my parents, and my father and my step-mum still live there. It isn't big, but it is quiet nice and has everything we needed. It's just right."

Arrecifes was given city status in 1950 and is known for its cattle ranches and farms – a million miles from the bright lights of the big cities.

Zaba lived in the family home with his parents – businessman, Jorge, and mother, Laura, who sadly died in 2000 – and his siblings. He said: "I am the oldest. I have one brother and a sister, Lucia. Gianluca is my little half-brother because my father re-married a few years ago.

"Gianluca is only five, so there is a 20-year age gap! He was born just as I went to live in Spain to play for Espanyol. It was difficult to bond together initially because I was like a stranger to him living so far away and seeing him once a year.

"I am only in Argentina for 10 to 15 days a year, so it's taken time for him to know who I am, but we are very close now. He can speak well now, so we talk a lot on the phone and I think he likes the fact his big brother plays for Argentina."

Zaba's grandparents lived in an even more rural setting than he did on a ranch out near the hills. He spent many happy hours playing at the ranch, riding horses and helping out on what was quite a large property. It is a time he clearly remembers with great affection.

"I went to see my grandparents in the summer and over the weekends as they have horses that I used to ride and it was a good place to be. The summers were long and hot and it was the perfect place for any kid to be. Over time, the size of the place became a problem for my grandparents and they rented their home out, moving closer to town and downsizing. Hopefully, I will own it one day when I am retired – that would be an ideal scenario because we could then keep what is a very special place in the family."

Zaba's love of football was never far away during his formative years, and he took every opportunity to kick a ball in Arrecifes.

"In Argentina, you have a lot of space to play on the street, or in gardens, or at the park," he said. "We played on any space we could find in our neighbourhood after school. I called on my friends and went to play. It was quite a safe area to live in, but I had to leave when I was scouted aged 10 or so.

"There are only a few football teams in Arrecifes and my junior team coach came to me to say I had quality and that I should try my luck in the city. My father agreed it would be best and so I joined Buenos Aires side San Lorenzo when I was 12 years old. It would have been tough to break into a team like Boca Juniors or River Plate and my father felt I'd have a better chance of progressing at a smaller club.

"It was a big change for me and I lived with all the other youngsters in a house owned by the club, but they didn't have a lot of money for the young players to live comfortably.

"The food was always the same: spaghetti, chicken, oranges – just cheap food. My parents knew it was difficult and were there for me whenever they could get to Buenos Aires. My father gave me a small allowance that meant I could vary what I ate and he would sometimes take me to restaurants to eat different types of food. I was very lucky that we had the money to do that."

Outings for the young Pablo didn't always end with eating, as football-mad Jorge eventually took Pablo to watch his first football match at his beloved Boca Juniors.

"My dad went all the time to watch Boca with his friends and one day he took me with him," he recalled. "I remember one of my dad's friends was an Independiente fan – the team Boca were playing that day – and as he was stood with us in the home section, he had to pretend he was a home supporter.

"Independiente won 1-0 and when they scored, the guy was very quiet! In Argentina we take sport very seriously and it would have been a bad idea to reveal his true colours – he'd have never made it out alive!

"It was a great experience as the Bombonera is a very nice ground, and I enjoyed it, especially the ticker-tape receptions they used to get – we should try it at City one day!

"I remember that my parents came to see if I wanted to move away from Buenos Aires. It was very difficult for me as I was only 12 years old. My father is a Boca Juniors supporter, but we decided that San Lorenzo was the better option as Boca is a top team and it is difficult to go there as they have so many top players.

"San Lorenzo was the first choice and so I went there for training. The manager seemed to like me and wanted me to stay, so I signed a contract and was off and running. I've played at the Bombonera twice and it is very exciting to see all the fans there and I think my father enjoyed seeing me play, even though it wasn't in the colours of Boca.

"One thing I'd love to do, but haven't as yet, is to go to what we call a 'Classico' between River Plate and Boca. I hope to go in the future as it will be a great game to witness."

Right now, Zabaleta is happy in Manchester and has no plans to move on anytime soon.

"I feel comfortable here and I want to stay," he said. "If you see the squad, it makes you feel positive as it gives us a lot of possibilities to win something this year, but for that we need to fight in every game, for our fans and for ourselves.

"Football changes all the time. I wanted to come and play in England as it was an ambition of mine. Now I am playing here and I'm really happy and have three years left on my contract. Now all we have to do is bring some silverware back to the club."

City substitution as Barry is replaced by Dzeko to give City more of an aerial presence and a goal threat...

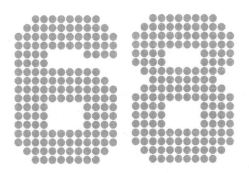

Red Dragon

Craig Bellamy was a decent bloke who came to City with a lot of baggage. He soon became a firm favourite and someone you wanted on your side rather than against it. The only chance I had to speak with him was when he was promoting a piece of artwork. We did it as a Q&A and I think because it is Bellers, it's worth including a snippet of it here...

The City fans have really taken to you – as have fans at most clubs you've been with – but they appreciate your work ethic and effort to the point that you've become a huge crowd favourite here. Have you found your spiritual home?

"I'm very happy here and because of the situation at this club at the moment, I've tried to embrace everything that's happening here. I've never looked at the players we've signed thinking it would be difficult for me to get a game. I looked around at the start of the season and just set myself personal targets. My first aim was to be fit because I knew that if I was fit, I could challenge for my place and take things from there. If I'm good enough, I'll play; if I'm not good enough, I won't – I just try and keep everything as simple as possible. I never try and do something I'm not capable of doing and just try play to my strengths. Basically, I don't feel nervousness before a game or nerves of whether I will play well, just nervousness of working hard.

"It's like a long distance runner training for a marathon – the pain you get before you set off because you know you're going to feel the same pain during it – that's the only nerves I get because I know I have to work extremely hard to stay in this team. I believe in myself and always believe things will hopefully go right on the day, but first and foremost I have to do as many sprints as I can, I have to cover as much distance as I can, because that is part of my role in the team.

"I try to keep things as simple as I can and I think the City fans have appreciated that as have fans at other clubs I've been with. They don't want me to leave and if I do, they hate me afterwards! It can all turn around, but I was appreciated at Newcastle, Liverpool, Blackburn and West Ham, but I'm old enough to understand that it can all change tomorrow. I just want to look back in future years with a lot of satisfaction of the part I played at this club and I hope City fans can do so as well."

This must be one of the best seasons of your career....

"On a personal level, yeah, I think it has been. From a consistency point of view, things have gone well since day one. This league is so difficult that consistency is not easy to maintain but, touch wood, it's rolled on and rolled on and I would be disappointed if I've not scored, created a goal or won a penalty or been a big influence in each game I've played this season. That's all I could ask for, really, so from a consistency level, I'd probably agree that this is the best season I've had in my career to date."

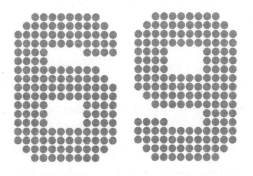

Carlito's Way

It took a while, but an exclusive interview with Carlos Tevez was finally arranged. We travelled to his house near Macclesfield and stayed for more than an hour. This was in 2010 and the only thing at that point missing from his cavernous mansion was his family...

It's hard to imagine the Blues without Tevez these days, with the word 'talisman' springing to mind when you think of his role within the team. A tour de force of energy, effort and burning desire, he is different from the majority of footballers in both his outlook and journey to becoming one of the best players on the planet.

What team wouldn't want to have Tevez leading their line? Well, there's one club not a million miles from us who decided they could live without his services, but more fool them. That particular club continue to be successful, but they don't look the same without the drive and determination Tevez brings to the table.

So when a player becomes so important to a team that their supporters can't bear the thought of life without him, the media seem to take a perverse pleasure in finding obscure quotes, twisting translations and making mischief when there is no real story to be told.

Body language is a massive clue to how a footballer is feeling and a quick glance at the goal celebrations during the 4-1 win at Fulham last month should tell you all you need to know about Carlos Tevez and his feelings for this club.

Beaming smile, eyes lit up and a joy in his manner that renders the rumours and speculation as the work of journalists working to an agenda rather than a basis in fact.

The City skipper agreed to set the record straight once and for all and invited this writer, our club photographer and, for good measure, one of the best translators in the business along to his Cheshire home for an interview to provide clarification and, hopefully, end the speculation once and for all.

So is he settled at City or is he desperate to return to Argentina?

"I feel very happy here, I am very comfortable here and I am very relaxed," he smiled. "I feel absolutely at home in England. Manchester City is my home; on the pitch there is no problem and I have made a lot of friendships within the club, so there are a lot of people I can share the great moments with.

"Off the field, I am like everyone else in that I need my family around me as well as my long-standing friends, but I think that is normal. When they are not here in Manchester, I miss them, but that is no reason to retire from football."

What father wouldn't pine for his two beautiful daughters? As Carlos says, he is no different from anyone else in that respect, but he accepts it all the same. Of course, the separation makes the reunions all the sweeter and the doting dad, who has a huge picture drawn by his girls taped to a window in his lounge, reveals the scene as he enters the arrivals hall at Buenos Aires airport on his return home.

"It's emotional. It's a great moment and when I see them for the first time, it gives me a huge lift," says Carlos, almost lost in thought. "After concentrating on the day-to-day life of a footballer; training, playing matches and so on, it's sometimes tiring. Your days are taken up in many ways; sometimes you stay at hotels the night before the game, or maybe you spend additional time doing rehab, which I have had to do a lot of recently due to a few little injuries I've been carrying. So it's great to put that to one side for a while and concentrate solely on your family.

"My daughters are beautiful. Katie is just like me in her character, but Floppy is just like her mother – her gestures, her mannerisms are just like her mum's.

"Time in Argentina is always family-based first and foremost with my girls. I also share time between my parents' home and my brother's home, but it's all about spending quality time with my daughters, my parents, my brothers and my mates."

Carlos was born in the unforgiving Buenos Aires suburb known as Fuerte Apache, with its name giving an indication of what the day-to-day life was life for the residents of this tough, embattled area of Argentina's capital city.

"Fuerte Apache is a totally different end of the spectrum from my life today," he says. "I don't have any family there anymore, but I do have some childhood friends and they always tell me that I haven't changed at all. I go and see them and hang out whenever I'm back.

"I'll always keep fighting during games and I've no doubt that is due to my upbringing as a kid at Fuerte Apache. Life was very tough. Some days you would find it hard to find something to eat, even a piece of bread. It was a day-to-day struggle and you would have to fight to get what you needed. I suppose I play like that on the pitch, too. It's in my nature to fight for every ball and never give up – it's how I survived as a kid and moved forward with my life."

While there is no doubt Carlos would grace any league in the world, he admits he loves England and the passion people have for the game over here. Spiritually and professionally, he is at home.

"The thing that sets England apart from anywhere else is that fans leave you to live your own life and you get a lot of respect from the fans, which is marvellous," he says.

"Away from the game, I must admit I don't do a huge amount in my spare time. I like golf and I try to play as much as I can, though I'm not very good. Otherwise, I just rest up and relax. I think about the game 24/7; I love football. As for Manchester, I don't go out very much. There is one Argentinian restaurant in Manchester. I have been there once and it was okay, but I'll eat at home more often than not."

One area of City that Carlos has tapped into is the burning desire the Blues fans have to see silverware arrive at the club. It's an ambition he shares and he draws inspiration from that sense of longing and hope and he desperately wants to be part of any future successes.

"I really like the desire the fans have to win something, and I sense that," he says. "It gives me a lot of strength. I know it is hard for people to go week-in, week-out; it can be expensive and it is not the main priority in life, but they make it their main priority.

"That motivates me and drives me on and, being the captain as well, it inspires me even more. Seeing our fans come to the ground in huge numbers makes me want to try even harder when I'm out on the pitch. I'm committed to help make this club a success."

As skipper, Carlos is also keen to show his relationship with Roberto Mancini is healthy rather than the negative coverage the player and boss are often associated with.

"Of course, I get on well with Roberto and I back him 100 per cent," he said. "I was disappointed that my substitution against Birmingham resulted in some of our fans showing displeasure towards him.

"What people didn't know was that I had played the previous three games going through the pain barrier and the manager knew that. I was very close to getting a more serious injury through playing when perhaps I shouldn't have, so his concern was for my well-being.

"I thank the manager for what he did and I would be very selfish to get annoyed by being taken off against Birmingham; he knows I am not right, so it is nothing but thanks to him.

"To criticise the manager was unfair because we need to be patient; there is a long way to go in the season. I am doing the best I can, but I am not totally fit at present, but I am doing the best for the team and will continue to give my all."

Despite the sterling work of Kolo Toure, Carlos was a natural candidate to become skipper this season. Always leading by example and playing with the passion and commitment of a natural-born leader, he admits being handed the armband is an immense source of pride, but he needed to be sure the transition of the captaincy was done in the right way before he took the role on.

"It's funny, you know, because I had mixed feelings," he reveals. "It was the night before the first match at Tottenham and I chatted with the manager. I was pleased on the one hand, but my first thoughts were for Kolo as I had been a team member under him, and suddenly to become captain and have that role taken away from a good mate of mine, it gave me mixed feelings.

"The first thing I did was go and speak to him to make sure things were right. He understood and was fine about it as he knew it was the manager's decision. This made me feel settled and I was very pleased from that moment because if I was captain and it was taken away from me, I would be upset, so it was the least I could do."

Carlos has been a crowd idol wherever he's played in England and he has views on each set of fans he's played in front of in this country and the unique relationship he's had with them.

"At West Ham we lived through such a tough season that year, we suffered together, we almost went down, but in the end it was all 'sweetness and light'," he says. "We struggled all year, but saved our skins at the end of the season, and we celebrated together. When you are on the rocks in the beginning, then succeed in the end, it makes things even sweeter. We stayed up with my goal at Old Trafford, so I will always have a place in my heart for the West Ham fans.

"With Manchester United, it was different, it was all high hopes and the club were doing well. Then it all changed with my departure to City and their fans changed their opinion somewhat!

"With City it is again different; there was a lot of doubt within the supporters initially thinking, 'has he just come here for the money? How will he play?' But I think I have since proved that I will die for the shirt and the doubts have gone away."

So, with the bond now set in stone between fans and player, what does Carlos think of the 'Fergie, Fergie sign him up' chant? He is open and honest in his view.

"It's not the song that needs to be changed; it's the attitude or the mindset of our fans. Let's not be thinking about Sir Alex Ferguson and Manchester United, we need to think of City and what we can do," he says.

"Let's win a trophy – we want to be great and we want to be a power in world football. The thing that would wind up Sir Alex more than anything is for us to win something and to start really achieving things. What we've got to do is not to devote any of our time to United, just focus on ourselves.

"I think it has been such a topsy-turvy season so far, with everyone beating everyone else. What we have to do is start believing that we are a big club, get our act together, concentrate and be strong enough mentally to go five or six matches with victories, whereas currently we will get a win, then a draw with the odd defeat thrown in.

"It's a case of thinking about it properly and getting our mindset right in order to get those half dozen wins in a row which will give us that belief that we can be champions.

"My message to our fans is, first and foremost, be patient. Think how City were doing three or four years ago and how thing have changed so dramatically. Everyone should realise that we all want the same things. The fans want to win trophies and so do the players.

"We want to become a bigger club and City is the team on the lips of people the world over. Be patient and be aware we are on the right road, though it won't happen straight away.

"We want to win the Premier League and the Champions League, so we all want the same things. We are almost there, so enjoy it and think how quickly we have progressed from where we were. It's coming..."

Sustained City possession is ended when Ferdinand intercepts a pass and clears downfield. A one-two between Zabaleta and Tevez fails to come off and QPR win a throw. The ball goes back to Kenny who is quickly closed down by Aguero, but he clears in time…

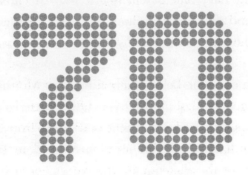

Legend

For City fans, he was the signing of the summer – further proof, if needed, that the club was heading in the right direction. It was a classic case of the returning prodigal son…

City were in Denmark on the day the news broke that Shaun Wright-Phillips was 'coming home'. The Blues needed to overturn a 1-0 home defeat to FC Midtjylland and the focus was whether the UEFA Cup campaign was about to end before it had really started.

There had been rumours that Mark Hughes was interested in

bringing SWP back to the City of Manchester Stadium and there were also indications that Chelsea may be willing to sell, but for City fans, it was just too good to be true.

Then news broke that Shaun was having a medical, and shortly after, there was confirmation the England midfielder had indeed become a Manchester City player once again.

Radio stations and websites were besieged with delighted Blues, ecstatic that SWP would be wearing the sky blue jersey once again, rather than the navy blue of Chelsea. Back in Denmark, City edged past Midtjylland after a penalty shoot-out, and a few days later, Robinho signed and the club was officially taken over – it was intoxicating, heady stuff.

There was a common belief that neither Jose Mourinho nor Avram Grant really got the best out of SWP. Often included in the team as cover for others, or forced to make the odd cameo from the subs' bench, the player that had left a legion of admirers back in Manchester only showed flashes of the all-action innovative winger he'd been at City.

Few doubted his ability and he was a popular figure with the Chelsea fans, but something wasn't quite right. He needed the belief and passion he'd been shown before his move to West London in order to get back to the very top of his game, and when the Blues logged a bargain £10m bid, he didn't have to think twice about returning north.

"I always believed that I'd come back one day," revealed Shaun. "It was just a matter of waiting to see when the perfect time would be and coming back this year was the perfect time.

"I decided I wanted to leave Chelsea and I'd always wanted to come back to City. I was just glad that everyone wanted me to come back when I did.

"The whole transfer went through so quickly. By the time we'd spoke about contracts and all the other details, I had to be on a train up here for my medical, so I never got time to hear what the fans thought or what their reaction was. At the time, I just hoped it was positive.

"The fact they stayed in the UEFA Cup through a last-minute own goal, then won a dramatic penalty shoot-out on the same day I signed, just made me smile. I've been here that long that I'm used to that being the way with City – it was always like that when I was coming through the ranks. We always liked to do the things the hard way, but hopefully the boss is slowly and surely getting that out of us now."

It was a dream return debut for SWP just a few days later, too, scoring twice as City thrashed Sunderland 3-0 at the Stadium of Light. With almost 2,000 travelling supporters in raptures, it was like their hero had never really been away.

"I've always thought that it would be great to return to City," he smiles. "My move to Chelsea felt like a long break where I experienced a great learning curve and improved my all-round game, but City were always in my future plans.

"The fans are fantastic and I can feel them willing to do well and it gives me the confidence to relax and play my natural game. I still consider myself quite young and it's weird to see things like that 'SWP-the Legend' banner hanging in the stand – but it's great, too! I try to give the fans back everything that they give me. I try to give 110 per cent in every game, even if things aren't going well for the team. That's how I played before I left and nothing has changed in that respect.

"I came to City when I was 16, so I've spent most of my adult years up here. For me, Manchester is like my adopted home, which is a great way to feel."

Adopted home or not, Shaun is a London lad and a stint in the capital did have its benefits on a personal level. So what are the negatives about returning to the North West?

"I miss being able to see my mum on a regular basis," he says. "My little boy and my family are all back in London, too, as well as a lot of my closest friends. My kids come to stay with me as much as they can, so they get to come up here, have some fun, have a laugh and they get to go to bed late which they think is great, though it means I am on the school run a lot more these days."

When Shaun left for Chelsea, his dad, Ian, was doing plenty of TV work, but these days he's a popular radio pundit for TalkSport. Ironically, Ian was inundated with City fans calling in when Shaun's signing was confirmed, though there was a slight twist. Most people start with "Ian, you're a legend, mate." The City fans began with, "Ian, your son's a legend, mate!"

Shaun smiles at the mention of this: "Well I always get told that my dad's a legend, so it's only right that he has to listen to it the other way around!

"Every now and again I'll tune in when my dad's on. When I'm driving or if he tells me that there is an interesting topic coming up, I'll listen in. It's right that he doesn't favour me in any way, though, and if I wasn't doing something right, then he'd be the first to tell me and that's the way it should be."

One thing Shaun does regret, however, was a comment he made earlier in the season about his habit of staying relatively injury-free. His dad once claimed his legs were made of rubber and Shaun himself hinted he was 'indestructible' in an interview. Of course, within weeks he was out injured and he ended the season sidelined for eight of the last nine games.

"Yeah, every time I'm asked about that I just say 'can we move on!' To be fair, the injury I actually had was one that has been playing up for the past three months and all the injuries I've had have been on the same leg, so we'll see what happens."

"Like I said, I've always wanted to come back, but I would have found it hard to play under Sven again. Being left out of the World Cup squad made me feel as if he didn't have any belief in me and so if he didn't have it at international level, I would have struggled to have played under him at club level."

So he's back home, enjoying life to the full and playing at his peak again. Did he ever imagine life would be this good when he was a kid?

"When I was growing up, I never realised that all this would come with playing football, but it kind of has done," he says. "I just love playing, having a laugh and not taking myself too seriously.

"I'm still the first to start laughing on the training ground when someone gets nut-megged because I just love football."

The corner taken reaches Tevez at the back post who directs a header towards the top corner before Kenny gets his fingertips to it...

Golden Silva

For City fans, it just kept getting better. A stellar array of names arriving at the club with money no object – the latest of which was Spain international, David Silva. The interview took place in the chairman's lounge where the cover pictures were also taken. In David's back pocket? A World Cup winners' medal – like you do...

If you believe everything you read in the papers, there were only two clubs in with a chance of signing David Silva this summer – Chelsea and City. Both sides were keen on adding creativity to their midfield and the Valencia playmaker fitted the bill perfectly.

With the Blues keen to tie up as many transfer deals as possible before the World Cup, it quickly became clear that wasn't going to be possible with a number of the potential targets Robert Mancini had identified.

Jerome Boateng was secured on the eve of the South Africa tournament, but Silva and Yaya Toure entered the competition as Valencia and Barcelona employees respectively. It was unusual, then, that Silva, not wanting any distractions before embarking on what would be a glorious journey with his country, decided to accept City's overtures while he was away with Spain.

A deal in principle was agreed and Silva announced he would be a Manchester City player when the World Cup finished, while thanking Valencia, already stripped of the services of the talismanic David Villa, for his time with the club.

"Firstly I would like to thank Valencia as a club and all of their loyal fans and my team-mates there and staff," he said.

"I enjoyed six years at Valencia. They discovered me as a footballer and they will always be a special club for me.

"The time is right for me to seek a new challenge and I am thrilled about playing in England with Manchester City.

"I believe the Premier League is one of the best competitions in the world and I want to bring success to City and win trophies for them."

Of course, there has been plenty of water under the bridge since those words were first issued, including the small matter of Spain's first World Cup win last month.

"So much has happened in a short space of time, my head is spinning," smiled Silva, who had stopped by at Carrington for his medical before arriving to sign his contract at the City of Manchester Stadium.

"It's still all a bit surreal and I've not had chance to absorb what happened in South Africa yet. What happened was incredible and to sing and celebrate in front of more than one million people at our homecoming is something I'll remember forever."

At least the sun is shining and as we continue to talk, his family are shown around the stadium with the thick, lush green turf already looking inviting with several weeks of the close season still to go.

"I haven't had time to look around the city at all yet," he grins. "All I've seen is the hospital where I had my medical – it was a very nice hospital, though! I'm going back to Gran Canaria for a rest after this, but I'm looking forward to coming back and having a good look around.

"I've heard a lot of good things about Manchester, so it will be fascinating to discover a new city."

David admits that the Blues are now firmly on the radar of the Spanish people as the club's profile continually rises around the world.

"Over the last few years, Manchester City's image has grown massively in Spain," he said. "The project here is getting more important with every year, and with me it's very exciting that I'm now part of it

"I think within two or three years it will be normal for City to be playing in the Champions League every year, so I hope we can be on a par and challenge the best clubs around the world.

"I decided to come here because it's a new personal experience and play in one of the best leagues in the world. It's a new challenge and I want to meet my team-mates and experience everything in what is a new life for me. I hope everything goes as well as my first visit to Manchester has because everybody has been very kind and helpful. I can't wait to get started."

It's like defence versus attack with QPR camped in their own half, defending their box as though their lives depended on it...

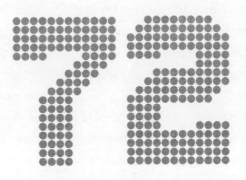

The Rock

Vincent Kompany was fast becoming the backbone to the City team and his vision for the future was revealed for the first time in this interview, conducted at Carrington...

If Vincent Kompany had his feet any firmer on the ground, it's doubtful he'd be able to move. Fast approaching a century of appearances for City, he's begun the 2010/11 season as one of the Premier League's best defenders – perhaps even Europe's – and must be one of Roberto Mancini's first names on the teamsheet.

Not that you'd guess it.

Kompany is old school and won't start patting himself on the back until there is silverware in the trophy cabinet – he probably won't even do it then because it's not how he does things. He wants to constantly improve and evolve as a player and, aged only 24, it's a frightening prospect for the strikers who he'll line up against in future weeks, months and years.

He'd be the first to admit he's probably one of the more serious members of the City squad, but he has a quick, dry sense of humour and is generous to a fault. Professionalism is the key word for the lad from Brussels; that plus loyalty and focus – possess any two of those qualities and you won't go far wrong with a player who doesn't take praise comfortably.

"I don't take praise and accolades too seriously," he smiled. "I take a step back from things like that because it's irrelevant in many ways. One moment you can be regarded as the best and have nice things said about you, but if you achieve nothing in the long term, it doesn't actually mean anything. That's how I look at it.

"If things are going well, it makes me want to work even harder so things remain at that level and then kick on again and improve. I want to maintain my standards but I'm always looking to get better all the time. I think that's how I can help the team – by being hard and disciplined about my own performances."

Perfectionists can be hard to live with, unable to lose the shackles of a misplaced pass or stop thinking about something they didn't quite get right, and Kompany admits he was no different, though he is changing in this respect.

"It used to be my weak point," he revealed. "I was too much of a perfectionist and it was probably doing more harm than good. It wasn't until I played under a manager who explained to me that it was okay to make a mistake and not be perfect. To stay focused on your game, no matter what happens, is more important, and learning that has helped me become a better player.

"I still do the best I can, but if I do make a mistake, I won't let it affect my game, and that has enabled me to progress because if I do something wrong, I'm able to put it out of my head and carry on. I've taken bits of advice from managers and coaches at Anderlecht, Hamburg and City, but I'm still developing; still learning.

"I don't think as a centre-half you always have to be the best player on the pitch every week – just the best man for your team, and that's all I try to do and nothing more. If people think I've had a good game, then great, but I'll only be really happy if I know I did a good job for the team."

Such is the esteem Kompany is held in as a defensive lynchpin, it's easy to forget that he was signed initially as a defensive midfielder with a view to seeing how things developed over a period of time. There was no grand design as such, but the ability to play at the back was always known and pondered upon under Mark Hughes' reign.

"When I first came to the club, I was told that I'd start in midfield and then see how things went," he said. "Then, if I was needed to fill in at the back, I would, but I might just as easily move back to midfield after that, so there were no hard or fast rules.

"I was fine with that because in football nowadays, it's a good attribute to be able to play in central midfield or defence and I was happy to keep that going. I knew we'd have a great team this season and the main thing for me was to get into the side because anyone who starts complaining about the position they play in has, in my book, got it completely wrong.

"I've had time to play at the back and had time to learn, but I'm happy to play wherever I'm asked because I don't think my performances are down to my position, just that I've been willing to learn and developed as a player, and the team will always come first for me."

With three different partners at the back already this season, it's interesting to see that City have remained defensively sound whichever duo are paired in the middle. Of course, the one constant (apart from the Carling Cup defeat at West Brom), has been Kompany. The Kolo Toure partnership had seen just three goals conceded in 10 games by mid-October, but Joleon Lescott and Dedryck Boyata have played, too.

"I've had great understandings with all three of them, and whatever happens, I always make the effort to make sure the guy who is alongside me feels comfortable playing next to me," he said. "That's important and all three defenders are very clever and have experience. We've trained with each other for a long time, so I'm not sure that if I wasn't among the pairing, the understanding would be any different because we know each other so well.

"We are all focused and we know have to play to the best of our ability to keep our places.

"I've been around in football for a long time. I've been through quite a bit, mainly due to injuries, and I've climbed up high again, so it would take a lot for me to experience something new in the game. I don't consider myself a young player by any stretch of the imagination.

"I would never want to use my age as an excuse for making a mistake, for instance – I don't want any of that. I've got enough experience to perform week in, week out at this level and I know what is expected of me."

Kompany was, of course, signed by Mark Hughes in the summer of 2008 and he admits there is a wave of uncertainty that ripples through the squad when a new manager comes in – and it was no different when Hughes was sacked and Roberto Mancini took over.

"It was difficult because when a trainer brings you into a club, you obviously feel that they really wanted you to play in their team," he said. "That's always a good feeling as a player and I think he's definitely a good manager, but whatever thoughts you may have at the time, it was important to move forward.

"The club is bigger than any individual and that's something we all understand, so when the new manager came in, it was up to us to be receptive to his ideas and now I think we are now seeing the results of the change. For me, one good manager has been replaced by another good manager and so far I've been lucky enough to learn from both of them."

One thing that is particularly important to Kompany is respect and honesty. If he puts the effort in on the pitch, he expects his club to be equally willing to go that extra mile. It's pettiness he can't abide and, in many ways, it was such an instance of bloody-mindedness that led to his departure from Hamburg.

After initially denying Kompany the chance to play in the 2008 Olympic Games because it wasn't a FIFA recognised tournament, Hamburg relented on the premise he only play in Belgium's opening two group games. But after being shown a red card in the opening match, he decided he wanted to stay and help his country to the next stage of the tournament. Hamburg dug their heels in and demanded his release and Belgium eventually conceded defeat. The damage caused between player and club was, however, irreparable and a furious Kompany returned to Germany feeling he'd been let down when he needed a little leeway.

"It was a reality check for me," he said. "It's often talked about players being loyal to their club, but it goes both ways and I've experienced being let down in this respect first hand. To not be allowed to play for your national team at the Olympics for silly reasons, and being treated like an object rather than a human being, is unforgiveable.

"I'd been at Anderlecht for 14 years before I moved to Hamburg and, as I say, what happened was a reality check for me. I left the club on good terms with the fans, players and the manager – it was just the men above I had a problem with.

"Here, at City, I feel so much respect for the fans and I think they have respect for me, and that's what I want to keep going."

The anxiety is almost too much to bear – there seems no way back for City despite the constant probing of the visitors' defence...

When The Boat Comes In

Jerome Boateng was one of those players who never really settled in at City. Injuries played their part, but he seemed almost agitated during his one season with the Blues – we never saw the best of him and vice versa. With not that much to talk about at club level, we spoke about his early life in Germany...

Berlin. A city steeped in history and at one point divided by a wall that split East and West Germany down the middle until the people of Berlin tore it down on an unforgettable night in 1989.

It was Berlin that young Ghanaian, Prince Boateng, decided was a place he wanted to better himself in, so he quit Africa in 1981 and headed for central Europe and a new life that would eventually lead to three sons and a daughter, all of whom went on to great success in their chosen careers.

Prince's attempts to study were thwarted and he was forced to find other work in order to put food on the table. After meeting a German girl, Catherine, the couple settled down and had two sons, Kevin and George.

Prince worked in a men's fashion store by day and was a DJ by night, specialising in Michael Jackson as he attempted to give his sons a better life. The strain was such that he eventually split up with his wife and later met an air stewardess who he fell in love with and later married.

The relationship led to two more children for Prince, Jerome and Avelina, though when Jerome was just two years old, his father left the family home and his mother raised him and his sister alone.

"I don't really recall my father being there, because I was so young," recalled Jerome. "He and my mother separated when I was small, but they remained good friends, so it wasn't as though I never saw him.

"We lived in an apartment in Wilmersdorf, which is a nice part of Berlin, but my half-brothers lived in Wedding, which isn't such a nice place. It was a bit odd for me because although I saw Kevin and George fairly often when we were small kids, I couldn't grasp that we shared the same dad.

"Obviously, as we grew up, I understood better."

With just a few years between Jerome and his two half-brothers, the boys enjoyed going to watch Hertha Berlin play with their father as well as playing in the parks at weekends, but the difference in neighbourhoods meant Jerome wasn't allowed to visit Wedding alone to have a kick-about with Kevin and George.

"I played football all the time, but my mum made me study hard," he continued. "All I ever wanted to do was play football – I wasn't interested in anything else. I practiced all the time and I used to get in trouble for watching a German TV show which featured games from England, Spain and Italy.

"It was on a 1am and my mum would get fed up with me watching it and then having problems getting up in the morning! I liked where I grew up – it was comfortable and I enjoyed school. As I got older, I sort of knew I was pretty good at football, and with Kevin and George being talented, too, we had some pretty competitive games in the park!

"It's funny because of the three, George was the best player. At academy level he was a great talent and could have gone on and enjoyed a great career, but he would be the first to admit that he made some poor choices as a teenager and the distractions off the pitch eventually led to him not fulfilling the promise he had."

Jerome and Kevin had no such problems and at last reunited as a family during their secondary school years, the boys became well-known for their talent with a football during their early teens.

"It was nice that we were together as a family," he said. "Kevin was picked up by Hertha Berlin and I followed not long after. We both were doing well and were selected by Germany, but eventually Kevin fell out with the hierarchy and he said, 'You know what? I'm going to play for Ghana instead.'

"For me, there was only Germany. I'm very proud of my father's roots and that I'm half Ghanaian, but I wanted to play for my birth country, and so we had the unusual situation of Kevin and I playing for different countries. Our father was very proud because he had the best of both worlds!"

Jerome reached a crossroads in his life in his mid-teens when he had to choose where his future really lay. He had two options, but felt he couldn't do both if he was to succeed in either.

"It was university or football," he said. "I needed to concentrate on one or the other and so I told my mother I wanted to take a year out of my studies. If I didn't make it, I'd go to university and get my qualifications, but Hertha Berlin signed me and my decision was vindicated."

Indeed. Jerome's progress was such that he worked his way through the ranks at Hertha Berlin from the age of 13 until he made his senior debut aged 17. Within a year, he was a first team regular, and at the age 18, Hamburg made a £1m offer that was accepted by the Berliners.

"I had to move out of my home for the first time, so it was a little strange, but I liked Hamburg," he said. "It's a very interesting city and I quickly settled in. They had players such as Rafael van der Vaart, Vincent Kompany and Nigel de Jong, and I soon felt at home.

"I remember playing City in a friendly in Hamburg when Mark Hughes was the manager, and then it was funny because both Vincent and Nigel left for City. I kept in touch with both of them from time to time and they both were really happy.

"I was sorry to see them both go. I understood Vincent's reasons for moving, and Nigel's, too. They were both really popular players and Nigel was really popular with the fans because of his style.

"Then, of course, we were all reunited in the quarter-finals of the UEFA Cup. The second leg at the City of Manchester Stadium was incredible and I just thought 'wow!' It was an amazing night and Elano was incredible, but we just hung on to go through. As soon as City came in for me, I remembered that night and didn't have to think too long about the move.

"City gave me the best feeling because they often phoned my agent and said they want me to sign for them. I spoke with other clubs, too, but I am young and the move from Germany to England excited me the most. And when I was younger, I always wanted to play in England."

Tevez brings the ball inside dangerously before slicing his strike high and wide after doing the hard part and making the space...

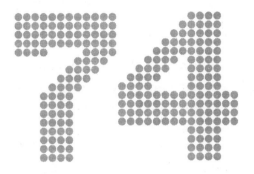

Toure De Force

Kolo Toure, one of the loveliest guys you could meet, completed his ban and returned to the first team fold having been forced to miss City's FA Cup triumph the previous May. We spoke in the home dressing room at the Etihad Stadium...

K olo Toure has thanked the club, his brother, family and City fans for standing by him over what have been an incredibly difficult past six months.

The Ivory Coast star is officially available to play for the Blues from today following the end of the ban imposed by the FA for failing a drugs test, and he is champing at the bit to get back out on the pitch and start playing football again.

In an exclusive interview, Kolo explains how he took a tablet he believed to be approved by the authorities, only to be told it was actually on a prohibited list – and his world was turned upside down.

"I remember it clearly," he said. "I was at home in my bedroom when the club doctor and Roberto Mancini came in to explain what had happened.

"It was a shock to see them there and I immediately realised the implications for my career, the club and my family. It was an awful moment because I didn't know what was going to happen."

In the interview, Kolo reveals how life became particularly difficult when his daughter came home from school after other children had asked her what her father had done.

"When people say drugs in Africa, it's not quite the same as here, when it could mean prescription drugs, so I had to explain to her what had actually happened," he said.

"It's been hard, but my family and the club have been amazingly supportive and I thank them from the bottom of my heart.

"Yaya has been incredible and as brothers, and this has brought us even closer. He was always there for me and kept me informed of what was happening at the club.

"I must also thank the manager, my team-mates, the staff and particularly Garry Cook and our Chairman, Khaldoon Al-Mubarak, for standing by me and helping me through this period.

"And I will try and repay our amazing supporters for all their good wishes, kind words and support. I feel totally recharged and as fit as I've ever been in my life.

"Hopefully, it will be like having a new signing because I am back and want to challenge for a first team place. I know it won't be easy because the team is playing so well, but I'll be pushing hard for an opportunity.

"I'm just so happy to be back and I will give everything I have to the team, this club and our fans. I can't wait to get going!"

City struggle to break through the QPR defence and resort to strikes from distance as Samir Nasri blazes an effort wide from 35 yards out of desperation...

Aleksandar The Great

Few players could compare with the dramatic background likeable Serb Aleksandar Kolarov had endured as a child...

Aleksandar Kolarov's home turf is Belgrade, one of central Europe's most historic cities, with the Danube winding its way through Serbia's capital, where the architecture and the views attract tourists by the coach-load. He and his pals played happily on the streets; impromptu daily games until dusk before graduating to more organised football if, as Kolarov and his brother Nikola did, they showed the talent that held the promise of a professional career. It would be the textbook, conventional "making of a footballer" story, but for politics.

Politics sometimes touches young footballers in the UK with the loss of a local playing field to urban development, or cutbacks that close the local sports centre. For Aleksandar, it's different. He smiles a wry smile: "I'm 25 and I have two wars."

The first of those was the break-up of the old Yugoslavia, a bitter and horrific conflict that had been simmering since Tito died in 1980. Without his dictatorial iron grip to hold together nations forcibly joined, Yugoslavia unravelled bloodily at the seams in the early '90s so that today, Serbia, Croatia, Bosnia and Slovenia are all separate countries. The conflict was enacted many, many miles from where Kolarov and company kicked a ball.

But in the second of Aleksandar's wars, NATO bombers rained fire on Belgrade. They waged war on his city.

It was NATO's way of putting pressure on Slobodan Milosevic's troops to withdraw from Kosovo, where independence had been declared. So from March 24 to June 11, 1999, Operation Allied Forces homed in on "strategic" targets such as factories, power plants and even bridges over the Danube. Inevitably, there were also civilian casualties.

Kolarov, at first reluctant to unlock the memories, says: "I was young and there was war. When you are a kid, you just want to play football, but you can't play football because you have bombs in the city. I was young, 14, but I remember everything…the bad stories.

"I don't like to talk about it – it was just a war, you know?" he says, his voice heavy with irony. "The first couple of days you have fear for something, then every day is the same, you know? There is bombing, life continues. Bombs fell near my house, the windows blew in. There was a military airport near my house, so that was a target. But nobody that I knew was hurt.

"People protested on the bridges; young people, but older than me, when they started to bomb everything. They just said, well, if you die, you die. They bombed bridges, everything. There were concerts on the bridges. I didn't go; we played football, though not at the academy – the trainers didn't want to be responsible for what might happen.

"It was three months – but I was young and we didn't have to go into school, so I was happy. We still played football in the street! Those first two nights we stayed in, afraid of the bombs, but then nobody did that any more. People slept normally in their houses – if it's your destiny to die, you die…"

He shrugs again and you remember that line from the Talking Heads' perceptive "Life During Wartime" – "This ain't no party, this ain't no disco, this ain't no fooling around…"

Kolarov confirms: "I was only 14, but the people of 20, 21, who wanted a night out, couldn't. You couldn't go to the cinema or the disco, because at nine o'clock, you'd hear a sound, the alarm, the siren, when the planes with bombs were coming. And there was nothing you could do. You could hear the planes overhead, you could see where the bombs dropped. You almost get used to it, it was… normal life. When you heard where they'd dropped the bombs, you'd go into your house and go to sleep. It wasn't hard to sleep after the first two days, you were so tired."

Kolarov is from Zemun, in the west of the city and a brisk stroll from any one of three bridges that straddle the Danube: "I was born in Belgrade but my family moved 20 kilometres away to a smaller place, Vojka, where my mother and father had work. I lived back in Belgrade from being ten, playing for Red Star. I stayed with my older brother Nikola and went to school in Belgrade."

He recalls: "I first started playing football when I was six years old. I used to play once or twice a week, and then from being eight, I went every day to training. Every day. We used to play in the streets and then go and play again on the pitch. When I was ten, I went to Red Star and started going every day to play seriously.

"In the street, there would be 20, 25… and one ball! You know kids.

We would put something down for goals, a sweater or something. When I was young, I played striker! When you are young, you want to be goalkeeper or striker, and I played striker. I did play in goal, but I was not so good. I wasn't tall for my age, just average. And you always want to score goals when you are young.

"I was at the Red Star Academy, and there were a lot of good players who are now playing in Italy, Spain, England. If we'd go to school in the afternoon, then I would play in the morning. Otherwise, if I'd go to school in the morning, I would play in the afternoon. Yes, you could get tired, but if you know what you want to do…I was a child, and I loved to play football with my friends. You have energy for these things at that age. But when I started at Red Star, I would be too tired to play again in the street. And I had to study for school. Like every child, I didn't like school too much, I liked to play football. But I was okay in school, normal.

"I was eight years in the first (junior) school and then four years in the second school. After this, nothing! I didn't go to college. I signed for a team in Serbia when I was 17, but not Red Star. I signed a professional contract for Cukaricki Stankom and started playing in the Serb championship. They were a small team in the second division, but we went up immediately to the Premier League. I went straight into the team. In the first 20 games, I played five or six, and then every game. I was full-back by then."

Belgrade has two major teams, Red Star and Partizan, and their rivalry in the so-called Eternal Derby has spilled over into hostilities in the recent past. Both clubs boast a huge, loyal following. Aleksandar, inevitably, supported Red Star as a boy. He admits: "When I was young, I dreamed of playing for Red Star, and maybe I will play for them one day – when I am 35! I used to go to every game at home. I know all the songs. I would join in the singing at every game, but once I started playing professionally, I couldn't go any more.

"Red Star and Partizan derbies were very, very exciting. Now it's hooligans. There are a lot of police in the stadium, but years ago it was just incredible to see the game between Red Star and Partizan. These problems exist in Italy and Spain and other countries as well, but they say we Serbs are the bad people. All those wars…"

Brother Nikola, a central defender three years Aleksandar's senior, went on to play for two teams in Bosnia, Olimpic Sarajevo – in the city that was infamously put under seige by Serb snipers at the height of the war – and Borac Banja Luka, another name that figures prominently in the history of that dark conflict.

Kolarov says: "From being seven or eight, I always wanted to play for my national team, and I worked very, very hard. Now, after ten years, I play for Manchester City and the national team. So it was worth it, all the hard work. From my generation, there are a lot of Serb players in Italy here in England. In my country, if you were going to school, everything was study or maybe you don't find work. You had to study. With sports, it's easy to say, but you can do a lot for your country. I think players who come from Serbia are very hungry to work, to do something, because every one of us has some story in their life."

His was certainly some coming of age. Aleksandar Kolarov's war will stay with him the rest of his days. But he insists: "I've never had nightmares, I don't think about it. It was just happening – you can't do anything about it at the time, you have to live with it. But some people in Serbia who lost parents or family members may have a problem. It's hard for them to forget."

Balotelli replaces Tevez upfront to give City another option, and Jay Bothroyd comes on for QPR replacing Zamora...

The Enforcer

Nigel de Jong – a fantastic guy off the pitch and a fierce competitor on it. But there was much more to Nigel than met the eye. With this in mind, the focus of the interview was his background and how he became the person he was today. Fascinating stuff...

Born on the wrong side of the tracks? Not exactly. Nigel de Jong comes from a good family but grew up in a tough neighbourhood where standing up for yourself was not merely a conscious decision, it was a necessity in order to survive the streets.

It may sound a bit dramatic, but that's how things were for Nigel as a kid. With his father, a professional footballer, splitting from his mother when he was very young, he quickly had to get used to being the man of the house – particularly as his mother's kidney condition meant continual use of a dialysis machine, rendering her virtually housebound.

It was a tough life and Nigel admits it made him focus on his family and responsibility. Further down the line, it would inspire him to become a multi-million pound footballer, a successful businessman and at the heart of a team we all hope will one day soon start to lift trophies.

"I was born on the west side of Amsterdam, it was not a typical part of Holland as such," he began. "There were a lot of different cultures there, with a lot of the Surinamese people, which is where my father is from. It's called Osdorp, and yeah, it's a tough neighbourhood, but you don't see it when you go over there.

"I was always doing something, either playing football or basketball with my friends. I still have a couple of friends from there I see on a regular basis.

"My parents separated when I was four, so my mother, Marja, was the main figure in the house. I had a little sister, too, Asheema. My mum had a kidney disorder, so she couldn't work and we were living off benefits. My mum had to be at home, spending a lot of time on a dialysis machine, so things could have been better for all of us, but we got on with things."

For someone who has been mercilessly pummelled in the press of late, Nigel's life and attitude to those he loves around him is deserving of far more respect. In fact, if the majority of his critics were prepared to find out just a little more about the man, they would discover someone who sacrificed his younger years to care for his family and make sure they led comfortable lives in the future.

"I think all the stuff that was happening when I was young made me more determined to do better for my mum," he continued. "I had to become the man of the house because I was always taking care of my mother and baby sister. It made me realise at a young age that I had to toughen up as I was taking on more responsibility than other kids of a similar age. The drive to succeed came from that."

Football was in his blood, though, and although he saw his father occasionally, his influence was always there, in his genes, and he began to develop into a talent from an early age, fuelled by his love of Amsterdam's connoisseurs of Total Football.

"Ajax have always been my team," he smiled. "My old man was playing for their rivals PSV, so I always watched them train as he played in the time of Romario and Ronald Koeman, so it was always nice to watch such great players train. I remember at a young age that I always wanted to play for Ajax. They had Patrick Kluivert, a young Clarence Seedorf and Edgar Davids, it was a great team. This was at the old Olympic Stadium. I used to go the games with my mates and my uncle whenever I could."

Nigel's father, Jerry de Jong, was born in Suriname in 1964 and he enjoyed a 17-year playing career with several Dutch clubs, representing the Netherlands on three occasions. He was just 19 when Nigel was born, but his son remembers his playing career with clarity.

"My dad was a right-back and winger," he said. "He was really quick and played for the Dutch national side a couple of times. He was quite a good player, to be honest. He then went to play centre midfield when he didn't have the pace anymore.

"I saw him in the summertime as he had his life as a footballer and I was always at school. So that was the only quality time we could have together.

"My mother was the type of woman who if I got slapped on the street, I had to go back and slap them back," he said. "I couldn't come back crying. I think that toughened me up. I was playing with the bigger kids as I had my gift to play football, and that toughened me up, too.

"I was always busy, either helping my family or playing sport; I did a lot of basketball and tennis. I was always doing something, but football was always my real passion. I was a right-winger at Ajax, but then the coach put me as a striker, where I scored a lot of goals, believe it or not! When I was 12 or 13, I went back to midfield and have never left since. I think I put too much into the defending part these days, but maybe goals will come at some point.

"If you're on the streets so much, people are going to recognise you, and you gain respect for being good at something. I used to just pick up a ball, run round to my mate's house and then go around the streets getting people to come out and play football. People used to challenge us on the streets to games of five versus five, and we used to fight not to lose. They were good, happy times."

Though his days weren't spent wiling away around the centre of the city, he occasionally went into the heart of the Amsterdam with his friends or on an errand of some kind.

"It doesn't matter if you go to the city centre or the suburbs, it is quite a mixed culture; everybody speaks English, and that's why tourists like to go to Amsterdam – for the multiculturalism," he explained.

"I was always used to that. When I was 12 or 13 years old, when you went out in the city, you just had to get used to there being people from lots of different countries around you."

Nigel's early promise soon saw him picked up by his boyhood heroes. "I was picked up by Ajax at six. There is a scouting network and you could go on a trial on a particular day and all the scouts would stand and watch.

"If you got picked, you'd then go through the various stages, and I kept getting through. In the end I was at the fourth trial stage and eventually I got a letter saying I was part of the Ajax Academy. That was a proud day. I can remember it as if it was yesterday."

As his football career began to take off, Nigel began thinking of other ways to secure his and his family's futuree Not satisfied with the prospect of a comfortable life as a professional footballer, he took the advice of a close family member and started to concoct various ideas for a business. The seeds, he admits, were planted from an early age.

"I always liked to play with numbers and my granddad told me to make sure everything was always organised in my life," he said. "It was my future, so I had to make sure that I could always be independent.

"I always wanted to do something if I had the money or the time for it, and I wanted to do a self-service restaurant. My career took off and then I moved to Hamburg, but the idea of business was always there.

"Then I met a guy who was in the car trade and I gave him the assignment to service an old vintage car and rebuild it. In that ten months I saw what was lacking in the market in Germany, so we sat down to see if we could offer something that wasn't already offered in the country.

"We started from scratch with classic cars, but decided that the market wasn't strong enough for that, so we expanded to luxury cars. We're now worldwide."

Not satisfied with finding ways of taking care of those he loves, Nigel has never forgotten his Amsterdam roots and the area he grew up in.

"I opened a football court in my old neighbourhood to make sure the kids still have somewhere to develop themselves," he smiled, almost embarrassed. "That Ajax team of Kluivert, Davids and others started out on the streets. I think that the main focus is to get boys back on the streets. It's difficult now with the PlayStations and Xboxes.

"I never had that as a kid. I only had a ball, but it's just the generation nowadays."

There's more to Nigel de Jong than the headlines that followed the unfortunate Ben Arfa accident. Much more...

Balotelli wins a free-kick wide on the edge of the QPR area; the attempt falls to Aguero. He beats his man and fires a cross in but Dzeko is denied by Kenny...

King Midas

Roberto Mancini arrived at City with a record of success and a desire to create history with his new club. Thirty minutes in his company and it was clear he wouldn't accept anything less...

If anyone ever doubted Roberto Mancini's pedigree, they should take a quick glance at his personal trophy cabinet, which hopefully rests on reinforced floorboards in his Italian family home.

With some 23 winners' medals from his playing and managerial career to date, not to mention his Italian Footballer of the Year and Serie A Player of the Year double, or his Manager of the Year award in 2007 while boss of Inter Milan.

Whichever way you look at his achievements, there can be no doubting that Mancini is one of life's winners.

Now he has been given the opportunity of bringing the glory days back to City and he is relishing the prospect of making the Blues a force in world football, and the good news is he has consistently delivered the goods wherever he has been.

Since taking over from Mark Hughes in December, Mancini has begun to mould a team in his image, though there is no fast track to overnight success, more's the pity. The Blues' first Italian manager wants to build an empire that will go from strength to strength and he is already targeting the Premier League title for next season.

And why not? The club has already demonstrated it can attract some of the biggest names in world football over the past couple of years, and there could well be more to come.

In choosing Mancini to lead City to the next level, the club's owners have chosen wisely, but there has been no real, in-depth interview with the Blues boss since he arrived late last year. Until now.

This writer has been fortunate to be able to speak to the manager on a weekly basis since January and he has never been less than polite, patient and engaging. The venue of the interview is his office at the City of Manchester Stadium, a plush room with a flat screen mounted TV, comfortable chairs and a smart refreshments area.

One could imagine Carlo Ancelotti dropping by for a glass of red wine after the match or perhaps Arsene Wenger stopping in for a quick chat and a healthy discussion about the referee's performance.

Relaxed and smiling as ever, Mancini takes a quick call on his mobile, informing the guy at the other end to act quickly regarding whatever the discussion concerned. "Si, si, pronto, pronto!"

Dressed in a stylishly casual way only the Italians and French can seem to pull off, the manager of Manchester City takes his seat as I comment about gaining a privileged glimpse at one of the club's inner sanctums.

"You've never been in here before?" asks Roberto. I say I haven't. He looks surprised. "Now you have," he grins.

If football is religion for millions of people around the world, Roberto managed to combine both during his days as an altar boy in his home town of Jesi (pronounced 'Yey-see').

Born on November 27, 1964, Roberto was raised a devout Roman Catholic by his parents, Aldo and Marianna. Football and the church crossed paths many times, but there is one story that perhaps shows that even as a young boy, his talents on the football pitch were already suggesting divine inspiration.

The tale goes that there was an important game for Roberto's youth team, Calcio, taking place at the same time as his first Holy Communion. Hearing the team were losing 2-0, the local priest – also a coach of the said team – asked Roberto whether he had his kit and boots with him.

On discovering the said items were in the changing rooms, the priest suggested he should maybe go and join his team-mates, by quietly slipping out the side entrance! Whether it's true or not, I don't enquire – it's such a charming story that it seems perfect to lead into Roberto's early days.

"Jesi is a town in Italy, not too far from the sea," he began. "It has a population of around 45,000 people, so it's not exactly small – it's not far off an average home game attendance at the City of Manchester Stadium, I suppose.

"My mother worked as a nurse and my father worked as a carpenter and also did masonry, so it was a nice steady home life."

The idyllic pace of life in Jesi meant that Roberto's father was always on hand to kick a ball around with his son and advise him during his formative football. Like most dads, he'd played himself, but not for any reason other than pleasure.

"My father was an enthusiastic amateur and he played, but not professionally," said Roberto. "He loves football and I think he wanted me to be a footballer because of the life it could possibly give me and because of the pleasure it had given him.

"When I was small, we used to go to the football pitch at the back of our home and play every day after school. We'd practice, practice, practice, and if he was busy, I'd play with my friends instead. They were very happy days for me.

"My father had a friend in Bologna and eventually I think he thought I might have a future in the game, so he told him that he felt I was worth a trial. Bologna had a terrific reputation for nurturing young talent and an academy that is not dissimilar to the one we have here at City.

"They gave me my chance to show what I could do, and after playing for just one hour, they decided they wanted to sign me. I was just 13, and that meant moving to their residential academy some 200km away.

"It was a very difficult period of my life because I was very young and was a long way away from my parents and friends. It was something I had to get through because obviously I wanted to be a footballer and that involves making sacrifices, but it was very hard, too."

Though there were numerous other famous Italian sides closer to his Jesi home, there was only one side Roberto loved as a youngster. Following in the footsteps of his old man, he supported the side known as the 'Old Lady'...

"As a boy, my idols were Juventus," he smiled. "They are one of the most popular teams in Italy and from around the age of six, I would travel with my father to watch them play every home game. It would take us 10 hours on the bus to get from Jesi to Turin, but I have very happy memories of those times.

"Up to around 13 years ago, there were only two channels in Italy, so football wasn't on TV all the time like it is today. It made going to the matches even more special, and so when I would go to the Stadio delle Alpi to watch Juve, I would get very emotional because it meant so much to me.

"We spoke about football all the way there and all the way back. I remember my first European Cup game for Juve, the first league game – everything! Great memories....

"All the team were my heroes rather than just one player. I couldn't just choose one. Dino Zoff, Roberto Bettega, Gaetano Scirea – all great players. I remember when they played City in 1976 in the UEFA Cup. I don't remember going to the game, but I know Juve won the second leg 2-0 to go through 2-1. I think Brian Kidd scored the winner in the first leg!

"I suppose that was the first time City came into my consciousness and I always remembered the sky blue shirts they wore, but there were many great Italy/England duels during the 1970s. The games between the national teams were always closely-fought and I remember Derby County, Arsenal and Liverpool always caused Italian sides problems."

Meanwhile, the teenage Mancini was proving to be something of a protégé and his club manager decided he'd seen enough in training to pitch the youngster in at the deep end after just three years at the academy. It was to be the start of a glittering playing career that would see his silky skills make him one of the country's most promising talents.

"I made my debut for Bologna when I was just 16 years old – very, very, young to be playing Serie A football – but I did well and scored nine goals during my first season. Despite this, we were relegated and I was sold to Sampdoria.

"In truth, I could have gone to almost any top club in Italy, including Juventus, because they all expressed an interest in signing me. Sampdoria had a wonderful chairman and I liked the challenge of going to a club who had never won any major honours before. In all honesty, I'm not sure why I didn't choose Juve considering my allegiance to them."

Roberto's choice proved to be inspired. He helped the Genoese club to become a major force in Serie A and Europe and for the first time, Sampdoria were crowned champions of Italy.

"I ended up staying for 15 years at the Marassi and during that time, we won everything," he recalled. "It's a fantastic thing to play for a club like Barcelona or Real Madrid, but to play for a team who has won very little and help them achieve great things is, I believe, better. To help change the history of a club is incredible and you will stay in the memories of all that team's supporters for many years."

Roberto was a success on the international stage, too, earning 34 caps for Italy over a 10-year period from 1984 to 1994, though being a flair player, he was perhaps underused by a succession of overly-cautious Italy bosses.

Mancini's playing style had elements of Gianfranco Zola, Teddy Sheringham and a dash of Brazilian magic thrown in. Some of his goals were world class and he was technically superb, with his team-mates at Sampdoria bringing out the best in him. Gianluca Pagliuca, Gianluca Vialli, Toninho Cerezo, Pietro Vierchowod and Attilio Lombardo – the names roll off the tongue.

"On a personal level, things couldn't have gone better for me," he said. "I hold all the club records with Sampdoria, from appearances through to goals, and the fans have never forgotten me and I doubt they ever will. It was an amazing time for all of us."

All good things eventually come to an end, however, and after 15 years with the same club, a parting of the ways seemed best for all parties. With 566 appearances and 171 goals, he remains a club legend, but he needed a new lease of life to see out his playing days. His move to Rome would prove he had something of a Midas touch...

After countless trophies and a European Cup final defeat to Barcelona, Mancini decided to move on while he still could.

"After such a long time with one club, by the time I was 32, I decided to play elsewhere and find a new challenge," he said. "In 1997, I signed for Lazio – another club who had never won anything – and during my three years in Rome, we won the Serie A, the European Cup Winners' Cup, seven trophies in all.

"I then became assistant manager to Sven-Goran Eriksson, but after six months, he was sacked because he'd agreed to become the next England manager, and so Lazio decided to make a change. That sort of spelled the end of my time with them."

Mancini has always had a great respect and a fascination for English football, so when an opportunity arose to perhaps have one last hurrah as a player, he accepted it willingly, albeit in the inauspicious surroundings of the East Midlands.

"Yes, I had always wanted to come to England, so I signed for Leicester City in 2000," he said. "Sven spoke with the manager of Leicester and asked if I'd like to come and play for them, so I did and I really enjoyed my time with them, brief though it was.

"I have very good memories of Leicester. I only played five games, but I enjoyed working for the manager and with the players. It wasn't long enough, but I made lasting friendships all the same.

"I took Robbie Savage out for dinner at an Italian restaurant in Leicester and introduced him to Italian cuisine. We had penne pomodoro and spaghetti and I don't think he's ever forgotten it!

"But after one month, Fiorentina contacted me and offered me the manager's job, which I accepted, so I returned to Italy. I would have liked to stay in England longer, but this was a chance to manage on my own for the first time. I stayed with Fiorentina for one year and we won the Italian Cup, but the club had major financial problems, and when the chance arose, I returned to Lazio, but this time as manager.

"I stayed there for two years and won the Italian Cup once again and also took the club into the Champions League, then I was offered the role as boss of Inter, which I accepted.

"We had to work very hard and in my first year we won the Italian Cup and qualified for the Champions League. The next year we won the Serie A title for the first time in 20 years, winning 17 games in a row at one point. I enjoyed great success and had many happy times at Inter, and by the time I left, we had won seven trophies in four years."

Roberto's record as a player and a manager is remarkable and it all bodes well for City. He's won trophies at every club he's been at – Leicester apart – and he seems to attract silverware like a magnet.

So how does a great player make the transition to become a great manager? It's a path trodden by a precious few, but though there are obviously elements adopted from other managers along the way, much seems to be due to instinct and natural leadership that perhaps cannot be taught.

"I have my own mind and my own ideas, but I have taken influences from people like Eriksson, Vujadin Boskov – who I worked with for many years," said Mancini. "Those two managers in particular were very important to me because they were different in so many ways and had a completely different ethos, were totally different characters, and I've taken a little bit of knowledge and added it to my own.

"I think the most important thing I try to instil in my players is that they must always believe that they can win – we need a winning mentality at this club because eventually, it pays off. It doesn't happen overnight and can take maybe six or eight months to really be absorbed, but if you are prepared to work hard every game, you will always have a chance of being successful. It's a simple observation, but very true – you can't win anything without working hard.

"I want to win a lot of trophies with this club. I think our fans are incredible and it makes me more determined than ever to bring them success – when we win our first trophy, it will be a very good moment for everyone, I think.

"For my part, I am taking English lessons every day. If you study intensively, you soon pick it up, though learning a new language at the age of 45 isn't easy! I have a basic grasp of English and it's important I always speak English when I'm here because that is the quickest way of learning.

"If I make the odd mistake, it is only to be expected because this is a new country for me and I've only been speaking English for the past few months. It has been a hectic six months and I'm looking forward to a rest now for a few weeks.

"I love being with my family, of course, and I miss them when I'm working. I will watch the World Cup on TV with my sons and just relax and rest as much as I can. Football will never be far from my mind, but it is a chance to recharge my batteries.

"It will be an interesting summer, but it would be nice if Italy made it to the final, but I think it will be difficult. When I return to Manchester, I think it is vital we have a good pre-season and I'm looking forward to it already. A lot of players will be at the World Cup and will maybe arrive back a little later, but we will have plenty of time together."

And what fate will befall the famous Mancini scarf? Roberto smiles at the mention of what has become something of a trademark over the past six months.

"I usually wear a scarf on the sidelines because I get pain in my neck if it's cold," he grinned. "I arrived in December and it wasn't so warm, so before my first game, our communications executive Vicky Kloss gave me her City scarf and that was that. I'm very happy that it became something of a fashion item."

And next season...?

"I'm not sure what I will do – it will be a surprise!"

Back To Back Boss

*Asked to speak with Roberto Mancini by a leading
football magazine, the Q&A format worked quite well at
the start of what would be a historic season for City
– here is a snippet of it...*

You've started the season brilliantly, but then so have Manchester United. How excited are you that the city rivalry also looks like being a Premier League title race?

"I don't know what will happen this season. The Premier League is very hard and there are many good teams, but it was important that we made a good start, which we have done – but there is a long way to go and we can improve a lot. I think we can win some trophies this season but as I say, we must improve in some areas."

Manchester United have been the team that sets the standards in recent seasons. How much have you judged the level City need to be at on the level United have been at? If you finish above United, do you think you will win the league title this season?

"I think if we finish above United, we will win the league for sure! United began winning many years ago and they have a winning mentality, so it is not easy to match them and be on their level so quickly. They are one of the best teams in the world, but we have a good team as well. What we need is time to improve because we have new players who need to settle in properly, but we are a young team and I think we will get better as we go along."

What's your relationship with Sir Alex Ferguson like? Is he somebody you have sought advice from over the years? Has he stopped giving you advice now?!

"I have a good relationship with Sir Alex and I have a lot of respect for him. For all he has achieved in football and all the trophies he has won over the past 20 years, he deserves the kind of respect he gets. He's a good guy and I like him – but it would be great if I could beat him this season!"

So you are helping change the history of the city…

"I am happy to help, but it is Sheikh Mansour and our chairman, Khaldoon Al-Mubarak, who have made all this possible."

And finally, United have been the successful team in recent decades. How have you persuaded players that your project is worth being part of rather than joining United?

"Because our team is continually developing and we are also now in the Champions League, which helps. Top players want to come to City because they can see what we are trying to do and that we have a very bright future. It was important that we won the FA Cup last season after so many years without silverware. Now we want to continue to win trophies, and I think we can."

Don't Believe The Hype

Painted as stubborn, fiery and temperamental, Mario Balotelli's reputation arrives several days before he does. Was there any truth, or is it easy to paint him that way? We chatted in the reception at Carrington for almost an hour – he later said it was one of his favourite interviews...

Mario rolls up in his white Gran Turismo Maserati, parks outside the Carrington main entrance and saunters across to the reception.

"Ciao," I say to him as he walks in. "I'll wait here in reception and we can do the interview when you've finished training. Sound okay?"

He nods. "Sure."

And off he goes. I've got two hours to decide what to talk to him about, so I have a look at some of the usual places to source material. Mario's website, a few YouTube videos and various articles British and Italian newspapers have prised out of him over the past few years.

Mario, generally, doesn't really 'do' interviews and after an hour sifting through the ones he has done, I'm not that surprised he tends to give them the wide berth.

'The Troubled World of Mario', 'I'm Not a Bad Boy' etcetera, etcetera…I got bored of reading them. It seems people are always trying to unravel the mystery behind the enigma. All deep, meaningful stuff aimed at getting to the 'real Mario'.

Of course, that kind of stuff can be interesting and has a time and a place, but it seems nobody will let him move on from his spats with Jose Mourinho or his occasional show of petulance on the pitch. When subjected to a torrent of racial abuse during a game for Inter a while back, Mario simply put one finger to his lips and advised his dissenters to 'shhhhh!' Maybe they and others should have listened.

So what if he has a high opinion of himself? So what if he's different and doesn't want to be painted as a stereotypical footballer?

He likes to go his own way. He's an individual and should be applauded for swimming against the current, not vilified at his every turn. Maybe he does attract the wrong headlines and attention from time to time, but it's worth remembering he's still only 20 years old and will make the same mistakes anyone his age might make. It's worth remembering he is also away from his family and friends for the first time, too.

Throw in a different culture, language and a new home before we even mention a new club and a totally different style of football to adapt to, and a picture starts to emerge, not of a precocious, troubled talent, but a young lad finding his way in life as well as coming to terms with life outside his beloved Italy.

It's almost time for the interview. I toss all the notes I've made over the past hour into the bin and scramble a few random questions down. I want this to be different for Mario and different for the readers of ManC.

Why re-hash old stuff? There's a millions things we can talk about other than the same old, same old. Besides, if anyone wants to know about his childhood and the fact he is the first black player to represent the Azzurri, it's all out there, already written and available on the World Wide Web.

Unerringly on time, Mario comes back through reception, goes out the door and drops a bag into his car. He returns, slumping next to me on the Carrington reception couch. No time limit is issued and he makes it clear I've got his full attention.

In all honesty, I score a bit of an own goal after checking he's fine to begin. "What makes you laugh, then?" Cristina, his sister and sometimes advisor, has now arrived and is sat one seat along.

"Why do you guys always ask the same question?" he says, shrugging his shoulders. "Why am I always asked about not smiling?"

"That's not what I meant," I counter. "I ask all the lads what makes them happy."

But I can see he thinks he's going to be answering the same things he's answered a million times. The problem is, I meant who makes him laugh and what does he enjoy away from football? Then why didn't I say that? Like I said, own goal. I may have been one down early on, but there was plenty of time left to turn things around.

"Maybe I should have said what do you like to do away from the game? Your interests and passions – that kind of thing. Do you like Xbox?"

Bingo. His eyes light up.

"Yeah," he smiles.

"Any good?"

"Better than you!"

I suggest I'd give him a run for his money.

"I play Pro-Evolution. That's my game. I don't play FIFA 11 because I've always played Pro-Evo since I was a kid."

Does he ever play as himself – and is the Mario on Pro-Evo better than the real thing?

"I don't know because I only ever play as Real Madrid – or occasionally Barcelona. I sometimes play for money – I know I shouldn't, but I've been known to stake £10 against my opponent to spice things up a bit.

"I have Call Of Duty, too, but I don't really play it that often. I don't like it as much. I also play Rainbow Six Vegas, which is similar to Call Of Duty, but again, I don't use those games very much."

He likes his electronic games fix, but while he likes Facebook, he's not only not keen on Twitter, he doesn't even know what it is. "Twitter? No, that's not for me. I like Facebook, but there are 1,700 people out there claiming to be me. That's quite a lot and there are lots of fake profiles, but there is only one official Mario Balotelli Facebook page. I update my page once or twice a week and it's a good way to keep in touch with my friends and family back home.

"I miss them all, but I don't want to talk about that because I'll jump on a plane and go and see them! I'm joking – I now have some good friends here in England, too. Micah Richards is like a brother and I see him socially a lot and I say we are twins."

I tell Mario, Micah says he is the better looking twin and he just shakes his head and laughs. "Twins are the same – how could that be?"

He adds he has lots of friends in the squad he sees outside training, and as the players begin to drift out towards their cars, it's clear he's a popular member of the squad with most stopping to chat with him or have a joke.

Before Mario arrived, I did get a tip off from Cristina about something very close to Mario's heart. He loves animals and dogs in particular, so talk shifts from games consoles and friends to a little character he's been missing since he came to England.

"What can you tell me about Lucky?" I enquire.

He smiles: "Lucky? Who told you about that? Yeah, Lucky is my dog, but he's still in Italy. It takes six months to bring a dog into England from abroad, so I'm still waiting. I plan to bring him back with me for the start of next season."

I ask where he found his faithful pal, knowing in advance he'd rescued him from a dog's home.

"He was a stray that was found wandering the streets, so they took him to the kennels. I was looking for a dog and when I went to the kennels, there he was. He's like a black Labrador – I think. I paid them some money and named him Lucky."

Surely, then, one of City's record buys has found the time to visit the Manchester Dogs Home in Harpurhey?

"Yeah, I've been," he says. "Only once, but I couldn't take one home. I love Lucky too much and it wouldn't be fair if and when he finally comes over."

I ask if anyone recognised him on his trip to North Manchester. And whether he drove there in his hardly inauspicious Maserati?

"No, I went in a Jeep and parked in the yard. I hadn't been in England that long so I don't think anyone knew me at that time. I like cats too, but not as much as dogs. I love them."

I tell Mario our family faithful hound came from Harpurhey's finest.

"His name?" he asks

"Paddy. He's not with us anymore."

"Dead? Was it the cats? That's a shame." We move on. I ask if it's true that he likes to visit Knowsley Safari Park near Liverpool, as was reported recently. "Yeah, I've been there," he says. "I was taken around in a Jeep – it's not a good idea, I think, to drive a white Maserati into the monkey enclosure.

"I liked it there and I fed the sea lions, got to see the lions up close. In fact, the zookeeper allowed me to get in the water so I could see what the sea lions could do and what exercises they make them do. I was very lucky because they gave a sort of private, customised tour of the park."

Mario shows me a couple of pictures on his phone of a lioness, sea lion and a monkey who appeared to have come too close. He is planning a visit to Chester Zoo in the near future, too.

Another of Mario's prized possessions is a quad bike, currently gathering dust in the garage of his city centre apartment. There aren't many opportunities to ride quads down Deansgate, so has he been able to use it?

"I have. Once. Around the apartment car park – that's about it. I need countryside to drive it properly, but I don't know when or if I'll be using it again."

It's been tough for Mario to settle in Manchester, but he's getting there.

"It's very different here," he says. "At first when I arrived, I was missing Italy and my family a lot. More than I ever imagined I would. I was very homesick, but I'm a lot more settled now and I'm getting used to being in England and living in Manchester. I'm here to play football, first and foremost. I have a nice view of the city and I'm doing okay. I'm getting around the city more and getting to know different places, and that has helped."

Talk of home and his family leads to Mario's school life where he showed tremendous promise from an early age and was encouraged by his father to play football for various junior teams. He excelled at junior level and discussed a possible move to Barcelona, but the fact he couldn't qualify for Italian citizenship until he was 18 scuppered that move and eventually Inter snapped him up.

"I went to a commercial school that mainly concentrated on sport," he recalled. "I studied Economics and languages – a bit of everything, in fact. I enjoyed swimming, athletics, martial arts and basketball."

I tell Mario his English is very good, but he shrugs it off. "It's not so good. At school, most people spoke English all the time and I used to listen – English, English, English, and I suppose I just picked it up because of that.

"I played football most of the time and got into trouble with my parents because I would play football with my brother in the house and we used to smash ornaments and things, but we just had to play. We lived in an apartment and used to play in the corridor outside our home. Coradi is older than me and he thinks he's a better player than me – no chance. My other brother didn't like football back then – he does now, though."

Can he ever see himself passing on his skills to children in some kind of coaching capacity?

"Me? No! Never," he laughs. "I love kids and I will happily play football with them, but I cannot teach them anything – it's just not me."

Rapidly switching direction again, I ask what each of his numerous tattoo represents and initially, with a little reluctance, Mario begins to explain what each design really means, but it's a task he warms to as he goes along, even revealing one of his tattoos is about his family – something sister Cristina had no idea about.

He points to his right arm. "This one is the happy mask and on my other arm is the angry mask. This is a lion because I have the same spirit as a lion and I have another, here (pointing to his left arm), that is friendship and family – these five characters represent my mum, dad, sister, brother and brother."

Cristina looks surprised to hear this. "He just asked me if I liked the new tattoo when he had it done – he never told me what it meant," she says – but she is clearly happy her brother has decorated himself in this way.

Mario explains why there is also a gun design around his family symbols. "It is a mafia warning," he smiles. "It means if anyone touches or harms my family, they will pay for it." He means it, too.

He also has a Champions League tattoo for his success with Inter, plus his initials behind each ear and signature on his upper arm. Fashion and looking sharp are clearly part of Mario's make up – as are designer shades, colourful footwear and a selection of intricately designed haircuts.

"I used to have a barber in Italy," he says. "He's still my barber but I use a guy in Manchester, now." He racks his brain. "It's erm… do you remember where I crashed my car into that BMW the first time? Right outside the shop."

It's Chester Road, in case you were wondering or fancied nipping in for a 'Balotelli'. While on the subject of roads and cars, I ask if his fortunes have improved behind the wheel after his accident last year, adding that it must be safer to drive in England than it is in Italy where the locals have a reputation for driving somewhat erratically. "Safer here than in Italy?" he protests. "No, you guys are crazy. Why does everyone else drive on the left and people in England have to drive on the right? It doesn't make sense."

I point out Australia, New Zealand, Cyprus and South Africa all drive on the right, too. "Yes," he agrees, with a hint of mischief, "but you are still strange, not everyone else! I like English people. You guys are different and like to do things differently, which is fine by me."

What about the City fans? He commented recently that their support warmed his heart, especially after the three goals he scored against Aston Villa over Christmas. Does he like the White Stripes tune that accompanies the song 'Mario Bal-o-telli, Mario Bal-o-telli!'?

"They have a song for me, too? I've never heard it, but I do concentrate on the game while I'm playing. I'm not saying I never hear the crowd at all, but I haven't heard that yet. I will listen out for it now. While on this subject, I'd like our fans to sing more at home and be louder.

"When we play away from home, our fans are very loud and never stop singing, but we need that at home, too, because that's what the players like. I like Blue Moon, but we like it noisy in our stadium, so that's my advice to them – more noise please!"

Finally, while Mario didn't seem to enjoy his time working under Jose Mourinho at Inter, he has a great working relationship with Roberto Mancini, his first boss at Inter and the manager who gave him his first break at senior level.

Mancini has said Mario needs to do better in recent interviews and speaks perhaps more harshly about his young charge than he does other players. A little less protective, in fact. Is this almost a father/son type relationship between manager and player?

Mario allows himself a wry smile. "Maybe a little," he says. "He believes in me and always wants to give my best, and he gets angry if he feels I haven't played as well as I can. He has a strong character and I am, too, so sometimes we clash and are a little stubborn, but it's fine with me because he's the best manager I could have right now."

Did he ever see his boss play? "Yes, he was a great player. But I'm better!"

On that note, I suggest I've kept Mario long enough. Forty-five minutes, in fact. He shakes my hand and says it was a pleasure before heading off at his usual breakneck speed towards the exit. He'll attract more negative headlines in the future, no doubt, and he probably won't deserve them.

When, and if, you see them, just remember: don't believe the hype – chances are it won't be true.

The History Boy

Sergio Aguero was the icing on Roberto Mancini's cake – with talent such as this, City's quest to win the title went from possible to probable…

It's fair to say that Sergio Aguero likes to make a dramatic entrance. The striker known back home in Argentina as the son-in-law of 'God' – since he married Diego Maradona's daughter – showed why his transfer to City could be a match made in Heaven with one of the most remarkable debuts in recent memory.

If anyone doubted his superstar status, or queried the record transfer fee that the Blues shelled out to prise him from Atletico Madrid ahead of Real and Juve, then that Monday night demonstration against

329

Swansea was all they needed. Half an hour off the bench was all "Kun" Aguero required to score two goals and give the kind of dynamic performance Roberto Mancini was anticipating when he urged the club's hierarchy to act this summer. "A photocopy of Romario," said Mancini. Tremendo Debut, blared El Diairo's headline back home.

Not for 30 years – when Trevor Francis marked his first game with two goals at Stoke's Victoria Ground – had City fans witnessed such a debut. But Aguero was only getting started. These were just the opening shots from a player whose declared aim is to snatch the accolade of world's finest from Lionel Messi. Aguero has fought his way up from severe poverty in the barrios of Argentina and his drive, just as much as his footballing ability and his hunger for goals, now pushes him to chase the Golden Boot as leading scorer for the season. Just for starters.

So with that, he harvested an impressive, clinical hat-trick against hapless Wigan – undone once more at the Etihad by an Argentinian, after Carlos Tevez's treble last season – and followed that immediately with two more goals against Fulham at Craven Cottage which should have secured another victory for Mancini's title chasers.

Back home in Argentina, Tevez is the people's player, ahead of even Messi who despite being the best in the world, is not seen as one of them, having decamped at an early age to the comfortable environs of the Nou Camp. But Tevez has a genuine rival in Aguero, who is seen as a younger version of El Apache and has the endorsement of his idolised father-in-law. "I'm proud of him because he is a wonderful boy," says Maradona. "He looks like me when I was a player. He is strong with thick legs."

Aguero learned his skills and ball control without a ball. Kun – nicknamed erroneously after a Japanese cartoon character Kum-Kum by his six siblings – and his boyhood pals often played their football with a bundle of rolled-up cloth in the shabby streets of his hometown of Quilmes, a shanty town of 60,000 residents near Buenos Aires.

Sergio, the second youngest of seven children, lived in a tiny home with a tin roof and no proper front door; a blanket would be draped across the entrance in an area where crime was an everyday fact of life. His father, Leonel, a taxi driver of Lebanese descent, earned £20 a week. It meant the growing family were always scraping a living, and Leonel and Aguero's mother, Adriana, often went without food so that the children could eat.

Now able to afford to dine in the finest restaurants Europe can offer, he recalls: "Sometimes we didn't have enough and we had boiled maté (twigs and leaves) with bread. At least it was something to fill you up. There were days when my father didn't have money for food and we slept hoping the next day something could be got from work. Life was very tough ... a lot of robbing. It was a difficult district.

"I still think about it a lot. It's something that goes with you as baggage in a way. I think of it even more when I watch TV and see people struggling to live. I was lucky. Although my neighbourhood was very humble, I always had my family and friends. But it helps me to remember the effort I had to make and the obstacles I had to overcome to reach this point. I had to sacrifice a lot, as my family did, and now it has paid off."

In those desperate narrow passageways between homes built from boards and tin, with little future for many, some youngsters were seduced by paco, a cocaine by-product that might be mixed with anything from rat poison to ground glass, but selling cheap and offering a temporary respite from the relentless poverty.

Sergio never succumbed to the dark side of the streets, but some were not so fortunate. He has said: "All the friends I had, I don't think any of them are at home. They're all in prison. If I hadn't got out of there, I don't know what would have happened to me. The ball rescued me."

And of his father Leonel: "I owe my life to my father. I remember that my first Christmas present was a ball. In the district where we lived, there weren't many kids who had one. I learned to play football in the streets. Every day of school, everyone came and played football. The street is a good school and you learn many things there – resilience, how to play against older players and how to put up with or dodge kicks."

That tough schooling, and the way he handled it against older, more physical opponents, came to the attention of Independiente, who signed him at the age of nine. By the time he was 12 – and Academy coaches should look away now – he was playing as many as five matches every Saturday. But he revelled in it, and in July 2003, a month after his 15th birthday, he broke the record to become the youngest player to appear in Argentina's top division. Previous holder? Diego Maradona.

Three years later, he made the inevitable move to Europe, being signed by Spanish La Liga outfit Atletico Madrid for £22million, the costliest signing in their history. It is a journey that many of his fellow countrymen make, although he admitted at the time: "At first I found it hard to adapt – the weather's different in Argentina, as is the pace of the game. But you soon get used to it. It wasn't as difficult as people said."

But that is only part of the story. Aguero was initially homesick in Madrid and according to some, developed a passion for expensive nightclubs, luxury cars and ... hamburgers. The already stocky striker's hamburger habit inevitably saw his weight increase, affecting his game, and it seemed that a player destined for great things had lost his way. Then, in 2007, he met Giannina.

Maradona's daughter, who is two years his junior, takes the credit as the stabilising factor in his life. The mother of their two-and-a-half-year-old son, Benjamin, her influence on him is so strong that it was reported he would not move to England without her permission. He says: "Giannina is the woman of my life, my support system. She grew up in the football bubble and knows all about it. That is an enormous help."

Luckily for Blues fans, Giannina shares his ambitions and was prepared to vacate their £4.5million house in Madrid, just down the road from Cristiano Ronaldo, in order to further Sergio's career. He says: "Ever since I got engaged to her, my wife told me: 'Look, I know football, I understand how it works. I will follow you wherever the game takes you.' That's exactly what happened.

"Manchester is maybe not an easy city to adjust to – but I'm doing well so far and the main reason is down to my wife and family. They understand that this is an important club that made a decisive bet on me for their new project. It helps when you feel wanted, not only at home – but at work."

Aguero finally signed a five-year contract with City on 28 July. Eighteen days later, he was announcing his arrival in quite sensational style before nearly 47,000 Etihad Stadium spectators and a transfixed satellite TV audience in the pubs and sitting rooms of England and Wales. He means business: and not only in the Premier League. Aguero has immediately bought into the adrenalin rush and sheer joy of the Blues' first Champions League campaign after an absence from Europe's top table of 43 years.

He says: "There is a very special feeling in Manchester right now. I am beginning to understand how much this competition means to City's fans. They believe we can go a long way in this competition and I think they are right. We have all the conditions in place to go much further than anyone might have expected just a few months ago. But we are starting to appreciate that for the City fans, who have supported the club in difficult moments over many years, it will mean most to them if we do well."

Sergio refuses to rule out a Premier League title with which to mark his first season in Manchester: "This season there is a real chance we can challenge, with the new players and the talent and the mentality within the club. City has been quite a big club for a while, but some really good investments have been made. If you look at the last three signings – me, Owen [Hargreaves] and [Samir] Nasri – it clearly shows a club investing in players with the aim of achieving something.

"As long as the group stays tight, like now, and we're playing good football, the results will keep coming. Hopefully we can win a lot of trophies for the club. I've never won a league championship anywhere, so I really want to do it here – and I expect to do it here. Let's hope."

Wright Man, Right Place

Shaun Wright-Phillips – the City fans love him, and as he celebrated a decade of service, it was another excuse to talk with one of my personal favourite players – and people – to have pulled on the Blue shirt...

Waiting in the players' canteen at Carrington, I feel a tap on my shoulder.

"What's happenin', D?"

I know who it is before I turn around to see Shaun, dressed in his civvies and ready for the interview. I've always got along well with Wrighty and knowing someone for ten years allows such informalities. The thing is, he's always been the same, from the first time I interviewed him back in 2001, to this most recent sit-down – he's always the first to come over and say hello at airports on when he saunters into the reception at Carrington, and he feels comfortable enough to let you know if he doesn't fancy doing something.

The day before, he sprinted down the corridor when he saw me coming through the door because he had to take one of his dogs to the vets after training.

"Wish you'd been that fast against Kiev," I shout.

The next day, I'm in the canteen and he comes to find me. That's the way he is and he takes his personality out on to the pitch every time he plays. Result? There haven't been many more popular players than Shaun in the Blues' modern era and the City fans love him as much today as they did when he first burst into the first team as a raw, untried teenager in 2000.

Former skipper Andy Morrison had a disagreement with Wrighty in training way back when, and he said that he loved the way he stood up for himself in a minor altercation in the gym afterwards. "He's got a heart as big as his body," said Mozzer. That's why he's in his tenth year with the club, though he actually joined 13 years ago in 1998, eventually becoming the first graduate from City's newly-formed Academy.

We sit down on the leather chairs in the Performance Analysis suite to dissect a career that has now spread over three different decades. Relaxed as ever, he settles himself in and we begin.

"I can still remember my first day in a City shirt when I was about 15," says Shaun. "It was against Port Vale at Platt Lane playing for the older age group with players called Michael Julien, Darren Garfield and Dave Laycock. They used to look after me. That was just a trial game, so I just turned up and got on with it."

Shaun was at Platt Lane because Nottingham Forest had just released him – a decision the club probably regret to this day. Though he was disappointed, he felt he had nothing to prove to Forest or anyone else.

"Forest had promised me a contract, but then they turned around and said I was too small and that I wasn't good enough," he continues. "It's different now of course, in regards to how big someone is, but at the time, that's how it was. I guess everybody's entitled to their own opinions. I think it was Steve Wigley and Paul Hart who decided I could go.

"It's not something I hold against people, but when you're young, you expect more of a chance instead of people saying that you're too small and not good enough. You never know how long it takes somebody to be nurtured. The guy that brought me here was called Kieran Rafferty, who was part of Forest's scouting network. He believed in me, contacted City and the rest is history. I still speak to every now and again."

One thing Shaun has never been short of is self-belief, and what could have been a devastating blow to his confidence turned out to be something he merely took in his stride.

"I knew I was good enough," he says casually. "My mum was really close to me and she came to all my games at Forest. My dad was like that as well, and my friends. Being released didn't faze me and it was never a thing of trying to prove people wrong.

"Bradley was also on Forest's books and my mum wanted us to stay together, so my brother had a trial with City, too, and ended up being taken on as well."

With Platt Lane little more than a Portakabin and few training pitches at the time, Shaun became one of Jim Cassell's first discoveries, but life as a trainee wasn't quite the same when he started out.

"When I was on trial, I would help clean the bathrooms, boots and suchlike. It was a good craic and a laugh. I'm not sure that still happens, but it should if it doesn't. It's good to still have that element in there as it lets young kids know that they haven't quite made it yet. It keeps their feet on the ground."

So what became of the Class of '98?

He smiles at the question: "That's going back a bit. There was Dickson Etuhu, who's now at Fulham. Terry Dunfield, who I think is playing in Vancouver somewhere. Rhys Day, Chris Killen and Chris Shuker, who's at Morecombe now. They are the main ones that have made it from the group I was in.

"The first time I got a sniff of first team action was in August 2000 when I played in a testimonial game at Old Trafford, I think for Denis Irwin's testimonial. A few days later, I made my debut against Burnley in the League Cup and my first league game was a couple of months later at Port Vale. Ian Bishop, Jeff Whitley, Nicky Weaver, Michael Brown, Andy Morrison, Richard Edghill, Richard Jobson, Shaun Goater were all in the City team around that time, so we had a pretty good squad."

Though he would leave for Chelsea in 2005, something we'll get to shortly, Shaun admits he feels he's been a City player all his life – he has for more than a third – and he will forever think of the Blues as home.

"Most definitely, that's how I feel," he says. "It doesn't feel like I've ever been away, it feels like I've gone through all the changes the club has undergone, seen everything and witnessed it all, from the Maine Road days to the Gillingham play-off final. It feels like I'm part of the furniture here."

Why does it feel that way? In these hire and fire 'em days, a player staying anywhere for more than three seasons is rare. Five is more uncommon still and ten is almost unheard of. What is the magic that has kept Wrighty a Blue for so long?

"The way the game is now, there tends to be a lot of changes in management and a lot of players move on, so I guess it's quite a rare thing. I think I've been really lucky. For me, the biggest pull has been the fans.

"They've been with me since I was playing as a schoolboy, all the way through the reserves, right the way through my career. They didn't even turn their back on me when I left for Chelsea, they've always supported me. When they came to Chelsea and when I returned as a Chelsea player, I always received a brilliant welcome. It's more like a family situation.

"The way I look at it is they always give good support and they always support the team with all their heart. I just try on the pitch to give it everything and 100 per cent every time I play because I know there's people out there who have supported me when things haven't gone so well, they've always been behind me. The most I can do for them is not to short-change them on the pitch, that's my outlook every time I cross that white line."

Shaun's first manager was Joe Royle, who loved talking about "the little fella." He played under Joe for a couple of years before he was sacked following the 2001 relegation from the Premier League.

"Joe gave me my chance, so it was quite a sad moment when he left," he says. "But football is a game that involves comings and goings. There are a lot of lows, but also a lot of good times, too.

"Then Kevin Keegan came in and it was weird at first. When he first came, I didn't play much at all; he kept me as a substitute and told me that I was a bit too small for the system that he was operating, which was odd because I think we were about the same height!

"He brought in players like Eyal Berkovic and Ali Benarbia, who taught me a lot about the game and the way I used to run without the ball. When they had the ball, I always knew where to run and how to do it. They helped me to create so many assists, it was unbelievable; they were fantastic team-mates and tutors."

When Shaun finally started to win Keegan over, he became a permanent fixture in the side, but without a goal in his first 20 or so matches, that was the one thing missing from the promising youngster's game. Then came the trip to Millwall, where visiting fans had been banned after previous trouble between the clubs.

"That was a bit weird," he recalls. "We didn't have any fans. That's one game that always sticks out to the fans, reminiscing about when I scored my first goal, but there were no away fans to celebrate with. It's a good memory to have.

"Darren Huckerby used to play me on the PlayStation and we would play Pro-Evolution Soccer. We played the night before in the team hotel and I beat him 3-2. I said wouldn't it be funny if we both scored the next day and we won 3-2? And we did. We were laughing about it together on the journey home."

There was perhaps an even more memorable goal Wrighty scored a few years later, too. With the Blues leading the first ever City of Manchester Stadium derby 3-1, the ball was played along the touchline to Shaun who picked it up, carried it to the edge of the box before unleashing an unstoppable drive that went in off the underside of the crossbar. Cue a wobbly celebration and pandemonium inside the ground.

"That will always top them all because it was the derby and we beat them 4-1," he smiles. "We didn't look like we would have a chance because we were struggling in the league, but it was just a fantastic result. The goal I scored at Old Trafford was a good one, but I still preferred the one at the City of Manchester Stadium.

"I'd put the 30-yarder at Highbury right up there, too. Joey Barton helped to create that goal with his enthusiasm to tackle shall we say! It was a good strike to be fair. There's so many happy memories from my 10 years here and hopefully there will be many more to come."

Of course, Shaun's time with City was truncated by the three years he spent with Chelsea. It was assumed by many that he'd asked for the move because of the circumstance around the move, but he reveals it was anything but.

"To be honest, at the time I really didn't want to leave," he says. "But I did in the end because it benefitted the club. We were in a poor financial situation, so it all happened in the end.

"I'd been a regular fixture in the City team and, obviously, I love playing football, so it was quite frustrating at times playing for Chelsea. At the time they were one of the best clubs in the world, so being a young lad, it was never going to be that easy and I had to fight for my place there.

"When I did play, I tried to give it my all and I even went on a run of games when Jose Mourinho got the sack, scoring seven goals in 10 games. It was a fantastic experience and I loved every minute of it. Overall, the pluses definitely out-weighed the minuses."

Deep down, he always hoped the chance to return 'home' would present itself, and when it did, he didn't have to be asked twice when Mark Hughes offered him the chance to come back in 2008.

"As soon as I knew that City wanted me, it was just a case of wanting to sort the contract out and getting it done as quickly as possible. I always believed one day that I would come back and I would love to retire in England at this club," he says. "'I've got my fingers crossed that this could still happen. That was always a thought in the back of my mind. Now I want to fulfil a lifelong dream and help win a trophy for the fans that have supported me throughout my career at City. It's my boyhood club."

Shaun's Second Coming, as it were, was away to Sunderland at the Stadium of Light. It was Boy's Own stuff as he bagged a couple of goals in a 3-0 win and he enjoyed the style of play he slotted quickly into.

"I'd say when I first came back under Mark Hughes, we were getting compared to Arsenal and Barcelona for our attacking premise, so I'd say it was on a par really with the Keegan era in that respect. I've enjoyed playing under all the managers, but I suppose Hughes' style at that time suited mine."

We've been talking now for a good half-hour and Adam Johnson pops his head around to ask what Wrighty is up to. "You'll get a testimonial interview when you've been here ten years," he tells him, laughing.

I know it's getting time to wrap up the interview, so I ask him to recall his best and worst moments from his decade as a Blue.

"That's tough, but some of my favourite memories include scoring my first goal for City at Millwall and also being a City player when I first put on an England jersey against Ukraine – and then scoring in the same game. It showed that I'd come from City but managed to create my England image by playing in a blue shirt.

"My worst memory was when I left. It was the hardest thing I'd ever done. When I left, I broke down in the car on the way down to Chelsea. It was a sad time for me. But when I found out that I could come back, I was like a schoolkid again, so I'd add that to my favourite memories, too."

Time has beaten us, though like any City fan, I could listen to Wrighty talk about his time with the Blues all day long. He hasn't quite finished yet, though. There's the future to consider and a personal message to the City fans.

"I just want to acknowledge how much they mean to me," he says. "I just hope that in the 10 years of playing for this club, I've shown my appreciation back. It's harder for me to give it back, I wouldn't know how to, but the 10 years I've been lucky enough to play in front of them have been fantastic. Long may it continue.

"To pay them back, I wouldn't just want to beat United and then lose in the final – we need to win it and if I could be part of the team that does that, I'd be a happy man. It would be incredible for the staff and fans who have been through the bad times if we could bring a trophy home for them.

"As for the future, who knows? This is my boyhood club and I would love to retire here. I'd like to play a part in helping the kids come through the club because obviously I've been through that and know what it takes to achieve those goals.

"I still give the same level of commitment to my game that I did when I was 18, and I hope I can stay here for many years to come."

Dzeko cuts inside again and fires an effort well wide and out for a throw-in — much to the dismay of the City fans...

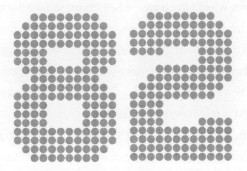

Play It Again, Samir

*Another part of Roberto Mancini's jigsaw was Samir Nasri
— a colourful character who wears his heart ion his sleeve...*

In a way, it was the unluckiest of memorable debuts. Samir Nasri, barely out of the Arsenal red that decorated his emergence as one of the best young playmakers in the Premier League, returned to North London in a City shirt and looked like he'd played with his new team-mates all his life.

Not only did he fashion the crucial first two goals of an eye-opening 5-1 victory over Tottenham, he linked up so well with David Silva and Sergio Aguero that the trio did as they pleased at White Hart Lane, teasing and toying with a defence that was made to look wooden at times.

Headline news on any other day. But not on 28 August. That super Sunday belonged to Edin Dzeko, the Bosnian hitman whose bravura performance brought him four goals, rapturous praise from previously sceptical commentators and writers, and, of course, such overwhelming acclaim that Nasri's debut was shunted into the "by the way" sidings with a "nothing personal" sticker by way of explanation.

Not that Dzeko wasn't grateful. "He's going to be a fantastic player for us," declared the striker, having feasted in the first half on two crosses he converted into the two goals that effectively pushed Tottenham to defeat before half-time. Samir, meanwhile, was already thinking as a team man: "We've sent a signal to the other challengers," the new No.19 informed a television interviewer.

Off the pitch, he's relaxed. On the pitch that day, he looked like a man in a hurry, legs continually moving and brain ticking over, a player looking to make up for lost time after his transfer from the Emirates to the Etihad rumbled on while he and Roberto Mancini had to bottle up their frustration at the delays. "It has been 40 days," said the exasperated manager at one stage, almost as if Nasri was out there, wandering around in some football wilderness. In a way, he was.

"It's a big relief," admitted the Frenchman when he eventually arrived with August drawing to a close, "because it was a long, long negotiation and discussion between the two clubs and now, finally, I'm a City player and that's what I wanted since the start, so I'm really happy.

"I was a little bit frustrated because I said to the (Arsenal) manager that I wanted to leave, but I stayed for the whole pre-season. I wanted to do the whole pre-season with Manchester City so that I could meet and know a little bit more about my team-mates. So, you know, it was a little bit frustrating."

Arsene Wenger, under fire from his own supporters and already reeling from the long-predicted loss of his midfield star Cesc Fabregas to

Barcelona, was understandably loath to allow his natural replacement Nasri to leave the Gunners just when he should be stepping into the leading role.

"The deal is a long way from being done," he stonewalled only days before Nasri cleared his locker, and not only picked the midfielder – with Nasri's blessing – to face Liverpool, with just an agent's demands holding up the deal, but also insisted he was ready to name him in the midweek Champions League game at Udinese that would have cup-tied Nasri for the group stages and doubtless triggered further haggling over the transfer fee.

In the end, the plane left for Italy without him after he'd trained, showered and changed, and instead Samir headed for Manchester, where his long-anticipated arrival ensured a warm welcome at the stadium from fans who had sensed that here was the missing jigsaw piece finally located from behind the big red sofa. Michael Russell's 90-second film of Nasri entering the offices to meet CEO Garry Cook and greet former Arsenal hero Patrick Vieira en route, became something of a YouTube sensation, quickly viewed by more than half a million people and even likened by one critic to Orson Welles' famous opening sequence in movie classic "A Touch of Evil".

Welles was a cinematic genius, but didn't deal in happy endings. Nasri has followed Kolo Toure and Gael Clichy from Arsenal – Vieira arrived via the scenic route after several years in Serie A – with a view to winning trophies and living happily ever after. So far, at the age of 24, and with three seasons in the Premier League to his name, he has won an Under-17 European Championship medal with France and the now-discontinued Intertoto Cup with Marseille a year later, in 2005.

Having winced through the Gunners' collapse in the Premier League last season, when City's Spring offensive found Arsenal's wilting resistance lower than at any time in recent years, Nasri realised that he couldn't wait forever if his dreams were to be fulfilled.

"What would make me happy? I hope titles," he nods. "I'm 24, everyone says I'm a good player, but I haven't won anything. I've played at a high level with Arsenal, but I have never won anything. This year, one of Arsenal's best players (Fabregas) left as well. No one has replaced him. When you join a team that has Aguero, Tevez, Silva, Kompany, you are confident of winning trophies.

"They are big players, and when you arrive at a club, you want to play with big players. The first game Aguero played, he came in, he scored twice and made an assist. I love this kind of player. Him and Silva, they're not tall ... they're like me. They have quick feet, good technique and they like to play, and when you play with players like this, you're always looking to have a connection with them. I have no doubts. I'm just happy to be there in the same dressing room.

"You know, in France, they call Manchester City 'The Galacticos', like it was with Real Madrid when (Zinedine) Zidane and Ronaldo and everyone were playing together."

"I wouldn't say I wasn't happy at Arsenal, but when you are at a big club, you hope to win things. Arsenal didn't have this mentality in the past. They brought in players, experienced players, but since the move to the Emirates Stadium, the transfer policy has been a bit different. The young players have good qualities, and in the future, I think they can do something."

The Arsenal connection at City has been discussed here before, and Nasri's arrival strengthens it. Kolo Toure's return to training after serving an FA suspension means that Mancini is now able to load three high-calibre ex-Gunners into his formation should he so choose. The Arsenal influence certainly had a bearing on Nasri's decision to head for the North West this summer.

He admitted: "I spoke with them (Kolo and Gael) a lot. They called me when I was on holiday. I spoke as well with Patrick (Vieira) because I've known him since the national team, so it was important to have advice from players who play for the club and know the club very well. They know the difference between Arsenal and Manchester City, and, for me, they make a big difference.

"Patrick is a legend in France, everyone loves him and respects him, and when a player like this, who played for Arsenal, Inter Milan and Juventus, tells you that Manchester City is the place to be because it's the club of the future – they want to win everything, they have a big, big project – then you have to listen to this guy, because when you see his career, you just respect everything he has done in the past."

Wenger, too, commands a deep respect from his fellow Frenchman, who made Premier League clubs sit up and take notice during a 2005/06 UEFA Cup run that saw an emerging Nasri put in two eye-catching performances against Bolton for a decent Marseille side that included Franck Ribery and Fabien Barthez. Wenger's French scouts, inevitably, were already comfortably on his trail by then, and he crossed the Channel in the summer of 2008 for a then-record Arsenal fee of more than £13million.

He says: "I will never forget what he (Wenger) did for me – he was like a second dad. He came to sign me when I was at Marseille. I was an international, but I have become the player I am now because of him and he always trusted me – even when I was injured, and I came back – he always gave me my chance. He was always there for me, he always talked to me. Now I saw the newspapers and everything, people are a little bit harsh with him, but you cannot forget everything that he has done for Arsenal and English football. I respect him a lot and I will always be grateful for everything he has done for me.

"I am a City player now and I think we can win one of the big trophies this season, I think we are the biggest challengers to United," he concludes. "Look at the investment over three seasons – you can see the squad has strength and quality players. World class players are not scared to come here, you can see that with Sergio Aguero. So I'm confident."

No Ordinary Joe

Joe Hart epitomized the confident, focused approach of the City players in 2011/12. There was a steely glint in his eye and an air of determination that left you in no doubt this would be our year...

"If you can keep your head, when all those around you are losing theirs and blaming it on you, yours is the Earth and everything that's in it, and – which is more – you'll be a man, my son!"

The poem 'If', albeit a truncated version, could certainly have been written about a goalkeeper and, in particular, Joe Hart.

City fans have watched him turn from promising teenager to a man over the past six years and now, as the poem says, the world really is his. Of course, say any of this to Joe and he'll likely dismiss it all and walk away shaking his head. He doesn't really do pats on the back and he'll also probably tell you there is so much more hard work to be done – and he'll be right.

The best never really arrive at their destination. It's a journey you continue to travel until things reach a natural conclusion which, in football terms, means retirement. So, at Joe's request, let's keep the plaudits and hyperbole to a minimum. For now at least.

When he signed for City in May 2006, he had just turned 19. The £600,000 paid to Shrewsbury Town seemed like a bargain at the time for a teenager who had been voted in a PFA divisional team of the year, won a similar place in a team voted by fans, and also won England Under-19 recognition. Recently, Sir Alex Ferguson admitted he'd been offered Hart for £100,000 and his decision not to proceed with the deal remains one of his biggest managerial mistakes.

Hart waited just five months before making his debut against Sheffield United in a 0-0 draw – the first of many clean sheets.

He could have been forgiven if he'd changed as a person and maybe let things go to his head, but he didn't. Whatever happens in his career, Joe will never forget he made his senior debut against Gravesend and Northfleet in the Conference and his feet are where they've always been, firmly planted on the ground.

"I didn't imagine it would be like this, but I didn't really imagine anything, I just turned up happy to be here," he said of his move to City. "Whether it was playing or out on loan, I didn't really know what was going to happen. I'm happy with how it's worked out and interest in the club has grown while I have grown, so it's worked out nicely."

Stuart Pearce may not be one of the most fondly remembered of City managers, at least towards the end of his tenure when the team were struggling in all areas on and off the pitch.

But it was Pearce who spotted Hart's potential, acted upon it and had the confidence to make him City's No.1.

"I spoke to him (Pearce) very casually at Carrington, he spoke a lot to my dad as I was quite young," Hart recalls of his initial meeting with the England legend.

"He took me up to his office. Paul Dickov was here as well, and he introduced me to Paul, which was amazing for me. He was cool, calm, really complimentary and very real in what he expected from me. It was relaxed and not too formal, that's just the way Stuart is.

"As for other teams, there was the usual rubbish of several teams being 'interested', but Man City were always the one for me personally. They were the ones who showed the most interest.

"It wasn't because of the geography, either. Not at all. That sort of thing doesn't bother me, I'd live anywhere. I don't think I really had the right to look for somewhere with a project when I was a 19-year-old playing in League Two."

The No.1 shirt wasn't just casually tossed in his direction, though. Hart needed to continue his education and was sent out on loan at Tranmere and Blackpool during the early part of 2007, and also won his first England Under-21 cap with Pearce now in charge of the team. Joe accepts the loan spells were crucial in his development.

"They were awesome," he says. "They've been there when needed. I've done a job for them and they've done a job for me. I'm not a guy to sit around and not play, so I was happy to play; if it meant dropping down a league or a standard I didn't care. I knew I would have to learn and go play elsewhere.

"It was quite easy to stay grounded because I moved from Shrewsbury to City, but I wouldn't say anyone knew I'd moved from Shrewsbury to City. I wasn't straight into the limelight or playing straight away. I was here to learn. It wasn't like I had done anything or achieved anything – I still really haven't. It was very easy to keep my feet on the ground. I was in awe of the keepers around me. I enjoyed looking up to them.

"David James was here very briefly, but he always wanted to move.

Nicky Weaver – a legend and a great guy. Andreas Isaksson was here, too, as was Kasper Schmeichel. Great keepers and a great time for me to learn from all of them."

But if things had been going well, they went into a different orbit in 2007 when Sven-Goran Eriksson made Joe first choice keeper at City, saying in so many words that he believed he was the future of English goalkeeping. Others agreed, and he was given his first senior England cap against Trinidad & Tobago in June 2008 as his career blossomed.

But with Eriksson gone within one season, and Mark Hughes the new man at City, things changed for Hart, especially when Shay Given was signed in January 2009.

Hughes wanted two top keepers competing for the No.1 jersey, but with Given thrown in immediately, and making a stunning debut against Middlesbrough, Joe knew opportunities were going to be limited.

"I felt like the door was closed here, so I would have to look elsewhere. I knew I wasn't going to go anywhere permanently, so I kept my options open. I had old heads advising me; they told me how it was going to work out, but I was young – I'm still young now – but in my mind, that was it and I thought my time with City was coming to an end. Shay was here – a brilliant goalkeeper – long-term, bought for a lot of money. So I had to look elsewhere. That's when Birmingham offered me the chance of first team football."

With a deal to spend the 2009/10 season on loan at St Andrew's, Joe left City while Given continued to flourish. Nobody could have guessed how good the move to Birmingham would prove and, more determined than ever, the custodian was outstanding for Alec McLeish's side.

"The goalkeeping coach, Dave Watson, was outstanding at Birmingham," he says. "He's really well thought of in the goalkeeping world and definitely an asset to Birmingham City. He's still there now and someone I still speak to. I take his advice a lot and he's someone I look up to and a good friend of mine, too.

"I think we just fed off each other. He's a very professional guy. He was a good goalkeeper, but his career was cut short through injury and I don't think he even made it to 30. I think my energy and passion for the game was combined with what he wanted and I don't think there were any limits, either. It didn't feel like he said 'you need to work on this', he knew that I wanted to learn everything and work on everything, and he could offer me that."

Ask any Blues fan – Birmingham that is – and they'll tell you Hart was a legend in his year in the Midlands. The accolades kept coming, too, and he was voted in the PFA Team of the Year, lost out to James Milner but was nominated for the PFA Young Player of the Year, and was voted Player of the Year by Blues fans.

Mark Hughes had been sacked by that point and Roberto Mancini had taken over. He watched Hart's progress with interest and towards the end of the season, when City's injury crisis struck at the worst time imaginable, attempts were made to bring Hart back for the last few games, but it wasn't possible.

"Towards the very end of the season, when I was at Birmingham, I met with Roberto and spoke with him. I wanted to hear what he had to say. In my mind it was maybe angling towards to what I had to do in the summer, because if I need to move, I need to move and do it quickly. He said he's watched what I'd been doing and that he'd had people watching me and he wanted me to come in and show what I could do back at City.

"I didn't really see it as me against Shay because it's not how it was. I played every game in pre-season because Shay was still injured with his shoulder, so I kind of had a run on him, if you like. I did okay and it meant a lot. I owe the manager a lot for playing me and I really appreciate that. I try to pay him back by playing my best every week and I'd do that for anyone, but I owe a lot to Roberto Mancini for letting me play at this club."

Heart Of A Lion

Pablo Zabaleta is someone every loves. Players, staff and fans all think he is a terrific bloke and it's a reputation well-earned. An unsung hero for so long, but not anymore...

Pablo Javier Zabaleta Girod, taking the air before a crucial UEFA Champions League match against the Spaniards of Villarreal, turned a corner to suddenly find his own unmistakeable image staring back at him as City fans brandished the billowing banner in gleeful tribute.

"Ah, the flag!" he grins, recalling his surprise and, truth be told, slight embarrassment to be the subject of such idolatry in a team laden with more celebrated stars. "I took a picture with the flag! I think when fans recognise some players, it is because the player is doing his job well. It makes me feel happy because I know that I'm giving everything for this team and this club."

And there is the Pablo Zabaleta philosophy in a nutshell. He is, perhaps, the ultimate team man, a quality recognised by successive City managers who might have more naturally gifted players available, a predator of a striker or a smooth operator of a midfielder, but nobody who will give an iota more for the cause.

Blood, sweat, tears, Zabaleta has shed them all. The cherished photo with the flag is vastly outnumbered by those of the wounded Argentinian being helped from the field of combat, his bloody grimace another badge of honour, but also a warning that he will be back in the fray as soon as humanly possible. There is never a white flag from Zabaleta.

When a tackle needs to be made, he is there to make it, and if it is a crunching challenge that leaves his opponent less willing to repeat the process too soon, so be it, and if he is sometimes a second or two too late against a speedier rival, then a yellow card is the price he reluctantly pays. Needs must, and taking one for the team figures high on Zabaleta's design for playing.

The pain and the blood are also part of the price he pays, and one of the reasons why Pablo Zabaleta has earned a place in the hearts of Blues fans. Putting your body on the line always strikes a chord with supporters, but the enthusiasm with which he hurls himself into the eye of the storm when the going gets tougher brings a certain inevitability with it. For Zabaleta, A&E doesn't just stand for Argentina and England.

"You never know what will happen, that's the thing," he shrugs. "It happens in football. This is part of the game. The worst one? Maybe last year against Stoke City, the game after the FA Cup final, I think it was with Rory Delap.

"I had one before that against Tottenham, the game we played for the Champions League position; I had an elbow from Peter Crouch which broke my nose, but I think the one against Stoke was worse. I had 12 stitches, it was a bad injury. But it was one of many!

"Christel (his fiancee) knows how I play. She's always saying 'try to take it easy sometimes!' But I say to her that when you're on the pitch, it just happens; when I go, I go. In the Premier League, I've had many problems with my nose and my head. Sometimes when you're playing against a team that plays long balls, many players in the Premier League are very tall, and when you have to jump with some of them, you'll get an elbow in the head or it goes head-to-head.

"But this is part of the game…it's our job. We need to stand up and need to carry on. I think it's in the personality of Argentinian players. Like Patrick Vieira says, all Argentinians are the same: very short but very strong!"

Zabaleta chuckles over his misfortunes and stitches and scars; a versatile, willing warrior whose attitude means that management and team-mates alike value his presence, whether at full-back or in midfield. A man who gives everything when called upon, but shows patience and wisdom when he isn't.

"As a professional, wherever you are, at any club, you always have to do your best. This is the best thing we can do for ourselves and for the club. When I came here four years ago, I felt the support that everyone here was giving me. The best way to pay them back is to give everything for the club. I always try to do my best – sometimes you can do better, but you need to always try your best.

"Maybe the fans recognise that I'm a player that never complains if I have to play or not, I can play in different positions and try to do my best for the team. I think if you're building a team like we're doing now, with this new team and new players, we need to know and we need to accept that we have 23 or 24 top players in the squad.

"I know I'm no manager – maybe one day I'd like to be – but I think that when you've got players who can adapt to different positions and always do their best for the team and don't complain, players like this help the team to do better. That's why when a player plays for many managers but stays for a long time at the club, it shows that the player is doing well.

"Sometimes, maybe only three or four players can play every single game, the rest maybe have to rotate. That's normal. There's so much talent in the team, and if we have to be on the bench for some games, we need to accept it and wish the best for the player who is playing in your position."

Blood, sweat…tears. Only once in four years of service since being plucked from La Liga and Espanyol by Mark Hughes has Zabaleta not been able to put City first. When news came that his father had been involved in an horrendous car crash back home in Argentina, he flew the 7,000 miles to Buenos Aires not knowing whether he would find Jorge alive at the end of a full day's journey.

He was preparing for a sixth round FA Cup tie against Reading when he took the call: "I was in the team hotel before the game and a friend rang me to tell me about the accident. He started with 'he's still alive, but it's better if you come here'. When you are so far away and people say that, you are thinking they don't want to say that he died because you have to travel 22 hours.

"I flew back to Argentina and was thinking the worst things. Fortunately, when I arrived there, I went straight to the hospital and saw he was alive. After three weeks, I came back to England. It was near the end of the season, so after the final game I went back home. I don't have my mum, so it made it more difficult. When I went there and my brothers saw me, it gave them support. When you have a problem like this, you want to be with your family.

"It was difficult at the beginning, he was in a coma for a month.

When it happens and you're so far away, it's difficult. I remember I went to Argentina and it was difficult to come back. But, in life, you need to be ready for moments like this.

"March the 12th was one year since the accident. He's progressing well. Obviously, it's not easy for him because he cannot work at the moment. He still has some problems in his leg and hand, but he's doing physio every day and he's putting in everything he has. He was 59 in April, so I told him he's still young and to get well!"

Typically, Zaba was back in England in time to play his part in two historic Wembley visits, collecting both a caution and a painful raking challenge from Paul Scholes that tore the flesh of his thigh and saw the United veteran sent off in the derby semi-final, then stepping off the bench for the last few minutes of the final as a replacement for Carlos Tevez. Zabaleta's season, nay City career, in microcosm, you might say.

He gets more chance to see his dad these days, having forced his way into the reckoning for the Argentina national team that once ignored his abilities. On one particularly frustrating occasion, Diego Maradona, then the manager, travelled to the North West to speak with Javier Mascherano at Liverpool and Carlos Tevez at Carrington without a word of encouragement or otherwise to Zabaleta, who had Inter legend Javier Zanetti blocking his path.

Now absorbed into the Argentina set-up as first choice, he said: "We're always trying to grow, you always have something to learn. Zanetti was right-back for Argentina for a long time so it was difficult to play in the team with him in that position. I learned a lot from him as a player and as a person, he was a great example. With a new manager, and since the last Copa America, I've been regularly starting for the national team. Now I need to keep working hard to keep my place."

There is an Argentinian enclave in Manchester these days consisting of Pablo Zabaleta, Carlos Tevez and "new boy" Sergio Aguero. Zaba admits it something that works for everyone.

"We spend a lot of time together. Sergio lives just five minutes away. He's a very funny lad – if you understand Spanish and hear everything he says, he's so funny. His personality is like this, he's very happy and positive for the team. I'm not surprised how well his first season here has been because I know him as a player and as a person. I knew before he came that he would do very well for the team. He's been one of our most important players this season.

"It's great for Carlos, for Sergio, for me. We play together for the national team and I played with them in the youth teams. For us, it's a new experience here. Whenever you leave your country, you learn a lot of things. The opportunity we have to be here in England, in the Premier League, is making a big impact in our lives. The culture is different, the football is different, we're really enjoying it here.

"I think it's very important for any player that has the chance to play here to learn English. I'm not saying we're going to speak the best English, but you need to try to learn because you need to learn to communicate with everyone. Not just the manager, but all the people around the club. I think some players are more focused on football and other players try to improve off the pitch."

It certainly sounds as though Pablo Zabaleta is here for the long haul if he has anything to do with it, although he is wise enough to be cautious when it comes to the question of committing himself for the rest of his career, tempting as that might be.

He said: "Manchester is one of the best places to be in the UK, and I'm really happy. Today I can say that I'm very well here, but I don't like to say (I'll stay for life) because sometimes you can say this and then after one year everything changes. Then people say, 'hey, but it's just been one year since he said he wanted to end his career here'. That's why I think it's a mistake when you see players who are in a good moment, or they have signed a new contract, and say they want to stay for their career.

"I think when you do this, it's because you're happy in that moment. I'm very happy here and I think this club has a great chance in England and in Europe to be one of the top teams. We're looking at a great future here and that makes me happy."

Those flag bearers of Valencia need have no fears that Zabaleta is looking to transfer his courage to a new cause any time soon: "I think for any player, when you finish a game and go home, if you've given everything for your team, then you can sleep well. You have to be honest. When you work, you need to be happy, you need to enjoy it. I love football, and when I go to bed, I can sleep well."

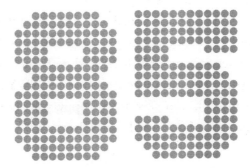

Believe

Sergio Aguero had the City fans eating out of his hand from the moment he scored twice on his debut against Swansea, but he was determined to end the season with the title – as he told me – he never gives up, no matter what. How prophetic would those words be just a few months later in May...

Well on his way to 30 goals in his debut season in England, Sergio Aguero couldn't have dreamed for a better first year with City.

True, a Premier League winner's medal would be the icing on the cake, but whatever happens, the hugely likeable 23-year-old has made a stunning impact and has become a huge crowd favourite in the process.

Life is good for the Argentina striker, who Lionel Messi believes is one of the best in the world, and who chanced his arm away from La Liga to find a fresh challenge rather than take what would have been an easier move to one of Spain's big two.

The language, the lifestyle and the climate would all have suited him and his wife and young son had he elected to move to one of Atletico Madrid's rivals, but he wanted to broaden his horizons and instead chose to sign for City.

Aguero's work rate and skill won him a legion of fans almost from the word go this season, with his stunning debut against Swansea getting him off to a flying start.

Even so, did he imagine he would become such a huge favourite among the City fans so quickly? "It's always gratifying to be considered an important member of the team by the fans," he said. "Hearing your name being echoed around the stadium…it's quite a rush. It makes me want to give even more when I go out on the pitch.

"But being held in high regard is only useful if it's useful for the team, so that we can reach our goals every season. The backing our fans give to me, gives me confidence and I try to pay it back by playing my best football.

"I was able to adapt quickly to the team and to the Premier League. That was all due to my team-mates, the club and the fans. We have had a great season, but there is so much more to come from this team. I've been told we've broken historic records and that's already an achievement. I've also learnt it's important to respect our progress, an on-going process. We want to win the title and we will continue towards that aim."

Aguero's style makes him a difficult player to mark or know what is coming next. Skilful, hard-working and technically gifted, the Blues' No.16 has scored some stunning goals, but has also been very close to some fantastic individual goals this season, beating three or four players and very nearly scoring the perfect goal. So is it fair to say we can expect even more from Kun next season?

"I hope so!" he smiles – a natural disposition for a player who is equally popular with his team-mates and staff. "I never hold back in doing my share for the team. If that sometimes means me attempting something a bit different, that's even better! I'm just as happy to take a lucky deflection or tap-in if it helps the team. Team goals are great for everyone, but if I can produce something memorable every now and then, you won't find me complaining.

"Every goal is special and I enjoy each one I score. I just celebrate in the way it comes out at that particular moment with nothing planned. That could be related to our Latin blood, right? Argentinian men are very passionate. And football is our passion, it's my passion. It's that simple."

Sergio's popularity is universal, and his bond with the City fans is evident every time he plays. But how does the backing in Manchester differ from his previous clubs in Spain and Argentina?

"Of course, I enjoy it," he says. "I was lucky to be well received at every club I've played for. It was the case at Independiente de Avellaneda, then at Atletico Madrid – and now here. The supporters of each team are different, but they all share the same passion for their team.

"It's true that they all express it in different ways, but the feeling is still the same. To me, having this kind of relationship is a privilege. It's comforting and inspiring for me."

A committed husband and father, Sergio's son Benjamin seems to have inherited his genes and those of his grandfather, Diego Maradona – Aguero's father-in-law. A video of the obviously gifted three-year-old has already had more than 2,000,000 views on Kun's official website.

"Benjamin is a blessing," he says. "He plays football all day and he loves it. It runs in the blood, right? But that's just something natural –

he takes the ball and asks anyone who comes home to play with him, with no pressure from our side. Ben likes watching the games and he goes to the stadium with my wife all the time. The day we gave him his first Manchester City jersey, there was no way to get him to take it off!"

Is the most famous footballer on the planet also now a City fan, then?

"Diego is now working in Dubai, so he has little time to travel," says Sergio. "I'm sure he'll come when he gets the chance. He's a man of football – he knows what is going on in every club in the world. That includes City as well, of course...

"As for moving to England, I feel we've adapted really well to living in Manchester and we haven't been here for too long, either. The staff of the club and my team-mates have been very supportive, especially Pablo Zabaleta who has been here for quite a while. Everyone has made us feel at home. We still would like to know the city better and maybe visit the outskirts more, but we don't have too much free time on our hands. But from what we've seen, we find it quite nice. We feel at home here."

Being Premier League champions would make Sergio feel even more at home, and he believes it will happen sooner rather than later.

"Why wait until next season if we can win it now?" he smiles. "We're fighting until the very end. We all want to make it and though it won't be easy, we believe we can win the Premier League this season. Winning titles is about never giving up, and we will never give up. I want to win it this season and then many more with City after that."

Words every City fan will love to hear.

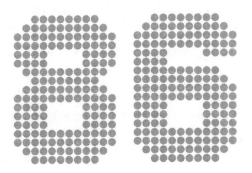

Zaba – Again!

No apologies for featuring Pablo for a third time…

Pablo Zabaleta says Tottenham is the biggest and most important game of the season so far.

The Argentinian defender, who is well on his way to reaching the 150-appearance mark for the Blues, is in no doubt the North Londoners represent a serious test of City's 100 per cent Premier League home record this season.

"I think Tottenham are one of the best teams in the Premier League at the moment, they're doing very well this season," he said.

"When they play with a strong side, they look like a really solid team. It's a crucial game for both sides, but one we need to try and get three points from to stay at the top of the table.

"The lads are all in great spirit and we know that we will have to be at our very best against Spurs and can't give anything silly away. It will be fast, competitive, but obviously, our way is to try and play attractive football and move the ball around quickly, so we won't change our style."

After remaining unbeaten at home for a year, City have suffered back-to-back defeats against Manchester United and Liverpool in cup competitions recently – Zabaleta says a third loss on the bounce is unthinkable.

"We can't let that happen," he said. "When we play at home, we feel more comfortable, and with our fans behind us, it makes the team stronger and that's maybe why we get more points at home.

"I think Spurs have a team capable of winning the title. They have a strong side and they have the same chance as the three or four teams fighting for the title have.

"The media have been talking about it being only between United and City, but that's not the case; Tottenham are right in there and are serious contenders."

Whether Zabaleta starts or is on the bench, he is well aware of the threat Spurs' wingers pose, but will be ready to go head-to-head with whoever he is asked to mark.

"Everybody knows that Gareth Bale is one of the best left wingers – not just in England, but in the world," he said.

"He's been doing well for many seasons at Tottenham and many top teams have been looking at him, but they will keep him and try to kick on.

"One of the keys to beating them is to try and stop their wingers, and Aaron Lennon is a very dangerous player, too. They have very quick, fast players, and whoever plays at full-back on Sunday will have to stop them.

"Having said that, I think they're going to miss Emmanuel Adebayor because he has been part of the reason they have done so well. We will be focused and ready – it should be a fantastic game."

Relentless

An interview with skipper Vincent Kompany was a must as the Blues began their final approach for the title – but even Vincent couldn't have predicted the drama ahead...

January is traditionally a hard month to get through.

Overspending at Christmas usually means belts are tightened, and festive excesses ensure belts are also tight, so with no holidays or much excitement, it's usually a month most people are happy to see the back of.

For City fans, January 2012 couldn't end quickly enough for other reasons. Highly contentious refereeing decisions saw the Blues lose Vincent Kompany, Gareth Barry and Mario Balotelli to suspension and concede three penalties.

Yaya Toure and Kolo Toure were denied permission to play in the FA Cup before jetting off to the Africa Cup of Nations until mid-February, while Roberto Mancini was vilified in the press for questioning decisions he felt were, at least, equal to offences his players were deemed to have made; Mario and Vincent were subjected to trial by media… it goes on.

All in all, it was a month to forget.

Losing Kompany, many feel, was the hardest sanction of them all. The inspirational captain effectively missed five games after being sent off so early against Manchester United, but he finally returned, refreshed and champing at the bit, for the last game of January, and now he is only looking at making sure his team continue their drive towards a first league title since 1968.

Officially installed as skipper on the eve of the 2011/12 campaign, Kompany is typically philosophical about his role in the side.

"I don't look at it as six months of captaincy, I think I've equally taken my share of responsibilities from when I joined the club for the past three and a half years," he said

In his absence, City won both league games, but dipped out of both the FA Cup and Carling Cup, though Kompany thinks there were positives to be taken out of each competition.

"I don't think there was any shame in the way we went out of the cups," he said. "Both were the kind of games that could have gone go either way.

"In the league, there's a belief in the team that we can become even stronger towards the end of the season, and that's important because from now until the end of the campaign is when you need to show your real strength.

"We're set up quite nicely for the finish, and we're sure we're going to get even stronger in the weeks to come."

City's Player of the Year for 2010/11 is the last to suggest the Blues' recent sticky patch is anything unusual and that all teams go through similar phases during a season. If anything, he thinks the opening weeks of 2012 proved that the squad has the resilience needed of champions.

"Ultimately, if we achieve anything this year, it's because we've got such a big squad," he said. "You always lose players at a certain times, but I feel we're going to set ourselves up for a strong finish. That's regardless of who's back and who's not.

"Coming out on top at the end of the season is what matters, but for this club, that's not the end of the road, it's just the beginning.

"It's not like we have based our season on just finishing top of the league; we're building something that's there to last. There's no reason we should look towards the end of the season with any more nerves than we did before because it's just a continuation of what we're doing now."

Kompany was never far from the action during his suspension and he was always straight down into the dressing room as soon as the final whistle went. He lived every minute and headed every ball as he sat and watched from the stands, but now he's back and hoping he doesn't miss another minute of the remaining matches.

"It was hard," he admits. "Players have stepped up, and that's important. It gives us even more self-belief when you see other players perform and you know that if anything else happens in the future, those players will be there. It makes us even stronger."

So when did Vincent Kompany become indispensable to this team? He answers in a manner you'd expect him to.

"Nobody is indispensable," he states. "If there's one lesson that I've learnt from being at this club for three and a half years, it's that nobody is indispensable.

"I always say the club is bigger than any individual, and that's so true. Once again, we've had two or three very good results in the league and this proves that we're strong enough to deal with any setbacks we may have.

"Going into February, we'd gained three points on our opponents, and we're heading in the right direction."

He won't be drawn on the sending off that caused such a discussion in football circles as to where the game, and the almost forgotten art of tackling, is actually heading. He wrote a succinct paragraph on his Facebook page and has now put the matter behind him.

"I've said my bit on it and to continue talking about it will bring back negativity," he said. "Right now, we're in a situation where we need to keep positive. We've got great goals and the biggest answer we can give to everyone is to win the title. Nothing else should be on our mind right now. Whether we've been treated fairly or unfairly doesn't matter. If we win the title, everything comes down to us."

Many believe that February and March is a chance for the Blues to pull clear, with a clutch of games against sides in the lower half of the table on the horizon. Kompany doesn't. He says: "I don't look at it this way. I always think that we can win all of our games. Right now it's going to be about consistency, and if we just keep doing what we're doing and don't get side-tracked with all the talk in the newspapers, teams will find it hard to beat us.

"We have the squad to achieve our ambitions. David Silva has been incredible, but who doesn't know that? Gareth Barry has been very important to us and Yaya Toure has been very influential... I can keep going on and going on. It's not just a coincidence that we're top of the league, it's because many players have done their job well, and if we want to mention names, we could go on forever."

But the race looks set to run to the last game of the season – on current form at least. Manchester United, perhaps driven on by thought of having to hand the Premier League trophy over to their noisy neighbours after decades of dominance, refuse to let the Blues out of their sights.

Does Kompany walk off the pitch jubilant having helped secure another three points only to hear United have also won again – and think, 'not again…'?

"I look at it the other way," smiles the skipper. "I think they must be thinking 'My God, they won again'. That's how it is now, we've set a relentless tempo for the rest of the league and that's put the pressure on everybody else.

"Whichever team has lost points so far has been punished, and we need to just keep doing what we're doing. I'm not looking too much at other teams because I feel that if we don't make any mistakes in our own games, we shouldn't have to worry about the other teams.

"And we can continue to become stronger. This team still has much more to give and we will as we mature. That's probably going to show more next year if we can compete in the Champions League. Then we're going to show even more that we're becoming a better team. This is just the beginning for us. Think of three and a half years ago where this club was at and the way we've developed to where we are now. It's already clear to everybody at the club that we're going to keep getting better."

As Kompany continues to improve year-on-year, and he is, correctly, talked about as one of the best centre-halves in the world, it is comforting to know that he considers Manchester to be his home. While it's a fact the previous incumbent in the captain's role perhaps didn't feel as strongly about the city he played his football in, Kompany does, and he gives an air of man who is settled both on and off the pitch. So much so that he recently sent out a tweet most Mancunians could relate to immediately.

"It was just a funny thing," he smiles. "When there were strong winds in the city and Beetham Tower was making that humming sound – the noise, the weather – surely if you're trying to sign a player you should try and avoid that day! But then again, if you live here for a while and then you go away, you miss it. I said I must be becoming a Manc and I suppose I am."

The proud father of 18-month-old daughter, Sienna, added: "If you become a dad, you change. It gives you that stability that comes with the responsibility. It puts positive balance into my life."

Kompany is just as focused and happy on the pitch, where he intends on creating history with Manchester City.

"I can't take satisfaction out of only winning one title," he says. "With the team and the potential we have at this club, I'd like to see us winning four or five titles in succession – being relentless, in fact. That's the way I've set the targets that we want; it might sound pretentious, but that's the reality. I'll be celebrating if we win the Premier League in May, but you won't see me being any different next year because the next thing you know, you end up losing everything you've achieved. That's not going to happen…"

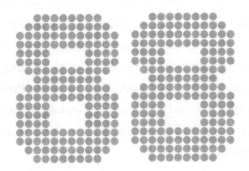

No Surrender

I spoke with James Milner after City's 1-0 defeat at Arsenal left the Blues eight points behind United with six games to go. We were in the tunnel at the Emirates and neither of us was in the mood to talk, but this brief interview encapsulated the players' never say die attitude perfectly...

James Milner says City's only aim is to win all the games that remain this season. The England midfielder says the Blues will keeping going until the end of the campaign, even though United are now eight points clear at the top.

After suffering late heartache with a 1-0 defeat to Arsenal, the message coming out of the Blues' dressing room, Milner says, is one of determination to not allow what has been a fine season to end on a flat note.

"We'll aim to win our last six games – as we would have done had we won here today, but it is going to be very difficult now," he admitted.

"Nothing has changed in that respect and we have to target 18 points and six wins so we can end this season on a high – we'll just have to see where that takes us, but I can promise our fans we'll never give in so long as the title is still a possibility."

Milner admitted the Blues' dip in form could not have been timed any worse, with dropped points against Stoke, Sunderland and now Arsenal in successive weeks.

"For two thirds of the season, we've led the table and played some great football, but we've not played as well as we can of late," he said.

"That we're not top anymore is down to us, and the fact we've not played very well is down to us, too. All we can do is try and get back to winning ways, starting with West Brom on Wednesday.

"We need to learn lessons from this season and take positives from it. We've hit a dip at exactly the wrong time, whether that's down to loss of form, confidence or fatigue, I'm not sure.

"We haven't performed to the sort of standards we set earlier in the season, and though the boys at the back defended magnificently today, we didn't keep the ball enough or create enough chances going forward.

"We need to learn from this, dust ourselves down and then go into the West Brom game in a positive frame of mind. There are six games left – it's not over and we will be giving everything to make sure we end the season as strongly as possible."

Blue Sky Ahead

Going into the final game, Joleon Lescott was confident the Blues could see the job through...

Joleon Lescott has responded to reports in the media suggesting City are expecting an easy ride against QPR on Sunday.

The England defender says the Blues' focus for the visit of Mark Hughes' side will be exactly the same as it was for Manchester United and Newcastle – and is unchanged no matter who the opposition is.

"I've heard a few things have been said about how we will approach the game and that we think all we have to do is turn up – but that's complete nonsense. We don't think like that about any team, and as professionals, we would never allow that to happen – that's why we are where we are.

"Every team we play represents a different challenge, and we will go out there with the right attitude and manner and try to get the job done."

Lescott added the occasion wouldn't get to the players ahead of what is, without doubt, the club's biggest game for 44 years.

"We have a fantastic squad with the likes of David Silva, Carlos Tevez, Sergio Aguero and Yaya Toure, who have all won major honours, so it's easy for them to focus for the big games and it comes naturally to them.

"For players like myself and Joe Hart, for instance, we've not really won anything major apart from the FA Cup, but we'll be equally focused on the task ahead."

Lescott revealed his ever-growing bond with the City fans reached new levels with the 3,200 travelling Blues at Newcastle giving him a rousing rendition of 'He's top of the league' – a song that could only mean one thing.

"I definitely did hear our fans on Sunday and it was what I had hoped to hear because it means we go into the last game knowing a win will secure the title.

"It's been a great few weeks with the five wins on the bounce and the way we've turned things around, but for us to start getting carried away now would be silly.

"It will be great to see Nedum (Onuoha) and Shaun (Wright-Phillips) and it will be a mad atmosphere, especially if we win and they end up going down.

"We just need to do what we've been doing in the last few weeks, give it our all and I'm sure we'll be fine."

16:47

End of normal time – the board goes up and there are five minutes of added time to play...

Unyielding

Yaya Toure – a man-mountain of a player and one of the best City fans have seen play for the club – he never stopped believing...

Yaya Toure is determined to win the Premier League for the City fans he believes are the best in the business.

Yaya, whose brace at Newcastle has put the Blues within 90 minutes of becoming champions for the first time since 1968, now wants to finish the job against QPR on Sunday to reward the backing he's had from the supporters.

"I came to City to make history, and that is my first objective – to help make a successful football club," said Yaya.

"I want to win it for our fans who have been amazing towards me

377

since the first moment I arrived. In fact, from day one, their support made me even more determined to give them something special back.

"Last year, we won the FA Cup and we have to continue like that and next try to win the game against QPR.

"We know it's going to be tough, but I believe in this team, I believe in the players we have, and we know we will have the same fantastic backing we've had all season from our fans.

"The job is not done yet. We have to keep going because QPR need the points, but it would be amazing if we win. It is for occasions like this I came to City – to make history – and I hope I will make history at the weekend."

Yaya was also keen to praise Roberto Mancini, who he believes is one of the best managers he's worked under, adding: "Full credit to Mancini – he is an unbelievable boss.

"He always believes in us and always tells us, 'Guys you have to believe in yourselves. The most important thing is you have to keep winning games and United can drop some points' – and he was right.

"Forty-four years is an unbelievably long time to wait for another title – it is too many years for the fans to wait. Now we have one game left and we have to deliver."

We Can Do It

When we were 2-1 down, I was saying to Mario on the bench 'We've still got time, we can still get another, they've got 10 men!' Then, when we got the second, I was like 'We can do it, we can do it!' A little bit of brilliance finished it off, it was just amazing. Being a Man City fan is never easy, I know that as a player. This season we've worked hard and we deserved the league. We knew it wouldn't be easy, but we got there in the end. I'm just so happy for the fans, the players, the staff...everyone involved with Manchester City, it's just an amazing day.

– Micah Richards

GOAL! Silva's corner is headed home powerfully by Dzeko to make it 2-2 – surely there isn't enough time left? Mancini urges his team to get back into position…

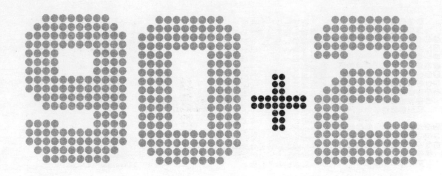

Bleed Man City

I can't sum it up in words, to be honest. I feel exactly as the fans feel, I bleed Man City the same as everyone else…

– Joe Hart

QPR kick-off, and with the news filtering through they are safe from relegation, the ball is kicked towards the City corner flag where Joe Hart begins another attack...

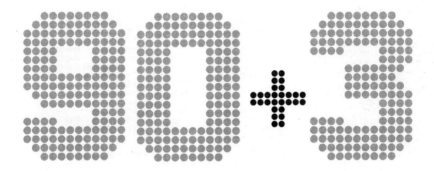

Just The Start

It's a great feeling, the best ever. I'm so happy that we can give this to the fans. Somehow, this whole project has become my own as well, I want this team to do well and for this club to achieve great things. This is just the start, I can guarantee you. Manchester is a place of miracles, but not just for the other side of town. Tonight it happened for us.

– Vincent Kompany

GOAL! City come forward with De Jong who plays the ball to Aguero 35 yards from goal. He plays the ball to Balotelli and receives it back before shrugging off two challenges and then burying the ball past Kenny to send the Etihad Stadium wild – City 3 QPR 2.

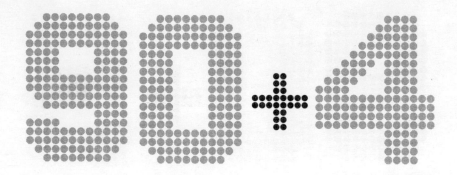

Incredible

It's good... five minutes from the end it was not good! Football is incredible. It's incredible because we did not deserve to lose this game, but we went 2-1 down. We wanted to win this title because we deserved this title. We dominated the season. The players were fantastic, they've had fantastic spirit all season and also today. It's fantastic to win this title because we've changed history after 44 years.

– Roberto Mancini

There is just enough time to kick-off, and as the ball is cleared to Hart, he holds on to possession before the referee blows for full-time – that's it, City are champions!

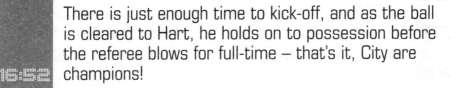

Fantastic Supporters

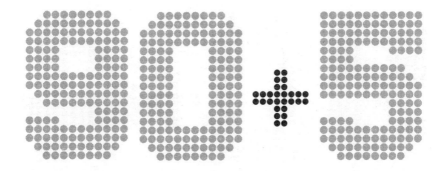

The only thing I can really say is that I'm really, really happy. The truth is we can barely believe it ourselves. We thought the Premier League had gone, thank God it worked out for us. We got two goals in five minutes, it was absolutely unbelievable. We have fantastic supporters. From beginning to end, they were right behind us. They've treated me very well from the moment I arrived and I love them loads. Let's hope this is the first of many titles. My personal objective is to keep improving as a player and win more trophies. This has given me even more confidence.

– Sergio Aguero